THE RED CORNER

THE RED CORNER

THE RISE AND FALL OF COMMUNISM IN NORTHEASTERN MONTANA

VERLAINE STONER McDONALD

MONTANA HISTORICAL SOCIETY PRESS, HELENA

Cover photograph shows men taking a break on the Bert Wagnild homestead near Outlook, Montana, July 1911. The men are (left to right): unidentified, Wagnild, Martin Knutson, Peter Sneen, and Carl Sneen. Courtesy Helen Wagnild Stoner.
Cover and book design by Diane Gleba Hall
Typeset in Adobe Garamond and Neuzeit Grotesk
Printed in USA by Creasey Printing Services
Unless noted otherwise, photographs in the text are from the Montana Historical Society Research Center Photograph Archives (MHS in credits).

Distributed by the Globe Pequot Press, 246 Goose Lane, Guilford, CT 06437
(800) 243-0495

11 12 13 14 15 16 17 18 19 10 9 8 7 6 5 4 3 2 1

LIBRARY OF CONGRESS CATALOGING-IN-PUBLICATION DATA
McDonald, Verlaine Stoner.
The red corner : the rise and fall of communism in northeastern Montana / Verlaine Stoner McDonald.
p. cm.
Includes bibliographical references and index.

ISBN-13: 978–0-9759196–7-5 (alk. paper)
ISBN-10: 0–9759196–7-9 (alk. paper)

1. Communism—Montana—Sheridan County—History—20th century. 2. Radicalism—Montana—Sheridan County—History—20th century. 3. Social movements—Montana—Sheridan County—History—20th century. 4. Social conflict—Montana—Sheridan County—History—20th century. 5. Sheridan County (Mont.)—Politics and government—20th century. 6. Sheridan County (Mont.)—Social conditions—20th century. 7. Sheridan County (Mont.)—History—20th century. I. Title.

HX91.M9M35 2010
335.4309786'218—dc22
2009051319

Dedicated to my mother, Helen Wagnild Stoner,
and in memory of my father, Vernon Stoner

CONTENTS

ILLUSTRATIONS

PREFACE

On a spring day in 1985, the hired man on my parents' farm was rummaging through the contents of an old trunk in search of an inner tube for a tractor tire. He found a number of serviceable inner tubes as well as something unexpected: a collection of yellowed newspapers that had gone unnoticed for years. One of the papers, dated November 2, 1932, was headlined, "Vote Communist Tuesd'y, Nov. 8." The masthead indicated that it had been published just miles away, in Plentywood, Montana.

Although I had lived in Sheridan County for most of my life, it was only with the discovery of these nearly sixty-year-old newspapers that I began to learn about the political firestorm that had swept through my community. When I attended school in the 1970s and early 1980s, the county's Communist movement simply was not discussed, certainly not in classrooms and never in polite conversation.

Later, when I began to learn about the Sheridan County farmers' movement and described it to a graduate school professor, a labor historian, he marveled at the peculiarity of this event. He said that historians know about the radical activities conducted in places like New York City, Chicago, smaller factory towns in the Northeast, and even in western Montana's mining communities. But in Plentywood, Montana? It was a quiet hamlet in the northeastern corner of the state, sparsely populated by farmers, most of them practicing Protestants—hardly the typical launching pad for a radical, left-wing political movement.

This book investigates Sheridan County's remarkable experiment with Communism, the conditions that made it possible, and the people who contributed to it. It reflects my academic training in the field of communication: my tendency is to focus on how the radicals formed their persuasive appeals, the ways in which they connected with their audience, and why, just as the Great Depression enveloped the country and their message should have resonated the most clearly, the Communists were rejected by the voters. Although the radical cause in northeastern Montana ultimately failed, it represented something extraordinary and ambitious, a political movement that made Sheridan

County unique among farming communities of the 1920s and 1930s. It put us on the map. We became what Ivan Doig called, in his novel *Bucking the Sun,* "the Red Corner of Montana."

For decades, during the McCarthy years in the 1950s and the Cold War, the people of northeastern Montana tried to forget their brush with notoriety. Thus, not only did I graduate from the Plentywood school system without having heard of the Sheridan County Communists, but I also did not know that my great-great uncle, Clair Stoner, was one of the early farm movement leaders. I am fortunate to have learned about my county's past in time to interview a few of the residents who lived through it, and I am glad that their story can now be told.

Verlaine Stoner McDonald
Berea, Kentucky

ACKNOWLEDGMENTS

This project, so long in the making, would not have been possible without the help of many associates, friends, and family. My work began at the University of Southern California in the early 1990s where the chairman of my dissertation committee, Tom Hollihan, and committee members Randall Lake and Steven J. Ross conscientiously guided the project that would become this book.

The completion of my degree made it possible for me to join the faculty of Berea College, an institution unlike any other, where I was eventually granted a sabbatical during which I wrote an early draft of the manuscript. Berea College also provided funding for my work at the Library of Congress and has always supported my aspirations as a teacher and writer. I also thank the Appalachian College Association, which provided a generous sabbatical fellowship.

I am grateful to a number of historians who have encouraged and assisted me. Bill Pratt has shared his observations, feedback, and materials since I first contacted him in 1992. At the same time, I read Lowell Dyson's *Red Harvest,* an excellent source on American Communists and farmers. Dyson's interview with Charles E. Taylor was invaluable to my work. I also appreciate Harvey Klehr's and John Earl Haynes's work at the Russian State Archive of Socio-Political History and Haynes's negotiations that brought microfilm copies of important Communist Party USA (CPUSA) documents to the Library of Congress.

Also critical to my work were the contributions of many local historians, writers, residents, and former residents of Sheridan County who generously shared their memories and perceptions of the radical period. I have turned time and again to what folks in Sheridan County reverently refer to as "the book": *Sheridan's Daybreak.* I am grateful to Magnus Aasheim for his efforts in editing both *Sheridan's Daybreak* and its sequel, *Sheridan's Daybreak II,* as well as the research on the old "Chicken Ranch" that Mags undertook on my behalf during the fall of 2002. I wish he could have lived long enough to see this project completed.

During the writing of this book, two other important contributors passed away: my grandfather, Ray Stoner, who talked to me about his experiences during the "Red days," and Carl Taylor. Carl and his sister, Ellen Taylor Syrstad, candidly shared recollections about their father, Charles Taylor, and their childhood experiences in Plentywood. I also thank everyone who agreed to be interviewed for this book as well as the contributors and section editors who worked with Magnus Aasheim on the *Daybreak* books. In particular, I am grateful to my mother, Helen Stoner, who has constantly encouraged and supported my work on the Sheridan County farmers' movement (and all of my aspirations), most recently by joyfully undertaking the task of locating photos for this book. And I would be remiss if I failed to acknowledge Bill Wirtz for sharing the newspapers he discovered in the old shop at the farm.

I appreciate the frequent and patient assistance of my friends in the Sheridan County Courthouse, Library, and Museum: Sheila Lee, Mary Lynch, Milt Hovland, Bernice Van Curen, Joanne Garrick, Pat Tange, and Doug Smith. Thanks are in order to Joe Nistler, Tim Polk, and Marvel Hellegaard at the *Sheridan County News* and Burl Bowler and Milton Gunderson at the *Daniels County Leader.* I also owe thanks to several colleagues at Berea College who have offered their encouragement and assistance: John Bolin, Stephanie Browner, Phyllis Gabbard, and Richard Sears.

I am grateful to Charles Rankin, who, as editor of *Montana The Magazine of Western History,* published my article on the *Producers News* and later offered the best advice I could have received: that I take my manuscript to the Montana Historical Society Press. Molly Holz has been a gracious, welcoming, and wise editor, and her staff, including Glenda Bradshaw, Diane Gleba Hall, and Christy Goll, has been most helpful. It has been a joy to work with Ursula Smith, who has my gratitude for guiding me through the copyediting process and for her meticulous, elegant work and delightful e-mails. I also thank David Emmons and two anonymous reviewers for their helpful comments on the manuscript.

Finally, I thank my husband, Andy McDonald, who has been my steadfast supporter since I began this research. His instant appreciation for the prairies and people of northeastern Montana when he first visited in 1985 helped me see my home from a new perspective. Later, Andy put his knowledge about political history and his gifts as a writer and editor to work in reviewing my manuscript. His unflagging encouragement, patience, good humor, and loving care for our daughter, Carlyn, made it possible for me to complete this project. I look forward to our next project and all of the adventures to come.

ABBREVIATIONS

AFL	American Federation of Labor
CCC	Civilian Conservation Corps
Comintern	Communist International
CPUSA	Communist Party USA*
FBI	Federal Bureau of Investigation
F-LP	Farmer-Labor Party
IWW	Industrial Workers of the World
NPL	Nonpartisan League
UFL	United Farmers League
WFM	Western Federation of Miners
WPA	Works Progress Administration

*The general term "Communist Party" is used throughout the book for the purpose of clarity. It is not intended to obscure the contentiousness of the party's history in the United States, which began in 1919 when two separate and antagonistic parties formed, the Communist Party of America and the Communist Labor Party, both of which operated mainly underground. In 1921, following a merger of the Communist organizations, the Workers Party of America emerged as a legal party front. In 1924, it became the Workers Party, and finally, in 1930, adopted the name Communist Party USA.

THE RED CORNER

When there was enough rain, the soil of the northeastern corner of Montana grew hard red wheat. When drought came, politics of that same coloration sprouted instead.

—Ivan Doig, *Bucking the Sun*

INTRODUCTION

The Peculiar Case of Sheridan County Communism

The headline appalled the residents of Sheridan County, Montana. When the *Producers News* published its March 4, 1932, issue, much of the nation was gripped by dark events unfolding at home and abroad. The infant son of American icon Charles Lindbergh had been kidnapped and was being held for ransom. The military forces of Imperial Japan were ravaging China. Meanwhile, 15 million Americans were out of work as the nation's economy teetered on the brink of collapse.

Remarkably, however, it was a local story that inspired the outrage of the residents of Sheridan County. Headlined "Bolshevik Funeral for Valiant Young Pioneer," the story was about fourteen-year-old Janis Salisbury, who had died just the day before from complications related to appendicitis. She was described as a bright, active girl, who was mourned by her parents and five siblings, including her identical twin. However, Janis would later be best remembered not for her short life but for her remarkable funeral, an event steeped in radical politics and devoid of the religious overtones so cherished by the citizens of her pioneer community.

Rather than being held in a church, Salisbury's funeral took place in the local Farmer-Labor Temple, a civic auditorium where political events, dances, and youth activities were typically held. Instead of a traditional homily, the event featured speakers from the local branch of the United Farmers League, which was affiliated with the Communist Party, and the local Communist youth group. The editor of the

Producers News, a member of the Communist Party, wrote a controversial account of the funeral, describing in detail the service, which featured hammer-and-sickle decorations, the singing of "The Internationale," and the pledge of allegiance to the "Red Flag" by the Young Pioneers.[1]

This editorial decision would have profound consequences for the *Producers News* and the Communist farm movement in northeastern Montana, which, in the 1920s, had achieved stunning political success. Three decades before Senator Joseph McCarthy tried to inspire hysteria in the hearts of Americans with the specter of creeping Communist control, radicals in Sheridan County had already accomplished what McCarthyites perhaps feared most: they had created a community where "Reds" occupied every elected office in the county and had sent a covert Communist to Helena as their state senator for two terms. Local youths could attend camps where they were actively indoctrinated with Communist ideals, and the radicals' newspaper flourished, beginning nationwide circulation in November 1931 as the official organ of the Communist Party's United Farmers League. In the year of Janis Salisbury's death, former sheriff Rodney Salisbury was on the ballot in an attempt to become the nation's first Communist governor. Sheridan County was, in the estimation of at least one historian, "one of the most class-conscious areas in the nation."[2]

From that perspective, it would seem that the dire economic circumstances of the Great Depression should have fed the continued success of Communism in Montana. At the time, wind erosion and drought threatened the productivity of once-fertile fields, crashing commodity prices crippled the agrarian economy, and distrust of big business was at an all-time high. Communism was in its heyday elsewhere in the United States. Yet the radical movement in northeastern Montana was faltering, and by the autumn of 1932 it was, for all intents and purposes, dead.

This book explores the remarkable rise and precipitous fall of Communism in northeastern Montana by examining the intersection of the many variables affecting radicalism's prospects: ethnic heritage, local and national cultural forces, material conditions, precursor agrarian and labor organizations, directives from outside leadership, political imperatives, and the popular rhetoric employed in the movement. The book thus offers an explanation for the peculiar events that occurred in Sheridan County during the 1920s and 1930s and argues that the Montana experience served as a grim harbinger of things to come for the Communist movement in America.

CHAPTER 1

Plentywood, Montana

"A New Metropolis in the Northwest"

Until the late 1800s, the plains of northeastern Montana were sparsely populated, save for the native people of the Assiniboine and other tribes who hunted bison on the region's windblown prairies. That changed when American railroad companies began their reach across the plains toward the Pacific. To fund their continuing westward expansion, the Northern Pacific; Chicago, Burlington & Quincy; and Great Northern railroads needed to attract buyers for the land along their newly forged rail lines, and they embarked on vigorous promotional campaigns to lure homesteaders to Montana. With the help of various government agencies and officials, the railroads thereby increased business while driving up the value of their land holdings.

Serving Montana's northern tier of counties, the Great Northern, like many other railroads in the United States, made use of so-called town site companies to promote the growth of new communities. In 1910, the Dakota and Great Northern Townsite Company of St. Paul advertised the town of Plentywood as "a new metropolis in the northwest." The display ad featured a sixteen-item list under the heading "What Plentywood Has." The list included two general stores, four lumberyards, two hotels, a newspaper, two banks, a millinery store, a law firm, and a doctor's office. A separate column, headlined "What Plentywood Wants," cited the need for a "first class hotel," a dentist, a tailor, a photographer, and confectionery, jewelry, drug, and shoe stores. According to the advertisement, opportunities were "ripe for the business or professional man," who was encouraged to "come early and get a little of the milk and honey of the land."[1]

The Plentywood ad was relatively truthful and restrained compared with many of the others distributed by the Great Northern and other railroads, which were, at best, wildly optimistic and, at worst, deceptive in their touting of Montana as a lucrative new frontier. Western railroad promotions had been abundant since the 1870s, but these campaigns became increasingly aggressive in the early 1900s. Promotional items included posters, pamphlets, and postcards as well as romantic stories of frontier life that appeared in national magazines such as *Sunset* and the *Saturday Evening Post* accompanied by drawings and photos of scenic landscapes. The Great Northern itself employed thirty-four agents who functioned more or less as recruiters; they visited fairs and circuses and gave illustrated lectures promoting the Northwest. In 1910, the Great Northern created a special advertising car to illustrate the attractions of its territory. Such promotions, coming on the heels of the Enlarged Homestead Act of 1909, fueled the subsequent land rush in Montana.[2]

PLENTYWOOD

A NEW METROPOLIS IN THE NORTHWEST

The town is new; the country is new; most of the people are new.

What Plentywood wants:	What Plentywood Has:
Restaurant	2 General Stores
Laundry	2 Hotels
Flour Mill	2 Banks
Shoe Shop	3 Blacksmith Shops
Harness Shop	4 Lumber Yards
Drug Store	3 Hardware Store
Confectionery Store	1 Livery Barn
Jewelry Store	2 Meat Markets
Bakery	1 Newspaper
Dentist	1 U. S. Commissioner
Cement Block Factory	1 Millinery Store
First Class Hotel	1 Coal Dealer
Auto Livery	1 Feed Mill
Implement Dealer	1 Barber Shop
Tailor	1 Doctor
Photographer	1 Lawyer

Reasons Why PLENTYWOOD Can support these lines of business

BECAUSE it is the natural distributing point for more than 30 FULL TOWNSHIPS OF GOOD MONTANA SOIL.

BECAUSE it is the terminus of the Bainville-Plentywood branch of the Great Northern Railroad, and furnishes a gateway for a vast country west of Plentywood still practically unsettled.

BECAUSE the territory surrounding Plentywood is settled by people who are real farmers. They mean business and expects to make their homesteads their permanent homes.

BECAUSE Plentywood is ideally located where an abundant supply of water can be obtained at a depth of forty feet.

Opportunities are Ripe

For the Business or Professional man. Come early and get a little of the milk and honey of the land.

For further information inquire of

Dakota & Great Northern Townsite Co., St. Paul, Minnesota, or N. L. Nelson, Local Townsite Agent, Plentywood, Mont.

Plentywood Herald, *April 22, 1910.*

The railroads were not alone in the effort to sell Montana to homesteaders; in that endeavor, they were joined by state government itself. In 1909, the commissioner of the Montana Bureau of Agriculture, Labor, and Industry prepared reports on the state's resources. The resulting 216-page booklet, *Montana,* was sent to every state and territory and many foreign countries. The book met with such success that,

Harvesting Near Plentywood, Valley County, in 1910
Northeastern Montana
VALLEY AND DAWSON COUNTIES
Marvelous growth of this section during past three years. The Great Northern Railway's new branch line between Bainville and Plentywood. Thriving trade centers. Fertile 320 and 160-acre Homesteads. Lower Yellowstone Irrigation Project. Fort Peck Indian Reservation.

"Harvesting near Plentywood, Valley County, in 1910." [*Montana: The Treasure State* (Great Northern Railway: n.p., 1911)]

in 1912, the bureau expanded and published it in hardback, with ample photos and illustrations. It was, in the tradition of all good homesteading publicity tracts, a remarkable work of propaganda.

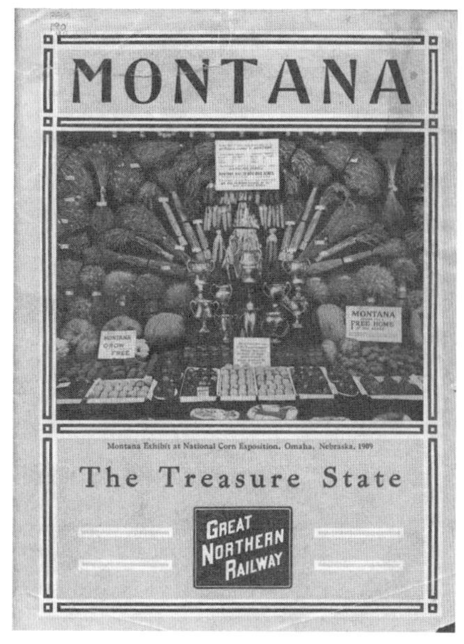
MONTANA
Montana Exhibit at National Corn Exposition, Omaha, Nebraska, 1909
The Treasure State
GREAT NORTHERN RAILWAY

The Montana exhibit at the 1909 National Corn Exposition in Omaha, Nebraska. [*Montana: The Treasure State* (Great Northern Railway: n.p., 1911)]

Short chapters of *Montana* provided details of the state's physical features, climate, mineral deposits, educational opportunities, and manufacturing, but agriculture was its primary focus. Readers were bombarded with production and valuation statistics that may have sounded impressive but were so lacking in context as to be virtually meaningless—yet they were strangely enticing. The book reported that "crops of hay, wheat, oats, flax, barley, potatoes and corn were harvested in Montana in 1910 from 1,579,000 acres." A lengthy paragraph detailing such minutiae as the acreage in timothy, clover, and "wild, salt, or prairie grasses" followed. There was an exhaustive discussion of possible calculi

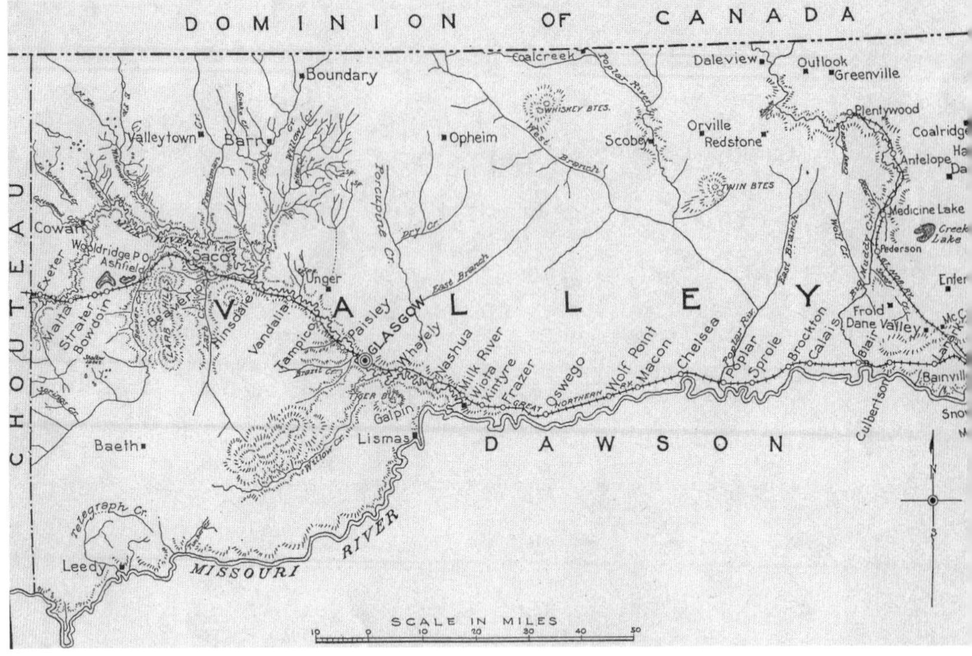

Valley County, 1912. [Montana Bureau of Agriculture, Labor, and Industry, *Montana* (Helena, Mont., 1912), 286]

for determining the number of arable yet idle acres in the state. The chapter concluded with the encouraging estimate that 28 million rich virgin acres awaited cultivation by homesteaders who could "secure a farm of these untilled lands which yield abundant crops." The message, backed up with the seemingly irrefutable evidence afforded by statistics, made perfectly clear to prospective homesteaders that brilliant opportunities awaited in Montana.[3]

To complement the impressive presentation of statistics, charts, photos, and illustrations, *Montana* included personal testimonials from Montana farmers and ranchers, beginning by quoting a recent immigrant who wrote: "I sold my land in Iowa for twice what I paid for land in Montana, and the Montana land yields twice what the Iowa land yielded." In an appeal to the nation's newest residents, many of whom had made their way to the United States during the great wave of immigration in the late 1800s, a letter by Marius Anderson offered testimony that Montana was indeed the new "Land of Opportunity." Anderson had come to the United States from Denmark in 1901 and arrived in Montana with a wife, two children, and fifteen dollars. By 1909, according to the letter, he valued his lower Yellowstone Valley farm of 160 acres and other holdings at between eight thousand and ten thousand dollars.[4]

Under the heading "Life on a Montana Farm" was a reprint from the *Rocky Mountain Husbandman* penned by R. N. Sutherlin of Great Falls, who had been writing and speaking about the state's agricultural resources for a generation. Referring to himself in plural form, Sutherlin wrote that he had been reviewing all of his previous flattering reports about Montana opportunities and that "while we are frank enough to admit that we may have at times used a little poetic license in our descriptions, we really believe all that we have said has been justified by existing facts." He stated that he knew "of no country with a more delightful run of seasons" and then described those seasons with more of the poetic license. He went on to claim that Montana's "soil is productive, our climate exhilarating, the water is fine, the air pure and develops a wonderful lung capacity." He mentioned that "thousands of contented, happy men and delightful lovely women grasp us by the hand wherever we go and assure us that the story the *Rocky Mountain Husbandman* tells is not a romance, but a fully verified truth."[5]

Montana included profiles of each of the state's then twenty-nine counties. The three pages devoted to Valley County (from which

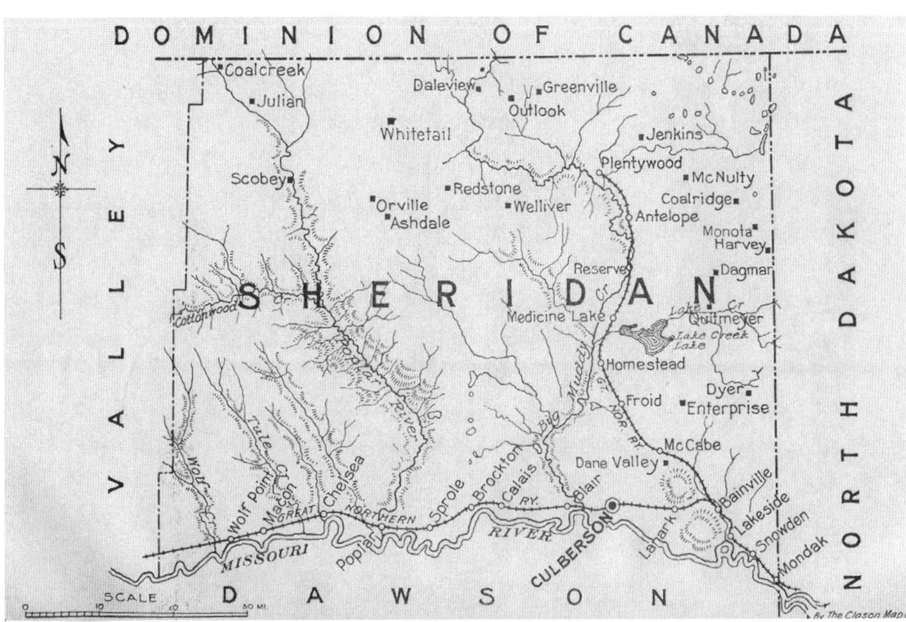

Sheridan County was created from Valley County in 1913; Sheridan County was later split to create Roosevelt County in 1919 and Daniels County in 1920. [Montana Department of Agriculture and Publicity, *The Resources and Opportunities of Montana* (Helena, Mont., 1914), 280]

Sheridan County would be carved in 1913) declared: "The lands are fertile, the climate good, and the rainfall sufficient for the profitable production of crops without irrigation when proper methods of cultivation are followed." It is interesting to note that the book failed to mention hazards such as the prairie fires ignited by burning embers from Great Northern locomotives that had devastated Valley County pastures and hayfields in 1901 and 1902 or the blizzards of 1903 and 1906 in which some ranchers lost their entire cattle herds.[6]

The publicity campaigns of the railroads and state government had tremendous reach and rhetorical power, but they were not the only appeals being made to potential homesteaders. Northeastern Montana was also promoted as the home of a religious colony by Emil Ferdinand Madsen, a former teacher at a Danish folk school in Tyler, Minnesota. In 1907, Madsen and his adult son loaded a railroad boxcar, called an immigrant car, with "household goods, machinery and animals, including horses, cows, chicken, the dog Rover and two pregnant pet cats" and set out for Montana.[7] Madsen was carrying out the vision of his friend, Pastor Henrik Plambeck, who had proposed planting a Danish Evangelical Lutheran settlement in the West. The previous year, Madsen

Valley County's "splendid vegetables" were exhibited at the Northwestern Development League's Land Show at the St. Paul Armory in St. Paul, Minnesota, in 1911.
[Juul-Ingersoll Co., photographers, MHS Photograph Archives, Helena]

Emil Ferdinand Madsen with his wife, Marianne Knutson, and daughter, Brynhild (Bonnie), circa 1910. [MHS Photograph Archives, PAc 77-94 VI-8.4]

had made a journey with six other Danes to northeastern Montana for the purpose of scouting an appropriate home for their planned colony.

Madsen's compelling narrative about his journey appeared in *Dannevirke,* a Danish-language newspaper published in Cedar Falls, Iowa. Madsen described what he saw in Valley (later Sheridan) County: "We stepped off the wagons and gathered in a cluster to enjoy the most glorious sight. Below us lay a large lake whose mirror-clear arms reached in over the prairie. North of the lake spread a level plain, gold painted by the sun." With great enthusiasm, Madsen described a bountiful garden and "splendid vegetables . . . equal to those I have seldom, if ever, seen" as well as nearly two feet of brown-gray loam that "when loosened is light and porous as a handful of ashes." He conceded that there were some rocks on the soil, but no more "than would be needed on the farm." Madsen named the colony in memory of Denmark's Queen Dagmar.[8]

Seeking colonists for the new settlement, Madsen implored readers to take "resolute action," to not take the time to write him a long letter but to simply "put sixty or seventy dollars in your pocket, go to the railroad station, and hurry out there." There was a hint of class consciousness in his invitation to all Danish people who "cannot carry

Midsommerfest *baseball game at the Danish Church, Dagmar, 1910.*
[MHS Photograph Archives, Helena, 946-674]

large debts, but who would like to get out of the claws of the employers and away from the city's clamor and discord" to join him in the Montana venture. Madsen's six companions signed their names as well and declared on their "Danish honor" that Madsen's narrative was true. Danes from Minnesota, Wisconsin, Iowa, and the Dakotas read Madsen's article, or talked to others who had, and began their journey westward. The colony began to expand.[9]

The Danes, however, were not the only Scandinavians in the region. Over time, many Norwegian émigrés found their way to the county in the hope of staking claims to land of their own. The influx of Norwegians owed much to the tradition of *odelsret,* which required that a family's land be given to the eldest son when a landowner died. Norwegians tended to have large families, which created difficulty for the siblings of the fortunate eldest son. Particularly in the late nineteenth century as land prices increased while wage levels stagnated, it became critical for Norwegian males with no property holdings to acquire land elsewhere, and often, it was in the United States. Like many others, they were drawn to the plains by the promise of owning land, the cost of which was said to be only their own labor.[10]

As it turned out, the ethnic and national backgrounds of Montana's new residents would play an important role in fostering the Sheridan County Communist movement. Many of the radicals had lived in Scandinavia and thus witnessed firsthand the influence of Socialist parties that existed in Norway, Sweden, Denmark, and Finland. Scholars have asserted that Scandinavians with socialist leanings were especially inclined to immigrate and identified "high correlations between the presence of Scandinavian-born residents and radicalism" in the United States during the 1920s.[11]

No matter what their ethnic or political background, many, if not most, northeastern Montana homesteaders practiced the Christian faith. In the Norwegian and Danish communities, worship services, Sunday school, and devotional meetings often began even before a pastor had been hired. The Dagmar Danes made the organization of a church the topic of their first meeting just weeks after arriving in 1907. In Antelope, a community settled primarily by Norwegians, residents built a Lutheran church even before they built a store or the Sons of Norway community hall. In fact, Antelope Creek Lutheran Church existed before the town was surveyed or platted.[12] Plentywood, too, was quick to build one Lutheran church and then another. As the story goes, someone in town remarked that the existing Lutheran church had been erected too far out in the countryside beyond Plentywood, and soon enough a new building was being framed just off of Main Street. And while Lutheran churches were the most abundant in Sheridan County, they represented only one of many denominations. A Pentecostal church opened its doors in Comertown; Adventist and Congregational churches were built in Antelope; and several Catholic congregations

Antelope, June 1911. [MHS Photograph Archives, Helena, PAc 81-69]

Plentywood from Riba's Hill, February 1912. [MHS Photograph Archives, Helena, PAc 81-69]

built houses of worship in the area, as did members of the Church of Christ, the United Methodist Church, and the Assembly of God.[13]

Churches functioned not only as religious sites, but as social centers for the community. Women's groups gathered there, and *Midsommer-fests*, educational programs, and socials of all sorts commonly took place within those buildings. The family histories in *Sheridan's Daybreak* recount ice cream socials and horseshoe tournaments, quilting bees, and community dinners, all held at the churches.[14] Until Plentywood built a civic auditorium in 1924, church buildings were used for most community activities.

The men and women who built the churches and communities of northeastern Montana arrived on the plains with more than what was packed in their immigrant cars. They also came with their ethnic and religious traditions, their experience of farming in the verdant hills of Norway, Wisconsin, or Minnesota, and their sometimes unrealistic expectations about homesteading in Montana. The Sheridan County that greeted them presented harsh living and farming conditions, and soon enough, many of these new arrivals would experience what they perceived as economic and social injustice. Taken together, these factors made the new Montanans of Sheridan County unusually receptive to some of the political narratives they would encounter in the future.

CHAPTER 2

"No Place for the Feeble"

Homesteading on the Northeastern Montana Prairie

It is difficult to imagine what must have gone through the minds of homesteaders as they stepped down from the Great Northern train at Culbertson after a long, difficult journey and first set eyes on the land that was to be their home. The dusty plain, with its stretches of western wheatgrass, likely appeared a forsaken frontier to transplants from the green hills of Wisconsin or the fjordlands of Norway. Culbertson, too, was probably a surprise. At the turn of the century, the hardscrabble cow town boasted thirteen saloons that stayed open around the clock, and shooting sprees and gunfights occurred with surprising frequency. The hotel accommodations were certainly rustic. Homesteaders who bunked overnight in the town's St. Paul House might have hoped that its name indicated a metropolitan sensibility, like that of the elegant St. Paul Hotel in St. Paul, Minnesota. On the contrary, after 1907, Culbertson's version had bullet holes in the lobby ceiling, put there by a band of cowboys who had ridden inside on their horses, guns blazing.[1]

The introduction to Culbertson, however, was just the beginning of the surprises that awaited homesteaders as they set about securing a land claim, meeting the requirements to prove it up, and adjusting to harsh living conditions. To find a homestead, settlers typically employed the services of a land locator who, for a price, would help them select a quarter-section (160 acres) before 1909 or, after the passage of the Enlarged Homestead Act, a half-section (320 acres). The locator might also accompany them to the claim. The location and

Seemingly endless prairie greeted homesteaders who came to Sheridan County in the 1910s. [Olson Bros., photographer, Library of Congress, LC-USZ62-37394]

quality of the property often depended on the skill and honesty of the locator. Although the prairie appeared fairly flat and undifferentiated, in fact, the elevation of Sheridan County ranges from roughly nineteen hundred to twenty-six hundred feet, and the topography is dotted by marshlands, alkali lakes, rugged shale escarpments, creeks, sandstone bluffs, and three sizeable lakes. A farm near one of the lakes or the Big Muddy River, the county's main waterway (which is most of the time more mud than river), conferred definite advantages. Good farm sites with all of the necessities—fertile soil, access to water, and some shelter from the winds that scoured the plains—were in short supply.[2]

After locating a claim, the homesteader submitted the necessary documents and paid a filing fee of twenty-two dollars at the U.S. Land Office. The law allowed homesteaders a period of six months before requiring them to reside on their claims, so many chose to return to their homes back east in order to save money for their move to Montana. Taking a leave of absence, however, was a risky decision since many settlers came back to Sheridan County six months later to find that a claim jumper had filed on their land. For instance, when he arrived in Culbertson in 1907, William Hass walked thirty miles north from the train station to claim land near Antelope. There, he paid a carpenter ninety dollars to build him a shack. When he returned the next year, he found a squatter on his claim; the carpenter he had hired asserted that a fire had destroyed Hass's shack. "If this had happened," Hass wrote, "the ashes of the fire had done a pretty good disappearing act in one year—no sign of them anywhere. Even the nails had burned up."[3]

Sometimes when they found squatters had taken over their hastily made claims, settlers fought back. For example, in the Volmer commu-

nity, a group of homesteaders formed what they referred to as a vigilante committee under the leadership of Hans Rasmussen (who would one day become a leading member of the Communist Party in the area). The committee would wait until the claim jumper was gone and then, under the cover of darkness, simply pick up his tiny shack and move it off their friend's claim.[4] Most settlers, however, did not risk the consequences of fighting for their jumped claims and simply took land in another part of the county. William Hass, for instance, decided not to enter into a dispute and walked another twenty miles northwest to claim land in what would become the Outlook community. His walk back to the train station took twenty-four hours, but his trouble was rewarded several months later when he returned to find that the claim was still his. Hass had chosen land with some of the area's best soil; he had no way of foreseeing that he would become one of the most successful farmers and richest men in Sheridan County, or that his future wife would be an active member of the county's Communist Party.

For a newcomer like Hass, erecting a shelter on a claim was a top priority, not only for protection from the elements, but as a way of demonstrating to claim jumpers that the land was unavailable. Yet another detail neglected in advertisements about the region was the lack of building materials. Trees were scarce and building supplies costly: in 1911, rough pine and fir lumber ranged in price from $22.00 to $30.00 per thousand feet; shingles were $4.00 per thousand; nails were $17.50 per keg. Furthermore, it was often inconvenient to travel to the nearest lumberyards in Culbertson or Ambrose, North Dakota. One bachelor homesteader found a creative solution: he used a wooden piano crate for shelter until he was able to build something more spacious. For those lacking piano crates, sod houses proved a popular option. Homesteaders used horse- or oxen-drawn plows to turn over the prairie soil, from which the chunks of sod were cut and stacked into thick-walled houses. Usually, the dirt-floored sod house had a roof of sapling poles covered with tar paper and then sod. Though sod houses were neither clean nor glamorous, they had the advantages of being warmer in the winter, cooler in the summer, and vastly less expensive than frame houses.[5]

Just as the scarcity of trees made building a log cabin out of the question, it also complicated the task of keeping warm, heating water, and cooking. If they could be found, old bison bones could be burned, but more common sources of heating material were "cow and buffalo chips"—dried manure. Manure was plentiful on the prairie, but it had some drawbacks as fuel. In addition to their pungent aroma, chips were populated with fleas, which rode into the house on the chips or on the clothing of whoever gathered them.[6]

The region's newest residents would also learn how unforgiving the prairie climate could be. Montana truly was, and is, a state of climatic extremes, where the difference between the highest and lowest recorded temperatures is 187 degrees (-70 degrees at Rogers Pass on January 20, 1954, and 117 degrees at Medicine Lake and Glendive on July 5, 1937) and where shifts of over 40 degrees in a few minutes and 103 degrees overnight have been recorded. Sheridan County is no different from the rest of the state in this regard. Subzero temperatures and driving winds characterize the long, brutal winters. The average snowfall is comparatively low by Montana standards, but the prairie winds are capable of stirring even a few inches of snow into tall, rigid drifts, which, depending on the objects in their paths, can become small mountains. Snow in Sheridan County often flies as early as October and as late as April, and at least trace amounts have been recorded in each month but June. The growing season averages 123 days, certainly longer than places like Butte (78 days) or Wisdom (21 days), but nearly a month shorter than Montana's "banana belt" in the Billings area (151 days). Although summers tend to be temperate, they occasionally bring drought or hail; flash floods and tornadoes have been known to occur as well, though they are infrequent.[7]

The homesteaders quickly learned about northeastern Montana's bitter and occasionally lethal winters. One killer blizzard began on New Year's Eve 1906 and continued through New Year's Day with winds in excess of forty miles per hour and temperatures dipping to 30 degrees below zero. The only good fortune for livestock caught in this storm was that most of northeastern Montana was unfenced range. Caught in a winter storm, cattle instinctively turn away from the wind and walk to

Ole Galland with his sod house and horse-drawn harrow. [Courtesy Marvin Wagnild]

keep warm, continuing to move until the storm has passed. When the 1906 blizzard subsided, two farmers discovered that their 300 head of cattle had "gone with the wind." At the end of a two-day trail ride, they found the 150 surviving cattle on the main streets of Williston, North Dakota, nearly one hundred miles away.[8] During the year of the Big Blizzard, as it was sometimes called, another farmer lost four thousand of his seven thousand sheep.

During these long and punishing winters, some farmers simply ran out of feed for their livestock, as John Egeland did in 1907. His cattle

James Lodahl and his sod shack, circa 1910s. [MHS Photograph Archives, PAc 77-94 VI-9.8 center]

had already been weakened by the tough winter when bad weather struck. Egeland wrote: "[F]irst came a sleet storm which was followed by a cold spell and one of the worst blizzards I have ever seen. It was too much for the hungry cattle and dead animals were to be found everywhere. That spring 'skinners' would remove the hides, let them freeze flat and would then haul them into town in a hay rack; they would be paid a dollar for each hide; the rancher didn't get much out of the deal but the dogs and coyotes lived well."[9]

In the summer months, too, farmers' fortunes hung on the vagaries of the weather. Drought was a constant worry, particularly in a place where irrigation is impractical, if not impossible. In a region that averages only thirteen inches of moisture annually, an inch of rain and the time of the season during which it falls means the difference between a bumper crop of wheat or a below-average yield.[10] Rainstorms, however, brought the possibility of hail, and with no reliable weather forecasts, homesteaders could only watch the western sky for suspicious, gray-white cloud banks forming on hot summer afternoons or evenings and hope for the best. Depending on when the hail fell and the diameter of the hailstones, of course, the garden and the fields might be largely unaffected or a season's labors could be completely devastated in seconds.

In the era before federal crop insurance, hailstorms were often catastrophic to a family's fortunes, as was the case for Frederick and Florence Blackmore, who watched from their house as hail pulverized their crop. Afterward, the couple surveyed the property, wondering how they would feed their family until another crop could be planted and harvested. Their children begged to use the hailstones to make ice cream, a rare summertime treat for people without refrigeration. The Blackmores conceded and made ice cream with strawberry jam, postponing their worries for the moment.[11]

Natural disasters came in other forms, and adding to a homesteader's worries were the firestorms ignited by lightning and sometimes by the ash spewed from passing trains. The gusty winds in the region made fire difficult to contain, and written accounts of the period are peppered with stories of prairie fires during which smoke blackened the sky to the point that chickens roosted during the day. Settlers plowed firebreaks religiously, but they were often inadequate barriers to the infernos that swept over the land.

Even if they evaded weather-related natural disasters, farmers still had to contend with grasshoppers and army worms as well as noxious weeds such as leafy spurge, field bindweed, and Canada thistle. And there was also the matter of commodity prices. During the mid-1870s, the first years that statistics were recorded for wheat production in Montana, the average price per bushel hovered slightly above one dollar. But by the time the new homesteaders were harvesting their first crops in the northeastern corner of the state, the price of grain had plunged. Between the years 1906 and 1912, for example, wheat averaged about sixty-five cents per bushel. In fact, from 1883 until the United States geared up to enter World War I, the average price never exceeded one dollar.[12]

Given all of these challenges, the new Montanans had to be hardy or they simply could not persist on the prairie. Even the endlessly optimistic prose of *Montana,* the handbook published by the Montana Bureau of Agriculture, Labor, and Industry, acknowledged that "[t]he task . . . of making a farm out of raw land is not an easy one, and Montana is no place for the idler, the penniless, the feeble in will or body."[13]

Whether they planned to farm or to take up some other occupation, the newcomers who arrived in Sheridan County during the first decade of the twentieth century would soon learn that their new home bore characteristics of the Wild West. Their introduction to the lawlessness of the prairie, if it had not begun upon arrival in Culbertson, might commence on the stagecoach ride to Plentywood. To get to Plentywood on the stagecoach, passengers paid three dollars per person and twenty-five cents per small package, a pricey option but more convenient than

Soren Larson rented George Harshbarger's steam plow to turn the sod on the Two Triangles Farm in 1912. [Henry B. Syverud, photographer, MHS Photograph Archives, PAc 77-94 VI-15.5]

walking. Soon, however, passengers would learn it was a safer alternative too as they saw the driver wore a gun belt with two revolvers and kept a rifle close at hand. Indeed, Sheridan County's proximity to the Canadian border, with its possibilities for eluding U.S. law enforcement, made the area popular with horse thieves, cattle rustlers, and outlaws of all stripes. The notorious horse thief "Dutch" Henry Ieuch reportedly gave Plentywood its name when he encountered a group of weary cowboys who were trying in vain to cook their dinner over a fire of cow chips. As the cowboys grumbled about their circumstance, Henry told them that if they traveled up the creek, they would find "plenty wood." The name stuck, as did Dutch Henry, who built a hide-out near Daleview and made it available to a host of other outlaws.[14]

Residents who lived along the stage route became accustomed to seeing plenty of tough characters, some of whom showed up at the homesteaders' front doors. Fortunately, most farmers and ranchers were not the outlaws' victims, but their reluctant hosts, allowing men to bunk overnight on their way to North Dakota with stolen horses. Kermit Ueland recalled, "The code was to ask no questions but give them food and lodging." According to Annie Ator, "Hospitality was extended without question to all travelers in the pioneer days. Men considered outlaws . . . were no exception." Ator's father even tended to the bullet wound of Tom Ryan, the robber who had been shot in a bank heist across the North Dakota line.[15]

As the outlaw era drew to a close by 1910, the growing town of Plentywood was developing characteristics many residents saw as a source of concern. In the early teens, the Great Northern employed about five hundred men as it built a spur line from Culbertson to Plentywood, while the Minneapolis, St. Paul and Sault Ste. Marie Railroad, known as the Soo Railroad, employed another five hundred in the nearby community of Raymond. With so many men in need of recreation, Plentywood developed a peripheral economy. Frank Livingston described the scene: "On Saturday night, many from both [the Great Northern and Soo railroads] flocked to one saloon in Plentywood and then the fights started. The saloon ran 24 hours and . . . several times I saw transients come tumbling out of the saloon into the alley. I was told the saloon had a big bouncer. Saturday night was no time to be loafing on a side of the street on the trail to the Red Light District. . . . There were holdups, stabbings, and drunken brawls regularly on the weekends."[16]

The red-light district consisted of three or four brothels in and around Plentywood. When they were not at work, the well-dressed professional women strolled the town's streets and shopped at Kitzenberg's Style Shop. According to the proprietor, Lillian Kitzenberg, they were willing to spend as much as two hundred dollars on a dress and often wore expensive perfume. One of the most infamous bawdy houses was the "Chicken Ranch" in rural Plentywood. The reputation of the ranch was well established among the worldly members of the community, but one family's experience reflects the innocence of many other locals. Word had gotten out about a chicken farm south of Plentywood, and Outlook resident Sadie Wagnild decided to replenish her flock by dropping in at the establishment. She was accompanied on the trip by her husband and small child, who later remembered seeing a glamorous young woman in full makeup sitting on a window sill and gazing out at the unlikely sight of a family pulling up to the brothel. It took only a moment for Sadie to realize her error, at which point she declared, "This is *no* chicken ranch!"[17]

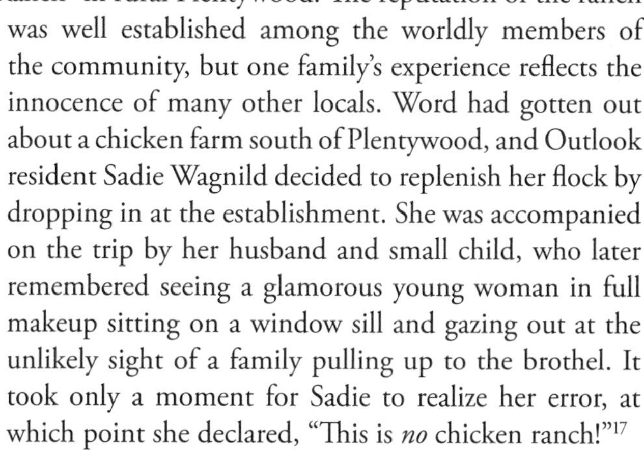

Although the prevalence of bar fights, muggings, and brothels might have indicated otherwise, law

The stage brought mail and passengers to Plentywood.
[Courtesy Mike Michels]

The Dagmar Record

Two Good Men Foully Murdered

SHERIFF T. A. COURTNEY AND DEPUTY SHERIFF DICK BURMESTER MURDERED IN COLD BLOOD LAST FRIDAY

THE SLAYED VICTIMS OF A "BAD" NIGGER.

As the news of the murder of T. A. Courtney and Richard Burmester flashed over the wire Friday afternoon the citizens of Sheridan county met with a shock from which it will take many days for them to recover. It was first impossible to realize the truthfulness of the reports, and as they were confirmed the citizens of the different towns, where these men were so well known, were thrown into a turmoil of excitement and every available auto was pressed into

bullet crashing through the neck severing the jugular vein and coming out the left shoulder, causing almost instant death as he fell to the ground.

Gave No Chance.

Like a flash the nigger turned the gun on Burmester, the first shot entering the right shoulder and passing through the lung, and as Burmester pulled his gun the nigger fired the second shot which shattered Burmester's right hand and knocked the gun from him. He then turned the

IN MEMORIUM

OBITUARY.

Thomas A. Courtney was born at Forest City, Minn., on the 19th day of March, 1877, and at the time of his untimely death was thirty-six years, two weeks and two days old

OBITUARY.

Richard Burmester was born in the little village of Idagrove, Iowa, in the spring of 1880, and was at the time of his death thirty-three years and a few weeks of age

Joe Dolin reported the murders of sheriff Thomas A. Courtney and deputy sheriff Richard Burmester in Mondak in the Dagmar Record, *April 11, 1918. Courtney's obituary is on the left and Burmester's on the right.* [MHS Photograph Archives, PAc 77-94 v4-71.435]

enforcement worked continually to contain the "Wild West" elements of Sheridan County. Plentywood's first peace officer, Ben Day, for example, was said to make regular use of his nightstick. According to the city's first mayor, George E. Bolster, Officer Day would "walk up to a tough, slug him, pick him up, toss him across a cart and take him off to jail." Bolster noted, "I needed someone like him to keep the town from getting too wild." Day served out his career in law enforcement only to be later gunned down in a fight. Indeed, a career in law enforcement was not without its risks. In 1913, just two months after being selected county sheriff, Tom Courtney and his deputy, Richard Burmester, responded to a routine request to assist officers in Mondak, in the southeastern part of the county. As they attempted to arrest a worker from the Great Northern bridge-construction camp who had been disturbing the peace, Courtney was shot and killed by the suspect, who then turned his gun on Burmester. The railroad dispatched a special train to take the critically wounded Burmester to the nearest hospital, but he died before the train arrived at its destination. The suspect surrendered and was jailed, only to be hanged and his corpse mutilated by an angry crowd.[18]

Taken together, the challenges and worries associated with living on the untamed prairies were enormous. Yet, despite these difficulties, homesteaders flocked to northeastern Montana. In 1900, Valley County, from which Sheridan County would later be carved, consisted of over 13,000 square miles and had roughly 4,300 inhabitants, of whom 2,253 were listed in the census as "white." By 1910, the population of Valley County had swollen to 13,630 (8,981 of whom were "native/white"), an increase of more than 200 percent in ten years. The entire county was considered "rural" (meaning that no towns had a population exceeding 2,500). By 1920, the population of Sheridan County alone stood at nearly 14,000. Plentywood, the county's largest town, could boast 888 inhabitants.[19]

These new Montanans were tempered by the hardships they endured: the unforgiving climate of the plains, the lawlessness of the frontier, and the vagaries of the agricultural economy. Those challenges, together with the social, cultural, and political backgrounds of the homesteaders, would make them especially receptive to the emerging farmers' movement of the 1910s and 1920s. The movement's message, grounded in the persuasive strategies of other farming and mining organizations in America, would be skillfully manipulated by local political leaders, setting the stage for the astonishing rise of Communism in Sheridan County.

Martin L. Rostad on his homestead at Coalridge, 1910. [Henry B. Syverud, photographer, MHS Photograph Archives, PAc 77-94 VI-10.C32]

CHAPTER 3

The Agrarian Myth and Prairie Politics

Precursors to Radicalism

In light of Cold War–inspired notions about Communism—totalitarianism, draconian restrictions on personal property and freedoms, military expansion—it is difficult to fathom how such an "un-American" movement could achieve widespread acceptance and success in rural Montana. However, the northeastern Montana farmers' movement, the culture in which it arose, and the types of rhetorical appeals it would use were well grounded in traditional and very widely held beliefs about the role of farmers in American life. Additionally, the Sheridan County Communists had the advantage of building on a foundation of homegrown populism and labor activism that had been established elsewhere on the Great Plains in the nineteenth century, which itself drew upon the ideology of the Revolutionary period.

In the early days of the Republic, American culture was rife with notions about what it meant to farm and to be a farmer, expressed in images that would undergird and enliven the message of the Communist Party in Montana a century and a half later. Indeed, the tendency to romanticize farm life dates back to the era of the Revolution. A contributor to the idealization of farming was St. John de Crèvecœur, a French immigrant who took up farming in New York and wrote *Letters from an American Farmer,* which became popular reading during the 1780s. Crèvecœur contrasted the excellent conditions in America with those in Europe, noting that the nation "from Nova Scotia to Florida" was composed, with exceptions in a few towns, of people who tilled the soil. These tillers, he said, were "animated with the spirit of an industry which is unfettered and unrestrained, because each person works for himself." He described farmers as having a "great degree of sagacity" and being "purified" by their cultivation of the land.[1]

Crèvecœur's sentiments were echoed by Thomas Jefferson, a gentleman farmer who is well known for his admiration of the nation's agricultural producers. Jefferson famously wrote, "Those who labour in the earth are the chosen people of God, if ever he had a chosen people, whose breasts he has made his peculiar deposit for substantial and genuine virtue." Moreover, Jefferson claimed, "Cultivators of the earth are the most virtuous and independent citizens." Benjamin Franklin, as well, praised the "industrious frugal farmers."[2]

Crèvecœur, Jefferson, and a host of other writers helped establish what historian Henry Nash Smith has called the myth of the "garden of the world," a compelling, poetic narrative about the vast virgin land of America's interior. Accompanying the "garden of the world" myth was the agrarian myth, which, as described by Smith and extended by fellow historian Richard Hofstadter, is a set of ideas leading Americans to idealize farm life and farmers as uniquely free, independent, honest, and good. The myth portrays the yeoman farmer as a moral, healthy, happy person, the ideal citizen of a democracy and someone called by God to work the land. The agrarian myth, Hofstadter writes, is "a kind of homage that Americans have paid to the fancied innocence of their origins."[3]

Amid the conflict over the expansion of slave-holding among newly admitted states and the Civil War itself, there arose a demand that free land be provided for citizens willing to create new farms in the West. The Homestead Act was passed in 1862. In the era following the war, the Desert Land Act of 1877 and the rapid expansion of the railroads made it possible for farmers to claim large plots of dry land on the Great Plains. This land sustained crops different from those usually grown east of the Mississippi, required more machinery to farm, and was farther from major grain mills and terminals. At the same time, farmers faced a constellation of issues related to their role in the market economy: it was now possible for farmers to purchase land, equipment, and seed on credit; they could produce crops for sale rather than merely for subsistence; and thus farmers would now have to accept all of the risks and burdens associated with this new brand of entrepreneurism. Agricultural production boomed with the proliferation of new technology and an increased number of farmers, but production exceeded domestic demand, and consequently, the wholesale price index for farm products

In the 1870s, when founder Oliver Hudson Kelley (front row, right) started the Grange, he envisioned a fraternal group that would promote farm cooperatives, engage in lobbying, and educate rural residents. [*History of the Grange Movement* (1873; repr., Philadelphia, 1969), following p. 15]

took a dive during the second half of the nineteenth century, declining 50 percent between 1865 and 1895.[4]

To say the least, the late 1800s were a time of profound change. With the rise of American industry, agriculture lost its role as the driving force behind the American economy. Metropolitan areas gained population and political power as workers left their rural homes. However, as the landscape of farming changed, the agrarian myth of old remained the same, and the resulting dissonance between the agrarian myth and the harsh realities of farming created fertile ground for a number of organizations devoted to education, reform, and protest in the rural Midwest and West. Throughout the early farmers' movement, activists called upon the symbolic vocabulary and images popularized by Crèvecœur and Jefferson a century before, and they fashioned persuasive appeals that would reappear, for better or worse, in the ideologies of future agrarian organizations.

The National Grange was the first of a long line of national agricultural organizations. Officially known as the Order of Patrons of Husbandry, the Grange was founded in 1867 by Minnesota farmer

Oliver Hudson Kelley, who envisioned a fraternal group that would promote farm cooperatives, engage in lobbying, and educate rural residents. The Grange also emphasized social interaction among country people, and Grange halls began to sprout up, serving as venues for lectures, town meetings, dances, and community potluck dinners.[5]

Meetings were central to the Grange's success, and the organization trained its masters and lecturers, both men and women, in Grange principles and practices. Grange masters were implored to enact "Good Grange Habits," including calling members by name, just as "the shepherd of a flock calleth his sheep by name," and being "A Live Wire" who "radiate[s] belief and joy in the Grange movement." Leaders were also directed to take the realities of members' lives into account. For example, they were instructed to always begin and end their programs on time, enabling members to return to their homes by midnight because "no farm family can profitably endure the strain of late hours for a series of years."[6]

Since a meeting was only as good as its program, program planning was to be undertaken with extraordinary care. The person responsible for planning programs, the Grange lecturer, played a key role. Like other officers, lecturers recited a creed, which stated: "I believe in a program for every meeting. I believe that, as a Lecturer, I should love to do my work. . . . I believe that even the entertainment features of the program should lead to thought. . . . I believe a Grange Lecturer must have hope; exert tact; plan far ahead; often show more confidence in members than they feel in themselves; keep her program disappointments to herself; *and smile.* I believe, finally, I should today resolve to beat my own record."[7]

According to Grange literature, program planning was an art. Each one was to include both serious and entertaining components, and lectures, music, recitations, and dramatizations were all recommended means of offering education and entertainment. During the Grange's early years, programs tended to focus on improved farming techniques, while women received tips on more efficiency in household economy and domestic chores. Thomas A. Woods notes that the Grange also made use of religiously oriented rituals that "taught practical and moral lessons" and encouraged members to develop virtuous qualities.[8]

Grange rhetoric emphasized the message of farmer empowerment. In his speeches, Ignatius Donnelly, one of the most effective and ideological of the Grange lecturers, described the Grange's mission as righteous and the organization as dedicated to improving farmers' lives. He explained that the Grange was a "fulcrum . . . from which to move the world" and that it would "wage eternal war against wrong and injustice everywhere." His position was echoed in one of the Grange's fight songs, whose lyrics proclaimed:

> Down with th' oppressor, up with our star,
> We will rally to the Grange,
> Our rights to maintain,
> Shouting the Farmer's cry of Freedom.

This call for social justice would frequently be made by later farmers' movements, including northeastern Montana's Communist campaigns.[9]

Granger rhetoric was also important in that it encouraged farmers to consider their role in the context of the larger economic system. If the agrarian myth of the yeoman working joyfully and independently was no longer consistent with the realities of late-nineteenth-century farming, then the Grange would promote an image of farmers as important and knowledgeable (or at least educable) members of the economic system who were standing up to assert their rights. Grangers also would not hesitate to identify those who would deprive farmers of their rights. In this effort, the Grange made occasional use of appeals that would become commonplace in farmer activism, that is, pitting the producers against nonproducers. As banners in an 1873 Grange Independence Day parade asserted: "This organization is opposed to railroad steals, salary steals, bank steals, and every other form of thieving by which the farmers and laboring classes are robbed of the legitimate fruits of their labor."[10]

For the most part, however, the Grange's approach was mild and rather ecumenical. It held that all classes of people were essential, that none should be privileged, and that farmers should concentrate mainly on improving themselves.[11] Although its language about oppressors and laboring classes would be repeated, notably in the 1930s-era Communist rhetoric in Sheridan County, the Grange's importance to future farmers' movements lay in its demonstration of the importance of creating a social realm, a sense of community, and a bond of identification with the people whom it sought to enlist.

As difficult times for farmers persisted and the Grange seemed to be making little headway in bringing about reform, its popularity waned. However, the organization did succeed in creating a positive climate and a membership base for a number of third parties that emerged in the Midwest at about the same time, one of which was the Greenback Party. As its name suggests, the Greenback Party concerned itself

Grangers articulated many of the concerns that later attracted Sheridan County farmers to radical politics. In this cartoon, the Grange farmer tries to awaken the public to the dangers of the railroad monopoly. [*Daily Graphic*, September 16, 1873, in *Granger Country: A Pictorial History of the Burlington Railroad,* ed. Lloyd Lewis and Stanley Pargellis (Boston, 1949), 82]

with monetary policy. It emerged in reaction to a post–Civil War plan to return to the gold standard, which the government had abandoned in favor of greenbacks as a means of financing the Union effort. The ensuing conflict was essentially between those favoring "hard money," who agreed with a plan to return to the gold standard and to diminish the supply of greenbacks in circulation (eastern bankers and speculators tended to fall into this camp), and those who advocated the retention of greenbacks (particularly those in debtor groups such as farmers). The Greenback Party's view was that "money was simply a means of keeping count of one's labor. It needed only government fiat, not intrinsic value."[12]

As a political party, the Greenbackers employed a more ideological rhetoric than had the Grangers. The image of the oppressor and thief,

Greenbackers claimed that a return to the gold standard would impose an additional burden on farmers and other working-class Americans like those portrayed here barely clinging to life in spite of mortgages, debt, taxes, low commodity prices, high transportation costs, and low wages. [*Review of Reviews*, November 1896, in John D. Hicks, *The Populist Revolt* (Minneapolis, Minn., 1931), 376]

present in some Grange rhetoric, found new life and centrality in the arguments of the Greenbackers. In fact, the Greenbackers portrayed the economic system in increasingly stark and adversarial terms, attacking "the money power," "the moneyed oligarchy," and "the bonded aristocracy." They were also less concerned than the Grangers with farmer education and self-improvement, concentrating instead on class consciousness. Specifically, the Greenbackers claimed that, with a return to the gold standard, banks and capitalists would be able "to compel the people to cultivate the earth, and to gather and market its productions mainly for [the capitalists'] use, reserving for themselves of the poorer kinds a bare subsistence." Some Greenbackers took the argument a step further, arguing that greenbacks, which had "freed the chattel slave" during the Civil War, would some day "free the wage slave" if they were retained. The idea of freeing people from economic slavery would be passed down to the descendant radical movements to follow.[13]

Scholar Paul Crawford notes that, although the Greenback Party held attraction for many in the agrarian movement of the 1870s, "only a small fraction of the farmers of the nation deserted the old parties to cast ballots as Greenbackers." Farmers' main concerns were related to the "immediate, tangible problems" that they faced in daily life.[14] As the Grange weakened during the 1880s and interest in the Greenback Party waned, the way was cleared for a new political party—the People's Party—that emerged to fill the void.

The Populist movement originated with various Farmers' Alliance groups, most notably with the Southern Farmers' Alliance, officially founded in 1877. The alliances were not explicitly partisan when they began but, like the Grange, served educational and social purposes. Also like the Grange, they relied on the power of oratory to recruit and motivate members. In 1884, for example, the Southern Farmers' Alliance employed S. O. Daws to travel and lecture throughout Texas. Daws spoke to farmers about the forces that influenced their plight, urging them "to stand as a great conservative body against the encroachment of monopolies and in opposition to the growing corruption of wealth and power" and to "lift the yoke of monopoly and oppression from their necks." Similarly, fellow lecturer Mrs. S. E. V. Emery spoke about the "crimes perpetuated against the people of the country through this infernal system of legalized robbery" and asked "[who] can fathom the greed of the money shark, or set bounds to the voracity of the civilized brigand?"[15]

The Southern Farmers' Alliance's lecturer system involved the selection of a lecturer by each local chapter. These individuals then delivered public addresses, developed their skills as educators and persuaders, and often went on to speak at district and state conventions. Rhetorical theorist James Klumpp notes that the result of the Farmers' Alliance's lecturer system was a "tradition of speaking that spawned a rich public sphere constructing the farmer's problems as public concerns." Although the lecturers traveled, they were always rooted in a home chapter and thus understood and addressed matters of concern in their own communities. The lecture system was a lasting contribution to farm activism.[16]

The Farmers' Alliance, and later the People's Party, added another element to rural activism with their camp meetings, a tradition borrowed from the southern Protestant evangelical tradition. Like tent revivals, these encampments would sometimes last for days; they featured music and lectures and allowed alliance members to "renew their spiritual commitment to the order."[17] Camp meetings were especially attractive in that farm families were often relatively isolated. Having an occasion to gather and socialize with their neighbors served as a strong incentive for many farmers and their families to attend these meetings, which became an effective way of winning or renewing the support of alliance members. And they served as an excellent example for organizers of later farm groups.

The growth of the Farmers' Alliance in Texas and elsewhere spawned third-party political action and resulted in the first convention of the People's Party in 1892 in Nebraska. The preamble to the Populists' convention platform claimed that "governmental injustice" had "bred two great classes—tramps and millionaires" and called for overcoming this "vast conspiracy against mankind" that "forebodes terrible social convulsions, the destruction of civilization, or the establishment of an absolute despotism." The platform advocated government ownership of railroads, telephones, and telegraphs and instituting an economy based on greenbacks and "free silver."[18]

As they would be in later movements, stump speakers were important to the success of the Populist movement, which benefited from the Farmers' Alliance lecture system that had developed forty thousand speakers across the nation. In his study of these "Populist spellbinders," Donald H. Ecroyd identifies the crucial role that orators played in furthering the Populist agenda, arguing that Populist orators, both male and female, made their listeners aware of the link between contemporary problems and their own plight and then showed that the solution to the problems could be found in the People's Party. "The Populist debater was a clever strategist," Ecroyd writes. "He did not permit himself to be forced onto the defensive. He took over the arguments of his opposition whenever possible—quoting opposition statements and pointing out inconsistencies in the opposition's point of view. The watchword was 'Attack!'" Employing themes made familiar by the activists who had preceded them, the Populists portrayed farmers as the members of a distinct class, one not to be confused with the wealthy, moneyed class of nonproducers who conspired to keep farmers down in order to profit from their toil.[19]

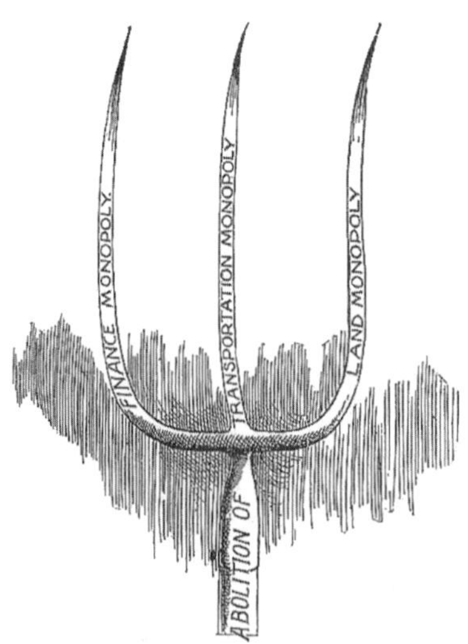

The People's Party and the Populist movement grew out of various farmers' alliances and relied on camp meetings and rousing speakers to generate support among rural residents. [www.projects.vasser.edu/1896/0319pa.jpg]

ROCKY MOUNTAIN HUSBANDMAN

$4.00 PER ANNUM.

A Journal Devoted to Agriculture, Live-stock, Home Reading, and General News.

VOL. 1. DIAMOND CITY, M. T., DECEMBER 2, 1875. NO. 2.

10 Cts. PER SINGLE COPY.

PUBLISHED WEEKLY BY R. N. SUTHERLIN, EDITOR AND PROPRIETOR.

AGRICULTURAL.

PREPARE FOR WINTER.

SMUT IN WHEAT.

Montana had twenty-three Grange locals by 1874. Although the organization languished in the state between the early 1880s and 1912, it did establish an important and long-lived Montana newspaper, the Rocky Mountain Husbandman. *The* Husbandman *masthead declared that it "is designed to be, as the name indicates, a husbandman in every sense of the term, embracing in its columns every department of Agriculture, Stock-raising, Horticulture, Social and Domestic Economy."* [*Rocky Mountain Husbandman,* December 2, 1875]

The traditions associated with the agrarian myth nurtured the Populist ideology. For example, the Populists longed for a return to an idealized bygone era when farm life was simpler and untouched by "money power" and when the status of the American farmer was revered. Populists distrusted the growing influence their urban counterparts were having on government, believing that East Coast bankers and "Wall Street millionaires" were conspiring to oppress and defraud the farmer. They blamed these characters for setting discriminatory freight rates and standards and for encouraging economic depressions, bankruptcies, and foreclosures.[20] Such rhetorical tactics were to resound in later radical movements and would be an essential element of northeastern Montana's political battles.

As for the actual presence of these farmer and political groups in Montana, the Grange could boast twenty-three locals in Montana by 1874. It established an important and long-lived paper, the *Rocky Mountain Husbandman,* in 1875, but the organization languished between the early 1880s and 1912. Farmers' Alliance branches also appeared throughout Montana, but the local chapters were slow to set up a state organization, and they consequently dwindled as the People's Party's influence grew in the 1890s. Populism drew strong support in western Montana, particularly in the mining areas where the Populist call for immediate improvements in working conditions had immense appeal. Historian Thomas A. Clinch notes that, in Montana, the People's Party's greatest strength was not among farmers, but among "urban trade unionist[s] or middle-class, intellectual advocate[s] of reform."[21]

Some of northeastern Montana's twentieth-century radicals had direct connections to these precursor movements. For example, although the Grange's best days were over before homesteaders came to northeastern Montana, its influence was apparent when one of its members, William Bouck, after being ousted by the Washington State Grange, kicked off his organizing campaign for a similar group, the Western Progressive Farmers, in Sheridan County in late 1925. In the 1930s, the Farm Holiday Association, founded by Milo Reno, also operated in northeastern Montana. Decades before, Reno's mother had been a Granger and a Greenbacker. The most notable example, though, is that of Charles E. Taylor, the man who would leave a mark on Sheridan County unlike that of any other farmers' movement leader. Taylor's radicalism was influenced by his father, who had been involved in nearly every agrarian organization of the nineteenth century.[22] The nineteenth-century farmers' movements provided a veritable textbook on methods of persuasion to be utilized in galvanizing rural activism. Whether in demonstrating the power of organization, emphasizing the value of excellent oratory, encouraging farmers to empower themselves, starkly defining the farmers' enemies, or mobilizing popular opposition, the Grangers, Greenbackers, and Populists clearly left a legacy for northeastern Montanans. However, they were not alone in the lessons they could offer. The effects of labor activism in western Montana would also be felt, albeit indirectly, in Sheridan County.

CHAPTER 4

Mountain Politics

Radicalism in the Western Mining Districts

In the same turbulent era that gave birth to the Grange and the Greenback and People's parties, the mining areas in western Montana and other Rocky Mountain states were experimenting with their own brands of activism. In particular, the rhetorical strategies of two organizations, the Western Federation of Miners (WFM) and the Industrial Workers of the World (IWW), would find their way to the northeastern corner of Montana—as would some flesh-and-blood members of the IWW.

The Western Federation of Miners was conceived by Ed Boyce and several other miners during the time they spent in a Boise, Idaho, jail following a strike in Coeur d'Alene in 1892; the union was officially organized a year later, in Butte, Montana. From there, it rapidly gained a foothold in the West, chartering locals from Arizona to western Canadian provinces, coordinating strikes, and providing such services as sick and widow benefits and medical facilities.[1]

Many Western Federation of Miners members had "learned their political lessons in Populist schools," and during the mid-1890s, some locals openly aligned themselves with the People's Party. During its early years, the Western Federation did not seem any more radical than other trade unions; in fact, the union was officially affiliated with the conservative American Federation of Labor (AFL) in 1896. However, the positions staked out by Ed Boyce and other leaders soon began to distinguish it quite clearly from the AFL. Whereas the AFL sought collective bargaining as a means for ironing out differences in factories and

Rhetoric later used by the Sheridan County radicals was also employed by the Industrial Workers of the World and the Western Federation of Miners. For example, William D. "Big Bill" Haywood, one of the driving forces behind the Western Federation, declared in a 1905 speech: "We are here to confederate the workers of this country into a working-class movement that shall have for its purpose the emancipation of the working-class from the slave bondage of capitalism." Haywood is the tall man pictured here in dark bowler and top coat (behind the boy in the stocking cap) leading a strike in Lowell, Massachusetts in 1912. [Library of Congress, LC-DIG-ggbain-10357]

mines, Boyce argued that "there can be no harmony between employer and employee." He also identified the current wage system as "slavery in its worst form."[2]

One of the converts to the Western Federation of Miners was William Haywood, later to be known as "Big Bill." A larger-than-life presence, Haywood became a driving force behind the organization. His past put him in good stead with the membership: he was a former cowboy, homesteader, and miner who had been injured in a mining accident. He cultivated his image as an outlaw and brawler, but he was also a gifted, forceful, and energetic speaker who eventually became famous nationwide.[3]

While he served as the Western Federation of Miners's secretary-treasurer, Haywood's opinions eventually shifted from promoting cooperation with the AFL to condemning it. He also took positions that often seemed at odds with one another, such as advising strikers to forgo violence yet proclaiming to fellow Socialists that sabotage would help bring about revolution. As Melvyn Dubofsky, a labor historian and one of Haywood's biographers, notes, the man was not troubled by the inconsistencies in his positions, and he made up for them with his tireless and effective efforts as an organizer and administrator. During Haywood's tenure with the Western Federation, the organization united with the Socialist Party of America, which had been formed by the fusion of the Socialist Labor Party and Socialist Democratic Party of America in 1901. The new party called for social and civil rights reforms, improved labor conditions and economic equality, and welfare legislation. Three years later, in 1905, Haywood and an associate from the federation attended the organizational convention of the new Industrial Workers of the World, a radical labor union, many of whose members were also Socialists. As the largest of several groups involved in the founding of the IWW, the Western Federation shared the greatest number of new members with the organization.[4]

Haywood gave a speech at the beginning of the 1905 IWW convention that sounded themes remarkably similar to those employed in early farm-activist rhetoric. "We are here to confederate the workers of this country into a working-class movement that shall have for its purpose the emancipation of the working-class from the slave bondage of capitalism," he said. As had much of the farm-movement rhetoric, the preamble of the IWW constitution clearly differentiated between the producing and nonproducing classes: "The working class and the employing class have nothing in common. There can be no peace so long as hunger and want are found among millions of working people and the few, who make up the employing class, have all the good things of life."[5]

At its 1905 convention, the IWW established an educational bureau, which produced the newspapers and periodicals that played an important role in spreading the organization's message. The IWW published over sixty newspapers during its first fifteen years, and IWW members, who came to be known as "Wobblies" for reasons that are unclear, mobilized their ranks to travel around the country, speaking on street corners or public meeting houses, selling or giving away pamphlets and other materials, and organizing the masses. Street oratory allowed the IWW not only to build its membership, raise money, and rouse sympathy for striking miners, but to counter the mainstream press's accusations about the Wobblies. The IWW also printed and distributed red song cards and directed that these songs be sung at street meetings in order to attract crowds for the speakers who would follow. Wobblies understood the value of creating a public spectacle as a means of attracting an audience.[6]

As the IWW message began to spread throughout the West, Wobblies met with resistance from the press, law enforcement, public citizens, and even the U.S. Army. Local officials recognized the power of street organizing and sought to undermine it by passing ordinances that prohibited street oratory. The IWW often fought bloody battles in their struggles for free speech, the first of which occurred in 1909 in Spokane, Washington. Wobblies who were arrested and fined frequently encountered terrible conditions in jail.[7] Yet the speaking continued. Free-speech battles were subsequently waged in Missoula, Fresno, San Diego, and elsewhere.

Although the IWW is remembered today mostly for its anarchistic and violent tactics, its rhetoric often relied on religious references, images, and claims. In his assessment of the parallels between the Wobblies' and American Protestants' use of music, as well as the religious claims and references in the IWW's newspapers, Donald Winters Jr. notes that "the soul of the Wobblies [was] nurtured by solidarity, rooted in class struggle and vitalized by religious zeal for the working class."[8]

Winters's observations about the IWW press are particularly relevant as they relate to the persuasive strategies later employed by farmers' movement leaders in northeastern Montana. Winters claims that the IWW press viewed religion as mainly a personal matter, although it at times utilized the character of Jesus, often portraying him as a hobo and rebel who stood up for the working class. Members of the Wobbly press also contrasted "pure" Christianity with American militarism and described what they viewed as the hypocrisy of organizations such as the Salvation Army and the Young Men's Christian Association.[9] These were positions that would be taken by northeastern Montana's radicals during the 1920s and 1930s as well.

However, if the IWW successfully adapted religious rhetoric to their purposes, some of their other strategies were less effective. Historian Aileen Kraditor notes that Wobblies sometimes "seemed intent on doing all they could to prove their enemies right." She cites examples such as Haywood's insistence on publishing inflammatory pamphlets, including one on sabotage, which he planned to publish around the time of the United States' entry into World War I. (The IWW executive committee overrode Haywood's decision.) In 1911, William Z. Foster, then a Wobbly, published a pamphlet that declared: "The syndicalist is . . . 'unscrupulous' in his choice of weapons to fight his every-day battles . . . with capitalism. He allows no considerations of 'legality,' religion, patriotism, 'honor,' 'duty,' etc., to stand in the way of his adoption of effective tactics. . . . With him the end justifies the means." Kraditor also notes that IWW rhetoric often insulted its working-class members. The editor of the IWW's *Industrial Worker* replied in print to the "apologetic, half-baked industrialists" who had asked that the newspaper moderate its language, saying that he had "no time to stop and 'patch fig leaves to hide the naked truth.'"[10]

In a sense, the lesson that northeastern Montana radicals took from the Wobblies was contradictory. In its religious appeals, the IWW showed sensitivity to prevailing cultural norms and values. Yet, at the same time, the organization often refused to moderate its calls for sabotage and other types of direct action or to present such calls subtly enough to be inoffensive. As northeastern Montanans would do, the Wobblies cast themselves as defenders of the voiceless working class. They launched appeals using speeches, songs, newspapers, and other printed materials in a way that created a compelling narrative and made the IWW position understandable to workers. Historian Salvatore Salerno notes that IWW "challenged the definition of American life imposed and diffused by government and business elites, while actively shaping a dynamic and revolutionary conception of workers' culture."[11] Yet, if Kraditor is correct, even as the IWW constructed a dynamic vision for workers, it was also capable of alienating current or potential members by using rhetoric in a way that belittled them, a habit the Montana Communists would manage to avoid.

In northeastern Montana, during the radical years, traveling Wobblies were comparatively welcome, particularly in certain quarters. Wobblies often passed through Sheridan County, where they were unlikely to be harassed by the radical sheriff, Rodney Salisbury, or his deputies. In fact, one Wobbly reportedly was recruited to deliver retribution to a local restaurateur who had withdrawn his advertisements from the radicals' newspaper, the *Producers News.* According to local historian Magnus Aasheim, the Wobbly visited the Elgin Café, planted a dead mouse in his soup, and caused a scene until proprietor Jim Popescu "barged into the dining area and put the maligner on the run."[12]

Other residents of Sheridan County had tangential relationships to the Wobblies. For instance, Ira Worley, who was involved in the

(above) Democrats nominated William Jennings Bryan and Arthur Sewall for president and vice president, respectively, in Chicago on July 10, 1896. Bryan also received the nomination of the People's Party. [Library of Congress, LC-USZC2-6263]

(right) In the 1896 presidential election, Valley County electors chose the Democratic and People's Party candidate Bryan over Republican William McKinley by a narrow margin. Here Bryan, second from left, shakes hands with citizens in Hamilton on a later campaign visit to Montana. [MHS Photograph Archives, Helena, 948-089 (detail)]

founding of the *Producers News* and served as the secretary-treasurer of the People's Publishing Company in Plentywood, testified on behalf of IWW members in a conspiracy case in federal court. Charles Taylor, editor of the *News,* raised money for the defense of IWW members who were arrested in Centralia, Washington, on murder charges in 1919.[13]

While there was a certain IWW presence in Sheridan County, Wobblies were not very influential in the northeastern Montana farmers' movement. Likewise, the influence of the Western Federation of Miners on northeastern Montana politics and political rhetoric was mainly indirect. During the early years of the twentieth century, when labor radicalism rocked western Montana, the political situation in the northeastern corner of the state was relatively unremarkable. In 1896, the first presidential election after Dawson County split to make Valley County (which would eventually be subdivided into Daniels, Roosevelt, and Sheridan counties), Valley's electors chose the Democratic and People's Party candidate, William Jennings Bryan, over Republican William McKinley by a narrow margin. In fact, all of Montana's counties but two (Dawson and Custer) went with Bryan in that election.[14]

For the next few elections, Valley County's Republican leanings coexisted, oddly enough, with a slow-growing Socialist contingent. In 1900, the majority of Valley County's electors chose the Republican ticket of William McKinley and Theodore Roosevelt, giving two votes to the Social-Democrat Eugene Debs. In the next general election, the county went overwhelmingly Republican, although Eugene Debs picked up nine more electors (for a total of eleven). This pattern would hold, with electors choosing Republican William Howard Taft in 1908 and Theodore Roosevelt in 1912 and awarding an increasing number of ballots to Debs in each contest. Socialism was apparently getting a tiny toehold in Montana's northeast corner at about the same time that it was peaking in the rest of the state. The Federal Bureau of Investigation

In the next few presidential elections, Socialism gained a toehold in northeastern Montana as the votes for Socialist Eugene V. Debs, who ran for president four times between 1900 and 1912, gradually increased. [Library of Congress, LC-DIG-pga-01130]

(FBI) took note of this development, reporting later that Marxists of one sort or another had been in the area "almost since the time this county was organized" in 1913. Indeed, there were several Socialist Party chapters in Sheridan County at that time.[15]

Judging by the voting records for 1916, the first general election year after Sheridan County's creation, the Socialists had made progress in the region. The Socialist candidate for president, Allen Benson, received 3 percent of Montana's total Socialist vote from the new county. In fact, only seven of forty-one counties in the state cast more Socialist votes, and all seven were more populous than Sheridan County. The Socialist candidates for governor, Lewis J. Duncan, and the U.S. Senate, Henri La Beau, did especially well, earning 8 and 7 percent, respectively, of their total votes in Sheridan County.[16]

In the mid-teens, the Socialist cause appeared to hold some promise in northeastern Montana. A number of events would intervene, however, including World War I and the patriotism it engendered, as well as the subsequent "Red scare" of the early 1920s. Perhaps the most influential, however, was the expansion into Montana by an organization from across the North Dakota line, the Nonpartisan League (NPL), whose activities would spread throughout northeastern Montana like a "political prairie fire," in the words of historian Robert L. Morlan.

In its efforts to organize and motivate farmers to improve their lot, the NPL employed the tactics inherited from the Grange and the Farmers' Alliance. Likewise, as the NPL marshaled public speakers and writers to promote the organization and publicize its goals, it carried on the traditions associated with both the agrarian movements of the nineteenth century and labor activism. However, the Nonpartisan League was different from all the organizations that preceded it in that it was the first to make significant inroads in northeastern Montana. As it made its way west, the NPL brought a new strain of radicalism, and Sheridan County would never be the same again.

CHAPTER 5

The Nonpartisan League and the "Old Time Socialists"

The Nonpartisan League was organized in 1915 by thirty-five-year-old Arthur C. Townley, a man of remarkable vision, charisma, and political instincts. Townley had run for the North Dakota legislature on the Socialist ticket in 1914, but he later left the party to work on a new project: rather than seeking election himself, Townley planned to recruit farmers to an organization that set its sights on capturing the entire state government. Like the Populists before them, the NPL's leaders endorsed political action that would reduce the domination of farmers by the railroad, grain storage, and milling conglomerates. Specifically, the NPL advocated state ownership of terminal elevators, flour mills, and meat-packing and cold-storage plants. It also urged grain inspections under the control of the state, provision of hail insurance through the state, and the establishment of farm credit banks that would operate at cost.[1]

The platform was not revolutionary, but the NPL's plan for enacting it was: the league differed from the People's Party in that it would not be a third party at all. The name of the Nonpartisan League would never appear on the ballot. Instead, Nonpartisan Leaguers would exploit the possibilities offered by the party primary elections that had replaced party caucuses and conventions as the means of nominating major party candidates.[2] A candidate of any party who demonstrated serious commitment to the farmers' cause could receive the NPL endorsement.

Arthur C. Townley organized the Nonpartisan League in 1914–15 to spur political action that would reduce the domination of farmers by the railroad, grain storage, and milling conglomerates. Instead of fielding candidates for office itself, however, the NPL endorsed candidates of any party who demonstrated serious commitment to the farmers' cause. Here Townley addresses a NPL meeting, probably at Glencoe, Minnesota, in 1917. [State Historical Society of North Dakota, Bismarck, B0921]

At first, the task of recruiting farmers to the NPL was not difficult, especially for a person of Arthur Townley's magnetism. He was not a polished orator—in fact, he was often quite profane—but he was enthusiastic, had a dry sense of humor, and knew how to get through to farmers. He also recognized the value of persuading farmers to invest in the organization: dues were originally only $2.50, but they were worth much more to the organization in terms of ensuring the new member's commitment to the cause. "Make the rubes pay their God-damn money to join and they'll stick—stick till hell freezes over," Townley said. As the NPL picked up steam and more recruiters were needed, a correspondence course instructed them in such matters as "Techniques of Persuasion" and "How to Arouse and Hold Interest."[3]

Historian Robert Morlan notes that one of the primary appeals of the NPL was its emphasis on the need for organization. Farmers were constantly reminded that they were the only unorganized group in the nation and that they would not wield any power until they organized. Townley also preached the importance of what he called psychology but what might today be called "audience demographic analysis." Organizers were enjoined to find out what interests, attitudes, and posi-

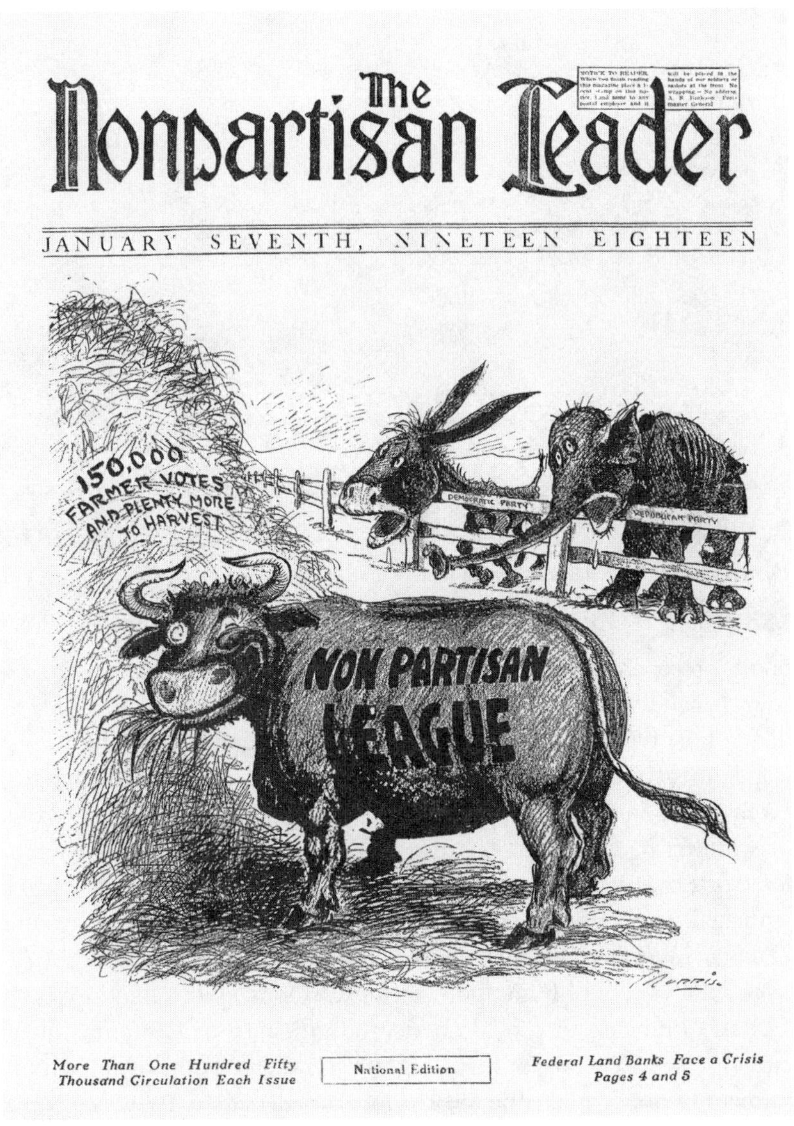

The Nonpartisan Leader

JANUARY SEVENTH, NINETEEN EIGHTEEN

More Than One Hundred Fifty Thousand Circulation Each Issue

National Edition

Federal Land Banks Face a Crisis Pages 4 and 5

Nonpartisan League newspaper, January 7, 1918.

tions particular target farmers had and then to "talk it," whether it was religion, prohibition, or hogs.[4]

The NPL also used a strategy that had proved invaluable to the Wobblies: publishing newspapers, a lot of them. In this, the IWW and the Nonpartisan League were participating in a common practice of the era. Historian Patricia Nelson Limerick notes that, even on the rugged frontier, where it seems more practical matters would have

Plentywood, 1913. [MHS Photograph Archives, Helena, 950-240]

taken precedence, newspapers appeared almost immediately when a town began to form.[5] Well into the twentieth century, most small towns had at least one weekly newspaper. In Minnesota and the Dakotas, the league took full advantage of small-town papers to spread its message. By investing in existing dailies and weeklies throughout North Dakota, or winning over editorial boards, the NPL eventually accumulated at least one league-endorsed paper in nearly every county. The league launched its own newspaper, the *Nonpartisan Leader,* in Fargo, North Dakota, in September 1915. Engaging and conversational, the *Leader* featured a variety of homespun stories, cartoons, photos, and jokes. It was also intended to provide news and guidance to league members and to serve as a means of rebutting the arguments of the organization's numerous opponents. The NPL soon broadened its influence westward, and later other *Leader*s were published in the states into which the league had expanded.[6]

In 1916, the Nonpartisan League placed Montana squarely in its sights. The *Montana Nonpartisan* began publication in Great Falls, which was also the home of the league's new state headquarters. In Montana, the NPL found ample support for its mission. Sympathetic newspapermen from Lambert to Inverness sought affiliation with the league and in the summer of 1918, labor activists in the western part of the state aligned themselves with the NPL's agenda, even opening the Nonpartisan Club in Butte. As the political prairie fire spread across

Montana, it began to attract attention beyond the Great Plains, even triggering a visit by former president Theodore Roosevelt, for whom the NPL "represented a clear and present danger to the republic," according to historian James F. Vivian. In fact, in October 1918, Roosevelt made an unexpected trip to Montana ostensibly to promote the Liberty Loan war bond effort. However, the focus of Roosevelt's speech, delivered at the new Billings civic auditorium, was not war bonds but a condemnation of the NPL. Roosevelt's invective notwithstanding, the league membership in Montana eventually reached twenty thousand, trailing only the Dakotas and Minnesota.[7]

The NPL launched its organizing offensive in northeastern Montana in the spring of 1918, sending Charles E. Taylor to Montana to start a new league paper, the weekly *Producers News*. Taylor and his wife, Agda, who was pregnant with their first child, packed up their belongings and set out for Plentywood, the Sheridan County seat. Nestled up against a ridge on the windblown prairie, Plentywood's name was slightly misleading: within the city limits, there were few trees to be found, except for those along Box Elder Creek. It was, however, the most populous town in the county, with roughly eight hundred of the county's nearly fourteen thousand residents. The town had been incorporated in 1912 and, by some accounts, was so crowded with newcomers and

Apparently the Great Northern celebrated its arrival in Plentywood in 1910 with the banner in this photograph that reads: "U LOOK GOOD TO US WE R GLAD WE CAME." [August H. Lindberg, photographer, Sheridan County Museum, Plentywood, Montana]

homesteaders in the early teens that foot traffic made the streets nearly impassable at noon on weekdays.[8]

Divided into quadrants by Main Street and First Avenue, Plentywood's downtown was anchored by four imposing banks at the main intersection and the busy Great Northern train depot one block to the south. The awnings of numerous Main Street businesses shaded wide sidewalks along which a busy stream of customers walked as they patronized the town's movie theater and its several hotels and cafes as well as farm equipment, hardware, clothing, and grocery stores. By 1918, the town boasted a municipal sewer system and a brick schoolhouse built for forty thousand dollars four years earlier.[9] Its dirt streets accommodated the Model Ts that were increasingly common as the 1920s approached. At the local baseball field, the Plentywood Pirates challenged teams from neighboring towns and counties. And, of course, the town's peripheral economy was thriving as well, with at least three brothels in business. As start-up prairie towns went, Plentywood was doing fairly well.

Charles Taylor, however, was not impressed. He later described Plentywood as a "Godforsaken little hole" that was "hostile as hell to us." Nonetheless, Taylor set up the *Producers News* printing operation in an old livery stable. Some farmers brought a wagonload of used typesetting equipment from a defunct newspaper office elsewhere in the county, and Taylor began to staff his paper. His first typesetter was "a wild eyed sort of fellow" who failed at his job. The next man was unreliable and often inebriated, but, according to Taylor, "he worked pretty good when he was sober."[10]

While finding a good typesetter presented some challenges, the posi-

Enjoying a Plentywood baseball game, 1910. [Sheridan County Museum, Plentywood, Montana]

tion of editor was competently filled by Taylor himself, a thirty-four-year-old dynamo who knew his way around a newspaper operation. He was tall and solidly built, weighing nearly three hundred pounds, with a full head of dark hair and even features. He brought to the job considerable background in the newspaper business and an inherited political ideology consistent with, if slightly more radical than, the NPL platform.

Taylor had been born into a family of twelve in Dodge County, Wisconsin, in 1884, and he came by his radicalism naturally. Both of his grandfathers had been abolitionists and Republicans, which Taylor described as "the most radical thing in the line of political parties then known." His paternal grandparents had followed politics and world affairs by subscribing to Horace Greeley's *New York Tribune.* In a 1965 interview, Charles Taylor traced some of the attitudes that prevailed in his family to the writings of Karl Marx, who served as a European correspondent for Greeley's paper throughout the 1850s.[11]

Taylor's father, Carlos, had held various jobs, homesteaded, and worked as an agent for the Farmers' Alliance. According to Taylor, his father had an "encyclopedic mind" but was "very impulsive, very sarcastic, and never got along very well with people because he had a way of telling them off, sometimes rightly and sometimes wrongly." He was, in short, "a rebel and contrary" who had taken an interest even as an adolescent in the Knights of Labor and the Greenback ticket in the 1870s. Later, Taylor's father became active in the People's Party.[12]

Taylor began school in a rustic log building in the woods near Lake Minnetonka, Minnesota, where his family had moved. By his own account, he was a mature and precocious child, often participating in plays and presentations at school, and even as a youngster, he was politically aware. For example, although he was only twelve during the election campaign of 1896, Taylor was "vociferous and vocal, and . . . was debating everybody around." He was saddened by the loss of People's Party candidate William Jennings Bryan and "thought the country was ruined."[13]

Taylor's interest in journalism also emerged at an early age. In addition to working on farms and in lumber camps beginning at the age of twelve or thirteen, he was intermittently employed by the *Aitkin Age,* a local newspaper, by the time he was fourteen. His duties as press-setter and cleaner often kept him busy twelve hours a day. In the winter of 1901, at age seventeen and with only an eighth-grade education, he took a teacher's examination and taught at a remote school near the present site of McGrath, Minnesota.[14]

The first years of the new century were rather unsettled for Taylor. He entered Hamline Preparatory School in St. Paul in the autumn of 1901, and within two years married the daughter of the couple with whom he boarded. After a two-year sojourn in Oregon, Charles and Mary Taylor returned to Minnesota, where their son, Francis, was born in 1904. According to a state census, the family was still intact in 1905, with Charles Taylor's occupation given as "salesman." But the couple divorced fairly soon thereafter, and Mary and the toddler went home to live with her parents.

The dissolution of his marriage was a "great emotional strain" for Taylor, which he sought to escape by leaving school and homesteading near Big Falls, Minnesota. It was during this time, around 1908, that Taylor made the acquaintance of Agda Lungren, with whom he would correspond for several years. The *Producers News* later reported that, during his time at the homestead in northern Minnesota, Taylor completed a correspondence course in law and was elected judge in Koochiching County. In 1909, having developed tuberculosis, Taylor left the homestead and moved to the drier climate of Buffalo, Wyoming, where relatives were ranching. At the time, Taylor was a professed Socialist and a "great admirer" of Eugene Debs, the three-time candidate for president on the Socialist ticket.[15]

In Buffalo, Taylor found few who shared his Socialist views, but he did land jobs in the newspaper trade. In 1910, when his health improved, he returned to Minnesota to help found a Socialist paper, *Port of Call,* in International Falls. That fall, he ran for the state legislature on the Socialist ticket, finishing fourth in a five-man race. However, Taylor's tuberculosis flared up again, and he returned to Wyoming, where he did newspaper work, taught school, and faithfully paid his Socialist Party dues. In 1915, he returned to Aitkin County, Minnesota, to farm with his brother and teach school in the town of McGregor. Then, in June 1917, ten years after his first marriage ended and roughly nine years after beginning his long correspondence with her, Taylor married Agda Lungren. When his brother entered the army and the farm was sold, Charles and Agda Taylor went to Minneapolis.[16]

The Nonpartisan League had been founded during the time Taylor was on his second stint in Wyoming. After his return to Minnesota, Taylor noted the NPL's tactics as the organization made inroads in his state, and he began thinking about "the plight of the farmer, how they were exploited by bankers and elevator companies every which way." He felt that the NPL held considerable promise for farmers. Despite having had no previous correspondence with the league's leaders, Taylor

(far left) In 1918, the Nonpartisan League sent Charles E. Taylor to Plentywood, the Sheridan County seat, to launch a new league paper, the weekly Producers News. [Courtesy Carl Taylor]

(left) Taylor's wife, Agda, accompanied him to Plentywood. [Courtesy Carl Taylor]

walked into their offices in early 1918, "told them who I was, offered my services . . . and they looked me over." Apparently they liked what they saw, for he was soon sent to Plentywood.[17]

Of all the Montana farming communities to which the league could have assigned Taylor, Sheridan County was one of the best and its selection a clever tactical choice. First, it bordered Divide County, North Dakota, where the NPL had already made significant inroads, electing a league-endorsed sheriff and publishing a weekly newspaper, the *Divide County Farmers Press*. More importantly, Sheridan County already had a fairly well-established left-wing faction of dedicated activists with whom Taylor could work. As an FBI intelligence report noted, "Almost since the time this county was organized there has been some type of Marxist movement in it. In the early days, old time Socialists . . . settled in this district." Among the Socialists who "manifested themselves" to Charles Taylor shortly after his arrival in Plentywood were such stalwart fellow travelers as Hans Rasmussen, Arthur Rueber, Clair Stoner, John Boulds, and Rodney Salisbury.[18]

Born in Denmark in 1871, Hans Rasmussen learned the masonry trade and attended architectural college in the old country before embarking on a series of moves. According to the *Producers News,* Rasmussen had "traveled more than any man in the county," even "crossing the pond" seven times after immigrating to the United States in 1898. He spent time laying bricks in Jamaica, the Panama Canal Zone, and several Central American countries, and finally moved from Seattle, Washington, to take a homestead in Sheridan County's Volmer community in 1908. He was a bachelor until the age of forty-two when he married Anna Johanna Mortensen, a twenty-seven-year-old Danish immigrant who had a homestead of her own.[19]

Early on in his tenure as a Sheridan County homesteader, Rasmussen had become involved in a type of farm movement, quite literally, when he led a vigilante group that moved squatters' shacks off claimed land under cover of darkness. In 1912, he ran for county commissioner on the Socialist ticket and was beaten at the polls by an almost three-to-one margin. Undeterred, Rasmussen made a bid two years later for the office of county surveyor on the Socialist ticket but was once again unsuccessful.[20] By the time the Nonpartisan League began to gain traction in Sheridan County, Rasmussen was one of its most seasoned and senior members, and he would be a loyal foot soldier in the farmers' movement until the bitter end.

Although he would not stay in Sheridan County as long as Rasmussen, Arthur Rueber of the Outlook community was another central player during the Nonpartisan League's early years. A cashier at the State Bank of Outlook, Rueber was about the same age as Charles Taylor, and like his colleague, had traversed the nation before settling in Sheridan County.

Rueber's rather sedate job at the bank was a contrast to his former occupation: all-purpose athlete and coach. During his college years at Northwestern University, Rueber had played football, serving as captain of the team during the 1905 season until a knee injury put him on the sidelines. The next spring, he signed on as a pitcher with the Little Rock Travelers, a minor league baseball team in Arkansas. But by April, the *Sporting Life* newspaper reported that Rueber had been released from the team, adding that he "apparently would have made good if he had experience in professional baseball leagues." He returned to football as head coach first for the University of Tennessee at Chattanooga and then Whitworth College in Washington before undertaking a new sport. From 1909 until 1913, he served as head basketball coach for the North Dakota State University Bison, amassing an impressive 42-6 win-loss record. Handsome and athletically built, Rueber remained involved in sports as a member of the Outlook baseball team after moving to Sheridan County.[21]

Rueber also had another strong interest; Taylor referred to him as a "big man in the Socialist Party" in Sheridan County who was "very strong" in his political convictions. Rueber and other members of the left-wing nucleus read the *International Socialist Review* and tried to stay informed about political issues, but Taylor noted that "out there in the country the rank and file didn't know much" about the finer points of socialism or what was happening in the Soviet Union.[22]

Following the tragic death of his four-year-old son and the closure of the Outlook bank in 1918, Arthur Rueber, his wife, Louise, and their surviving son moved to Plentywood. Two years later, in 1920, their home would be the site of a clandestine meeting at which Sheridan County's Communist group would officially coalesce. In the mid-1920s, Rueber joined Charles Taylor in a business venture that took them both out of state. From that point on, Rueber called Minnesota his home.[23]

During the years Rueber lived in the Outlook community, one of his neighbors was Clair Stoner, a native of Iowa who had come to northeastern Montana to stake a homestead claim with his two brothers in 1908. By the following spring, a contingent of Stoners—Clair, John, and Grant and their families—was farming near Outlook. Later an uncle and a sister and her family also came to call Sheridan County home. However, it was Clair who was drawn to the radical cause.[24]

Stoner's daughter, Lucile, remembers him as an ambitious person who poured himself into his work on the farm. Like others who tried to scratch a living out of the prairie land, he found the conditions in Sheridan County challenging, reporting that he "dug quantities of rock, broke the sod, fought army worms, grasshoppers, hail, drought and wind." He had no hobbies and was not actively involved in a church. It was his abiding interest in politics that filled his free hours. According to the *Producers News,* he was "actively connected" to the Nonpartisan

Among Sheridan County's radicals was Outlook farmer Clair Stoner, shown here with his dog, circa 1914. [Courtesy Ray Stoner]

Rodney Salisbury joined the Sheridan County Socialist cadre early and played a central role in the movement during its existence in northeastern Montana. [*Producers News*, September 23, 1932]

League from the beginning, and his daughter recalls that for both Clair and his wife, Doshia, the league was "like their religion." Although the Stoners eventually left Sheridan County for the tamer environs of Great Falls and then California, Clair would play a significant role during the county's NPL years.[25]

Equally strong in his fervor for the farm movement was young John Boulds, a North Dakota transplant originally from Centralia, Missouri. In 1912, at the age of twenty, Boulds homesteaded near Plentywood, toughing it out on his land for seven years before giving up the farm and moving into town. As described in an FBI intelligence report, John Boulds was a "man of slight build" whose education had ended with grammar school. He married Vivian O'Toole, "a very devout Catholic," and all of their children were raised and married in the church. One of their daughters, Mona, has described her parents' marriage as "a true love story"—in spite of her mother's opposition to John's radicalism and the disapproval of it that the family sometimes perceived among members of the Plentywood community. Although Boulds would never run for public office or take a leadership role in the NPL, he was apparently a dyed-in-the-wool Socialist and would persist in his political efforts long after many of his radical colleagues had left Sheridan County.[26]

The last member of the early Socialist cadre, a man who would play a critical role in the movement during its entire lifespan in northeast Montana, was Rodney Salisbury. Salisbury was born in Wisconsin in 1888, the first of eight children. He left school after the fourth grade to help support his family on the homestead they had taken in North Dakota. According to his daughter, Camilla Salisbury Kelly, his paternal grandfather recruited him as a boy to perform in a road show in which his grandfather "played the fool to attract an audience. Arriving at a small town he would use the outdoor toilet and profess to be unable to get out and the grandfather would kick the door and yell until someone released him. By then a small crowd would have . . . gathered and [Rodney] would dance for quarters and dimes on the station platform."[27]

Salisbury met Emma Ryan in 1912 in Brinsmade, North Dakota, and they eventually married and moved to Raymond, Montana, where their first child was born in 1914. As a pacifist, Salisbury intended to refuse conscription during World War I, even if it meant imprisonment. He was saved from such a dilemma by the birth of his twin daughters, Janis and Jardis, which exempted him from service. By 1925, the Salisburys had six children, and Emma Salisbury, an early supporter of Margaret Sanger's campaign for birth control, decided she would have no more.[28]

Rodney Salisbury was a slender, rather delicate-featured man, something of a contrast to Charles Taylor, but he was no less radical. Charles Taylor sang Salisbury's praises as an activist and a person who could carry out organizing tasks with finesse and efficiency. "But he was an extremist and kind of a Wobbly type," Taylor noted, apparently meaning that Salisbury, while earnest in his belief in reform, was willing to bend or break the law if it served the cause.[29]

His political ideology was not the only source of Salisbury's controversial reputation; over the years, and especially during his tenure as undersheriff and then sheriff, his lifestyle and alleged criminal activity would attract attention around the county and from the FBI. Like Taylor, he was condemned by Joe Dolin, the editor of an opposition newspaper, the *Pioneer Press*, who accused him of accepting bribes from "blind pig" operators during the early years of Prohibition. Later, he was said to be directly involved in bootlegging. Although the *Producers News* rejected these accusations, Salisbury's daughter later noted, "I do believe that he may have been a bootlegger because he was a scofflaw. . . . Rodney also believed that the laws are the instrument of economic repression of the working classes." This assessment of his character seems to be borne out by Salisbury's later life. In the late 1920s, he began a second family with the wife of the Plentywood miller and was eventually accused of, but never formally charged with, burning down a grain elevator, profiting from a brothel, and participating in the robbery of the county treasury.[30] His real or rumored activities aside, Rodney Salisbury's dedication to seeking progressive change was unrivaled.

And so it began that, in 1918, the "old time Socialists" of Sheridan County, along with their new de facto leader, Charles Taylor, undertook the task of promoting the Nonpartisan League agenda in northeastern Montana. They would use a number of strategies, some of which were reminiscent of nineteenth-century farmers' organizations, and put their newspaper to work in ways that would vitalize the radical movement.[31]

CHAPTER 6

Marketing the Farmers' Movement

The Nonpartisan League and the Producers News

For Sheridan County, June 26, 1918, was a day at the beach. Instead of completing the usual weekday routine of housework and farm chores, families loaded up their Model Ts for the drive to Brush Lake, east of Dagmar, to attend the Nonpartisan League's first annual picnic. The 280-acre oasis on the prairie had sandy beaches, a concession stand, a dance pavilion, and ample parking for the NPL's guests. The NPL's paper, the *Producers News,* had been touting the occasion for weeks, promising that farm families could enjoy swimming, boating, ball games, races, and "the very best music that can be secured," including a chorus that would sing "the patriotic airs." The festive occasion would feature a free barbecue and bean bake, with refreshments provided by the Red Cross, which would "realize a neat sum" from their sale. Another key selling point was the planned appearance of Jeannette Rankin, who, by virtue of her election the previous autumn, had become the first woman to serve in Congress. Despite Rankin's failure to appear (her telegram of apology was printed in the *News*), six thousand people reportedly attended the picnic.[1]

As the picnic attendance reveals, 1918 was a good year for the Nonpartisan League in Montana. The league's organizing effort in the state had begun only two years before, but already its ranks had swelled in both eastern and western Montana. In Sheridan County, the organization's growing success could be traced to the efforts of the "old time Socialists" who had undertaken the task of promoting the Nonpartisan League agenda using all the resources at their disposal, including many

Nonpartisan League meeting, Brush Lake, 1919. [Charles Edward Russell, *The Story of the Nonpartisan League* (New York, 1920), opp. p. 304]

of the organizational and persuasive strategies pioneered by early agrarian movements and outlined in league literature.[2]

In particular, Nonpartisan League organizers capitalized on the promotional value of social gatherings, community events, and oratories by speakers who had regional and even national political reputations. For example, Jeannette Rankin made her long-awaited appearance in August of 1918, giving speeches in Plentywood and Brush Lake, accompanied by Charles Taylor and Clair Stoner, among others. Usher L. Burdick, a North Dakotan who was at that time the head of the U.S. Grain Growers Association and whom *Time* magazine later described as being "a great success with small groups of farmers when he rips off his coat and speaks in unvarnished and unrehearsed language," spoke in Plentywood in 1921.[3] That same summer, the prominent Socialist and anti-war activist Kate Richards O'Hare, whom the *Producers News* identified as a "famous woman orator and humanitarian," also made a visit. According to the front-page article, thousands turned out to hear her "famous lecture" in spite of the fact that the venue was not ideal: she spoke outdoors in a cow pasture under the "burning hot sun for two hours and ten minutes." The cow pasture was her assembly hall because, according to the *Producers News,* some "smart alecks" had "made a general nuisance of themselves running about town trying to work up sentiment to stop the meeting" and prevent the event's promoters from renting any local halls.[4]

Arthur C. Townley was a popular speaker at Nonpartisan League events. Here Townley's plane arrives at Medicine Lake for a circa 1920 appearance. [Henry B. Syverud, photographer, MHS Photograph Archives, Helena, PAc 77-94 VI-33.16]

Nonpartisan League leaders themselves drew large crowds. In 1920, Arthur Townley was the main attraction at the annual NPL picnic. By that time, his presence was in such demand at NPL events across the northern Great Plains that he had begun to fly in a small plane between his many engagements. On July 3, at the landing strip at Medicine Lake, a huge crowd, many of whom had never seen a plane in flight, waited patiently for Townley. According to Magnus Aasheim, after several hours of anticipation, "Finally a speck appeared in the sky. . . . Immediately, there were cries, 'There he comes, there he comes!' From the applause one would have thought this was the coming of another Messiah." Townley was then driven from Medicine Lake to the picnic at Brush Lake.[5]

Even more integral to the Nonpartisan League's efforts to build a coalition of like-minded farmers, however, was the *Producers News* and its flamboyant editor, Charles Taylor. Indeed, as a strategist, editor, and storyteller, Taylor was, in many ways, masterful. He assembled his paper as an appealing mix of local, state, and national news, political opinion, cartoons, and the sort of society columns typically found in small-town newspapers of the era. A one-year subscription to the full-size, six-column paper that appeared every Friday cost two dollars. Conversational and lively, the *News* shared various characteristics with other Nonpartisan League papers, but the *Producers News,* along with its charismatic editor, would leave a mark on its community and radical politics unlike any other NPL paper. This achievement was accomplished, in large part, due to Taylor's skill as a rhetorical tactician. He used his newspaper to simultaneously politicize, catalyze, and build identification with farmers. To be sure, the *News* was always a political tool for relaying the league's agenda, but the editor never failed to make it readable and entertaining.

In his choice of editorial topics and news stories, Taylor demonstrated a keen understanding of the farmers and workers and their need for organization and representation. In this, he was consistent with Nonpartisan League practice, which countered the tendency of farmers to be independent minded by emphasizing the importance of "sticking together." One way Taylor and the NPL built solidarity was through the acquisition of the People's Publishing Company, which had been organized by Sheridan County Socialists and which was the official publisher of the *Producers News.* The People's Publishing Company commenced selling stock at five dollars per share. According to Taylor, there were a thousand stockholders in the company; his stated goal was for each member of the local league to be a stockholder in the paper.[6]

Within a month of the first issue of the *Producers News,* it was already under attack by the pugnacious Burley Bowler, the editor of the *Antelope Independent* who had an interest in the NPL himself and would eventually edit one of the league papers in neighboring Daniels County. In the May 13, 1918, issue, Bowler printed accusations that the *Producers News* was a Socialist paper and was not officially endorsed by the Montana Nonpartisan League. In response, the *News* ran an acknowledgment of the Socialist origins of the People's Publishing Company but noted that

Incorporated Under the Laws of the State of Montana

NUMBER 308

SHARES One

The Peoples Publishing Company

Plentywood, Montana

Capital Stock $20,000.00

This certifies that John S. Smith is the owner of One Shares of the Capital Stock of The Peoples Publishing Company transferable only on the Books of the Corporation in person or by Attorney on surrender of this Certificate and after the Board of Directors have had an opportunity to purchase same.

In Witness Whereof the duly authorized officers of the Corporation have hereunto subscribed their names and caused the corporate seal to be hereto affixed this 1st day of July

SECY. PRES.

SHARES $5.00 EACH.

Stock certificate for the People's Publishing Company, Plentywood, Montana.
[Courtesy Leonard Smith]

While Charles Taylor was editor, the Producers News *masthead carried the slogan "Paper of the people, by the people, for the people By Peoples Publishing Company, Publishers."* [*Producers News*, January 11, 1929]

THE PRODUCERS NEWS

Paper of the people, by the people, for the people
By Peoples Publishing Company, Publishers

CONTINUING—The Outlook Promoter, The Outlook Optimist, The Dooley Sun, The Antelope Independent, The Sheridan County News, The Pioneer Press and the Sheridan County Farmer.

CHARLES E. TAYLOR, Editor and Manager

"most if not all" of the Socialists had joined the league. Next, Taylor called an emergency stockholders meeting for the purpose of electing a board of directors. The *News* reported that "great interest was shown in the election of the board of directors, which demonstrated the fact that the farmers are alive to the necessity of a real Nonpartisan paper owned and controlled by the farmers themselves." As further evidence that his was the only true league paper in Sheridan County, Taylor published a letter in his next issue from the manager of the NPL's public relations office in St. Paul, indicating that he was "more than pleased with the character" of the *Producers News.* In the same issue, Taylor also printed a letter from the state superintendent of the NPL in Montana, granting the *News* his "unqualified endorsement." This was only the first instance of the sparring between Taylor and Burley Bowler that would continue for nearly two decades.[7]

Another common accusation against the *Producers News* was that the paper did not represent farmers but was Taylor's personal mouthpiece. In response, Taylor repeatedly claimed that he did not exercise control over the paper, but that it was "all in the hands of the farmers." (Although Taylor later revealed in an interview that he and his associates, rather than "handing everything down" to the farmers, "always worked on a policy of making it appear that everything came from the farmers.") Taylor's choice of words is important: the appearance of farmer control was the goal. In fact, the newspaper belonged in a very real sense to the Nonpartisan League, and its editorial policy reflected the views of that organization. Symbolically, however, the paper was for the farmers—the *News* belonged to the "producers"; it was a product of the People's Publishing Company, and its masthead reinforced that message by announcing that it was "a paper of the people, by the people, for the people."[8]

Early on in his editorship, Taylor began to establish himself as one of "the people" by announcing that he was from "old American stock," that several of his ancestors had defended the United States in wartime, and that he was a proud contributor to the Liberty Bond drive and the Red Cross.[9] Part of his strategy in this case may have been a response to the political climate, which was dominated by the patriotic fervor that had swept the nation after the United States entered World War I in 1917. Nationally, the Nonpartisan League had been contending with accusations of disloyalty during the previous year, and it was clear that Taylor did not want the Sheridan County organization to be similarly tarnished.

While Taylor could not resist disparaging the "Arm Chair Patriots" whose "contribution to the nation is not risking your life or exposing your precious hide anywhere there is danger" but instead reporting suspected traitors to the Department of Justice, he also declared in print his support for President Wilson and offered, "At any time we can be of service in any capacity in defending the ideals of Democracy either at home or abroad, we are awaiting our call." Truth be known, Taylor had not favored U.S. participation in the war but perhaps decided that the better part of valor was to withhold this especially controversial opinion from his readers.[10]

Taylor was also adept at gauging the mood and unspoken concerns of his audience, particularly those who had not served in the military. At the end of World War I, with troops returning from abroad, the editor made a point of praising those who had planted crops "to help feed the country in its hour of terrible ordeal." Later, he wrote a column, "The Patriotic Farmer," in which he identified farmers as the unsung heroes of the war who had made the sacrifice of staying home and who had "stood patriotically at their posts of duty." His flattering portrait of farmers likely served a purpose beyond generally ingratiating himself; it may have been aimed at assuaging any guilt felt by farmers who stayed home during the conflict and sold their crops at war-inflated prices while other Americans suffered in the trenches of Europe.[11]

Taylor also used his rural background to win farmers' support. In 1922, when he was running for the state senate as a Republican (with the Nonpartisan League endorsement), he published a sort of proclamation of his pedigree, noting that, although he was not currently farming, "He was farming when he came here, grew up on a farm, came from parents who are farmers, and expects to be back on a farm just as soon as he can go back with the hopes of having half a chance to pay out on one, which no one can do at the present time."[12] The statement was slightly disingenuous in implying that the only thing that prevented Taylor from farming was the profession's lack of economic viability. In fact, Taylor had spent most of his adult life as a teacher and newspaperman.

The NPL's goal of establishing interest and identification among farmers was furthered by the editorial approach of the *Producers News.* During Sheridan County's homesteading years, newspapers served as a source of entertainment as well as news, and the *News* embodied the kind of playfulness that was accepted practice in the West. Part of the paper's appeal was its earthy, colloquial, and humorous editorial approach. While the *Producers News* was a more professional publication than most of the other local papers, its news and editorial columns were informal by contemporary journalistic standards. Contractions and abbreviations (such as "tho") were commonplace; colloquialisms were abundant. For example, like many NPL papers, the *News* described the misdeeds of "big biz" and "the old gang." It claimed that some of the opponents of the farmers' movement liked to "howl" about the farmers' paper and "start a rumpus about religion" to divert attention from the real issues. It was also reported that farmers' movement foes made "a vow to get Charley Taylor's scalp." Couched in such colorful language, references to religion and the description of threats against Taylor would become part of the *Producers News*'s regular fare in the coming years.[13]

Taylor also enjoyed a good play on words. In one of his first *News* editorials, he described "'pay'triotic" industrial lords profiting off the backs of patriotic farmers, and the "lip patriots" who were all talk and no action. The Sheridan County Loyalty League—a local branch of the Montana Council of Defense that often spread propaganda, suppressed freedom of the press, and surveilled citizens—became the Lunacy League, while supporters of western Montana's mining companies became the Kopper Krowd. Some of Taylor's wordplay became the stuff of local legend. A Plentywood attorney who had advertised himself to the predominantly Scandinavian community as a *Norsk advokat,* or Norwegian lawyer, became in Taylor's references, the *Norsk abekat,* or Norwegian monkey. In another case, a corpulent opponent of Taylor's by the name of L. S. Olson was nicknamed Lard S. Olson.[14]

Indeed, the personal attacks printed in the *Producers News* could be vitriolic. Like other editors and columnists of his time, Charles Taylor was able to get away with the kind of writing that would invite a storm of libel suits later in the twentieth century. Burley Bowler, editor of the *Antelope Independent,* who had questioned whether the *Producers News*

Political cartoon, published by Charles Taylor in the Producers News, *August 29, 1919.*

was the legitimate organ of the NPL, was the first object of Taylor's wrath. Using Bowler's given name as an adjective, Taylor wrote, "The 'Burley Bowler' naively asks whether the editor of *The Producers News* is not a socialist. In answer we will venture to inquire whether any of the 'Burley Bowler's' ancestry were afflicted with lunacy? If there were any of them so afflicted we are very sorry, for they say it is inherited and that the descendent of such a one is subject to an attack at any moment. Take good care of your self, dear boy, a little too much exertion of a delicate mind is likely to break the silver cord, which no doubt would cause considerable commotion among your 'thousands' of readers. Be awfully careful."[15]

Among Taylor's other targets were Joe Dolin, a competing Plentywood newspaperman, whom Taylor assailed as a "contemptible, lying, bar-fly, booze-fighting" grafter and thief; Fred Ibsen, a local businessman who he likened to a pharisee; and Dr. J. C. Storkan, who would eventually file a criminal complaint of libel against Taylor and start his own paper to oppose the *News.*[16] Taylor's penchant for responding to questions about his ideology with personal attacks was a preview of the tactics later seen in Communist newspapers elsewhere around the country, including the *Daily Worker.* Critics of the party line were accused not only of being misguided or wrong, but of being traitors, capitalist puppets, or criminals. Still, by applying a mix of earthiness, humor, wordplay, and occasional outright abusiveness, Taylor captured widespread attention. Just as importantly, he began to establish identification and unity among the Nonpartisan League leaders, members, and farmers in northeastern Montana. While Taylor's use of humor and other rhetorical flourishes in print was deliberate, another rhetorical strategy, whether intentional or not, also served the ends of both the NPL and Taylor himself. It involved the creation of a veritable cult of personality around editor Charles Taylor.

Taylor lived in a time and place in which farmers in northeastern Montana faced daunting and relentless challenges. Into this milieu came the strapping young editor of the *Producers News,* whose lively style must have come as a welcome distraction for county residents facing hard times. In the 1980s and 1990s, when they reminisced about the radical period, Sheridan County residents remembered Charles Taylor vividly. By all accounts, he was flamboyant, powerful, confident, and rather extraordinary. He was described by local residents as "a real character," "a charming and brilliant conversationalist . . . not easily forgotten," and a person who could "practically hypnotize an audience." Even Burley Bowler, writing about Charles Taylor in the *Daniels County Leader* in 1967, described his former nemesis as "big-hearted," "charming," and "a man with a brilliant streak." According to one historian, within a few months of his arrival in Sheridan County, there was "a Taylor legend, an almost superstitious faith in his capacities. Even his enemies swore he could solve any problem, out-argue any man." These strong and lasting impressions may be partly due to the *Producers News*'s larger-than-life portrayal of its editor, created in part through Taylor's own braggadocio.[17]

However, it is important to note that these were impressions formed in later years. Judging by the headlines during his first year in Plentywood, Taylor had indeed moved to a place "hostile as hell" toward him. Capitalizing on this sentiment, he was able to turn the hostility to his advantage by recounting his exploits on the front page. Headlines in December 1918 announced "Editor Taylor Is Assaulted," and the accompanying story reported how he had been attacked by a local businessman, who had entered the newspaper office, punched Taylor, and generally made "a hoodlum out of himself." Taylor asserted, however, that the businessman had "got the worst of the encounter and beat it out of the office." In the same issue, an editorial, probably by Taylor himself, boasted that the editor was not intimidated by such shows of force. Just one week later, the editor was "Again Assaulted," this time by a defeated candidate in the recent election, who had participated in the "indoor and outdoor sport of taking a wallop at the editor of the *Producers News.*" The stories alleging assault and battery made for good copy, but they also served Taylor's political goals and aspirations by casting him in the role of the martyr—a lone crusader who was willing to fight courageously and selflessly to serve the honest farmers of the county. It was a theme Taylor would reprise time and again.[18]

Most of Taylor's fights were verbal rather than physical. His protracted conflict with *Pioneer Press* editor Joe Dolin began shortly after Taylor arrived in Plentywood. When Dolin received the county printing contract, allegedly under unfair circumstances, the war of words between the two men began. It would continue for several years. Under the heading, "Personal 'Pie-Near,'" Taylor ran an editorial accusing Dolin of making insulting attacks on him in the columns of the *Pioneer Press.* Yet, Taylor concluded, better to be attacked than praised: "We know of no greater insult that could be heaped upon us in any way than to have anything complimentary or even reasonable said about us in that contemptible, degenerated, debased, and scandalous mouthpiece of private infamy and public indecency . . . the 'Pioneer' Press."[19]

Not only competing newspapermen but even a local judge dogged Taylor. In the summer of 1921, Judge C. E. Comer ordered the county attorney to investigate whether the editor was in contempt of court as a result of articles he had written about a case before the court. Taylor responded in characteristic fashion, playing the martyr by noting that "if in his prolonged fight to bring thieves and bank looters and county robbers to justice, things have been said that the court can construe into being contempt, [Taylor] presumes that he will have to take his medicine." The case dragged on through the summer and fall of 1921, with the district court finally dismissing the charge in March of 1922.[20]

The *Producers News* portrayed the contempt-of-court case not just as a personal vendetta against Taylor, but as an attempt by the judge to protect his cronies from the newspaper's scrutiny, a take on events that was consistent with the paper's reporting on the physical attacks on Taylor shortly after his arrival in town. At that time, the newspaper identified a "conspiracy by certain parties to intimidate the editor of the *Producers News.*" It went on to predict that "the farmers are going to take the necessary precaution to see that this 'rough stuff' is abolished; for in a game like the above, two sides can play. However, the farmers are not looking for trouble, but if the worse comes to worse, they are able and will take care of themselves."[21] The important subtext of all of the persecution tales was that Taylor, the *Producers News,* and by

Although much of the rhetoric in the Producers News *had a playful quality, divisive class politics was a staple of the newspaper. This cartoon is a good example.* [*Producers News*, August 3, 1928]

extension, the NPL were fighting the good fight on behalf of, and with, the farmers. It was a constant theme in the paper.

From the beginning, Taylor practiced the tried-and-true strategy of naming the enemy and was a keen reporter of the various robbers, grafters, and foes of the farmer. The adversary thus identified, Taylor and the NPL could then play the role of unceasing advocates for farmers in the fight against their rivals. Building this sense of rivalry and diametrically opposed interests was part of a long tradition of "producer ideology" practiced to some degree by the Grangers and with increasing vigor by the Farmers' Alliance and the Populists. The producer ideology held that farmers and workers constituted a particular class that was distinct from a nonproducing class composed of merchants, bankers, and speculators, who were said to live off the honest labors of the producers.[22]

Historian Robert Morlan notes that many NPL newspapers relied on "a hymn of hate directed at the Chamber of Commerce" as a means of capturing readers' interest and signifying the differences between businesspeople and producers. The *Producers News,* likewise, contrasted the opposed parties: the "patriotic laboring farmer" with the local merchants and businesspeople who were "Mainstreeters" and "small town kaisers." The incumbent officeholders, especially those with ties to local banks and businesses, were labeled "the old gang." Appeals to a sense of producerism were clear when Taylor applauded the stockholders in the

People's Publishing Company for being "alive to the necessity of having a paper that will at all times fight for [the farmers'] interests and the interests of all useful and producing people; a paper more responsive to the actual doers than to the interest of those whose way of living is by doing the doers." In the *News,* one was either producing or "doing the doers."[23]

The 1918 election season proved the point. The race for the state senate was between Republican Henry Lowe and Clair Stoner of rural Outlook, who was running as a Democrat with the NPL endorsement. While acknowledging that Lowe was "a fine man personally," the *News* referred to him constantly as "Banker Lowe" as a means of contrasting him with "Farmer Stoner." In one issue, the paper asserted that Lowe "sometimes farms when he is not farming the farmers." Voters were asked, "Now who do you want for senator? Banker Lowe or Farmer Stoner? If you want the League program[,] vote for Clair Stoner, the farmer. If you want things just as they are, or a banker and a 'Kopper' program, vote for Henry Lowe, the Banker." In spite of the *News*'s best effort, Lowe went to the senate.[24]

Taylor portrayed bankers like Lowe, businesspeople, and Main-streeters in general as meddlesome and arrogant. He excoriated these opponents of the Nonpartisan League for trying to tell the farmer how to farm: "For years the farmer has been told what he should do to be successful, how much more he should raise, how he should diversify . . . how to 'get down to business.' And now he is getting down to business in real earnest and he wants to have a say in making the laws he has to do business under [and] he becomes a 'sucker,' a 'traitor' and other vile things in the eyes of the same fellows who have so long been trying to teach him how to run his business."[25] This invective foreshadowed what would become common fare in the *News*: stories pitting Main Street against farm and, eventually, "capitalists and Wall Streeters" against "the toiling masses." Although much of the NPL's rhetoric in the *Producers News* had a playful quality, divisive class politics was a staple in the newspaper, even at the beginning.

With its controversial content, colorful editor, and tendency toward muckraking, the *Producers News* quickly became the most widely read of the county's many papers and, according to historian Lowell Dyson, "the most important [Nonpartisan] league paper in Montana."[26] The Nonpartisan League made a strong case for radicalism during the late teens and early 1920s, and Sheridan County voters were persuaded by its arguments. In the 1918 county elections, local candidates endorsed by the NPL and running on the Republican ticket were elected almost across the board, with the exception of the races for superintendent of schools and state senator, in the latter of which "Farmer Stoner" was bested by "Banker Lowe." It is interesting to note that, although she was not affiliated with the Nonpartisan League, Jeannette Rankin, who had been the sole congressional opponent of the United States' entry into the First World War and was then running for the U.S. Senate, received a plurality of votes in Sheridan County, an occurrence in only two other counties, both bordering Sheridan County. Rankin's margins of victory were greatest in Dagmar, Outlook, and Raymond, all of which would figure prominently in the future electoral successes of the radicals.[27]

Even as they promoted the Nonpartisan League, Charles Taylor and several of his NPL colleagues had a covert agenda. In an interview four decades later, Taylor admitted that, in the early 1920s, he was "under cover. I wasn't advertised as a Communist" even though he had indeed joined the Communist Party. He also described himself as "the boss" of the 1920 clandestine strategy session that served as the founding of the Communist Party in Sheridan County. Taylor and Rodney Salisbury, along with Arthur Rueber and Hans Rasmussen, agreed that they could take "a step to the left" with the ultimate goal of leading "the masses into a Communist Party." He described the members of Sheridan County's "left-wing nucleus" (presumably including himself) as having always been far out on the left wing, opposing World War I, admiring the Russian revolution, and being true believers in the basic tenets of Marxism. Taylor confessed that they had only gone "into the Nonpartisan League as a strategy." Now they aimed to transform farmers' positive sentiments toward the Nonpartisan League into support for a farmer-labor coalition. There was a precedent for this approach in the rhetoric of the NPL. Arthur Townley frequently urged workers to unite with farmers in their fight for reform and so did Charles A. Lindbergh Sr., the Nonpartisan League candidate (running as a Republican) for Minnesota governor in 1918. Lindbergh was the first person to be described by the press as a "farmer-labor" candidate.[28]

As historian Lowell Dyson notes, references to farmer-laborism animated the enemies of the league because they "sounded a shade too close to the Bolshevik slogan of a 'workers' and peasants' government.'" Mainstream newspapers such as the *Kansas City Star* went on the offensive, for example, wishing luck to the NPL's "Anti-Bolshevist" opponents in the 1918 election. In Sheridan County, Taylor decried this sort of backlash and signaled his true convictions in a *Producers News* response to Montana's 1918 Sedition Act, which outlawed criticism of the government and served as a model for the law's federal version.

"Charles E. Taylor as candidate for U.S. Senate on the Farmer-Laborer party ticket." [*Producers News*, September 30, 1930]

He alleged that "in the wild ranting about bolshevism, Americanism, wicked foreigners, red rascals and what not, we are likely to forget that most of what the general run of so-called radicals advocate is needed by the people for continued prosperity and happiness." His indictment of "wild ranting" notwithstanding, Taylor and his colleagues would take care to remain under cover for a while longer.[29]

As Taylor and his colleagues inched toward the left, the Sheridan County farmers' movement remained outwardly allied with the Nonpartisan League. The 1920 general election season demonstrated, however, that the area's voters were already becoming interested in the Farmer-Labor Party (F-LP). That political organization had emerged as the Minnesota Farmer-Labor Party in 1918, later joined with other state and local organizations to form the Labor Party of the United States, and eventually changed its name to the Farmer-Labor Party. The F-LP nominated Parley Parker Christensen as their presidential candidate in 1920. He did not fare well in the rest of Montana, receiving less than 7 percent of the state electors' votes, but in Sheridan County, he captured roughly 23 percent of the electors. In another notable race during the 1920 election, the NPL endorsed one of its own, Clair Stoner, who ran as a Democrat for the state house of representatives. In this election, no "banker" could defeat him and Farmer Stoner won the seat.[30]

While the surreptitious but steadily leftward advance continued, the northeastern Montana farmers' movement flourished. After fewer than four years of organizing in Sheridan County, the Nonpartisan League put forth a broad slate of local candidates for the election of 1922. In fact, farmers' organization members sought election to almost every county office. Included on the ballot were Charles Taylor for state senator and Clair Stoner for reelection as state representative. Rodney Salisbury, then the undersheriff, ran for sheriff, and Hans Rasmussen threw his hat into the ring for county surveyor. The entire NPL-endorsed ticket was elected in November, by modest margins in some cases and landslides in others.[31] It was a momentous occasion: the radicals now controlled Sheridan County's government, had representatives in Helena, and would be the dominant influence in local politics for the next few years.

The 1922 election also showed that, once again, some of the rural precincts, which had a high proportion of Scandinavian residents, were overwhelmingly pro-league: Raymond, the home of Rodney Salisbury, gave roughly 80 percent of its votes to the NPL candidate in most contests. The tally in the largest of Outlook's three wards was similar. While Charles Taylor garnered two-thirds of the votes for state senator in the three Outlook wards, he captured only 36 percent of the vote in the three wards of his hometown of Plentywood. Similar results occurred in the comparatively urban wards of Westby and Medicine Lake. A city-country voting divide had emerged.[32]

In late December 1922, the *Producers News* announced that, after a rousing send-off at the train station by a large crowd, Representative Stoner, newly elected Senator Taylor, and their families had departed for the state capital. The article indicated that readers could expect a weekly letter "telling us how they do things in Helena." However, such letters were not forthcoming. During the 1923 legislative term, from January 1 until March 1, there were only a few reports on Taylor's and Stoner's experiences out west. Perhaps both men were distracted, Stoner by his involvement in the new Montana Wheat Growers Association (of which he would be elected director in June 1923) and Taylor by plans for an important conference in Chicago slated for July 1923.[33]

Planned as an ecumenical meeting of labor and farmer organizations and intended to create a stronger alliance of farmers and workers, the Chicago meeting, as it turned out, took an unexpected turn when Communist delegates packed the convention and seized the opportunity to form what they called the Federated Farmer-Labor Party. News of this development quickly reached the Sheridan County radicals, and by October, the *Producers News* reported that an official call for a state conference to organize a Montana Farmer-Labor Party, signed by "twenty-seven prominent farmers and labor leaders" including Senator Charles E. Taylor and Representative Clair Stoner, had been issued. In the same story, Senator Taylor boldly predicted that "the entire membership of the old Nonpartisan League will join the new party en masse." Taylor cannot be faulted for this boldness. After all, in just four years, the radicals had been rewarded for their audacious actions with astonishing political gains. In fact, Taylor's prediction about the migration to the Farmer-Labor Party was about to come true, and the Sheridan County radical movement was set to begin its next phase. Charles Taylor was stepping onto the national stage.[34]

CHAPTER 7

Bait and Switch

Communism Creeps into Sheridan County

It was not every day that a Sheridan County, Montana, resident was featured in the *New York Times,* let alone on page 1 above the fold, but that is where Charles Taylor's name appeared on June 18, 1924. The *Times,* which was covering the national convention of the Farmer-Labor Party in St. Paul, reported that Taylor had been elected party chairman and noted that Taylor's candidacy was supported by the leaders of the "Bolshevist forces" at the convention, William Z. Foster and Charles Ruthenberg. The reporter added, however, that Taylor, "an old Nonpartisan Leaguer, is no Communist."[1] In this assertion, the writer could not have been more mistaken.

Taylor, in fact, had been a Communist since 1920 and was at the forefront in launching the new Montana Farmer-Labor Party, even as he was serving his first term as a state senator, ostensibly as a representative of the Nonpartisan League. The NPL had been struggling for various reasons, not the least of which was increasing intervention from law enforcement. Like the Wobblies, league organizers were often harassed, as was the case in Miles City, Montana, where an organizer was beaten severely and the charges against his assailants dropped by the local justice of the peace. The league was not helped by the 1919 conviction under the federal sedition laws of its founder, Arthur C. Townley, who was charged with conspiracy to discourage military enlistments during World War I. (Townley briefly served time in 1921.) Another sign of the NPL's decline was the termination of its newspaper, the *Leader,* in the summer of 1923. The league was essentially out of business.[2]

Communists, at both the national and local levels, saw an opportunity to step into the void left as the Nonpartisan League faltered. The American Communists had first coalesced in 1919 when the left wing of the Socialist Party of America voted to accept Vladimir Lenin's invitation to join the Communist International (Comintern) and had formalized their status by establishing the Workers Party of America in 1921, but the move to recruit farmers was a significant change of direction. In its early years, the party had given relatively little attention to rural residents, perhaps because most American leaders were themselves from urban backgrounds. Following the Third Congress of the Communist International, which called for a united front in advancing Communism, however, the American Communists slowly began to broaden their appeal.[3]

The Communists' ensuing maneuvering would give birth to, and ultimately doom, the national Farmer-Labor Party, whose purpose was to unite farmers and workers in a common struggle

"Foster's Red Group Easily Dominates St. Paul Convention," the New York Times *declared on June 18, 1924, and noted "State Senator Taylor of Montana Wins, 7 to 1, in Contest for Permanent Chairman."*

FOSTER'S RED GROUP EASILY DOMINATES ST. PAUL CONVENTION

First Test of Strength Shows That the Communists Are in the Majority.

MAHONEY IS VOTED DOWN

State Senator Taylor of Montana Wins, 7 to 1, in Contest for Permanent Chairman.

DAY IS SPENT IN WRANGLES

Delegates Get Tangled Up on Precedure and in Trying to Count Complicated Votes.

By ELMER DAVIS.

Special to The New York Times.

CONVENTION HALL, ST. PAUL, Minn., June 17.—While the first day of the Farmer-Labor Progressive convention here, which has been so vigorously denounced by Senator La Follette and the American Federation of Labor on account of the participation of Communists, did not bring any downright test of strength between the reds and the pinks, the reds seem to have it.

This conclusion, indicated by the volume of applause for Communist leaders and Communist sentiments earlier in the day, was made certain when a motion to adjourn till tomorrow was made this evening by Joseph Manley, son-in-law of William Z. Foster, who is the Communist leader here, and carried by a good majority, though anti-Bolshevist leaders wanted to prolong tonight's session.

Foster had previously been chiefly instrumental in defeating William Mahoney of St. Paul, organizer of the convention, for the Permanent Chairmanship. But State Senator Charles E. Taylor of Montana, who was elected, had a good deal of support outside of the Communist sympathizers and Mahoney had lost a good deal of his to improve the conditions of working people. The Communists' first effort to form such a party occurred at a July 1923 convention organized by John Fitzpatrick of the American Federation of Labor in Chicago. Fitzpatrick envisioned an alliance that would include everyone from the United Mine Workers to conservative organizations such as the Farm Bureau, and he issued over thirty thousand invitations to the Chicago meeting. John Pepper, a leading Communist and advocate of a farmer-worker coalition, saw Fitzpatrick's convention as an opportunity to gather more organizations beneath the Communist tent. To that end, he ensured that Communist operatives packed the convention and then voted to create what they called the Federated Farmer-Labor Party. In outrage, Fitzpatrick and his cohort walked out. It turned out to be a hollow victory for the Communists; only a fraction of the groups at the convention ever officially affiliated with the Federated Farmer-Labor Party, and most of those already had ties to the Communists. Even the chairman, William Z. Foster, concluded that the organization was little more than "a united front with ourselves."[4]

Despite the paltry gains at the Chicago conference, the Communists continued their efforts to align with farmers. In its October 1923 report to Comintern's executive committee in Moscow on the topic of agricultural work, the American arm of the party noted that it had "for the first time carried on work among the farmers during the past three months. We have had two organizers at work in North Dakota during August and September." The party also reported that "[i]n Montana there will be formed on October 23 a state Farmer-Labor Party which will have the backing of the whole labor movement and will be entirely under our leadership."[5]

By this point, Charles Taylor had been engaged in building a clandestine Communist organization in Sheridan County for nearly three years. He was also, by his own recollection, in "constant contact" with the representatives of the party's executive committee in New York. In addition, Taylor had also allied himself with William F. Dunne of the Butte Federation of Labor, who had guided his own Socialist local into the Communist Party a few years before.[6] Not surprisingly, Taylor was at the forefront of bringing the Farmer-Labor Party to Montana. In October 1923, Taylor, Clair Stoner, Sheriff Rodney Salisbury, and the former county superintendent of schools, William Moe, traveled to Great Falls for the event. According to a FBI report, the meeting was attended by "former Nonpartisan Leaguers . . . Labor leaders, Communists and IWW's" and that William Dunne, the "leading spirit of [the] organization," had "engineered the entire meeting." Oddly

William F. Dunne, Butte Labor Party. [George R. Tompkins, *The Truth about Butte: Through the Eyes of a Radical Unionist* (Butte, Mont., 1917)]

enough, Taylor's nemesis, Burley Bowler, who was now with the *Scobey Sentinel* in neighboring Daniels County, also attended. Bowler, incidentally, was already, or would soon become, an FBI informant, and he later claimed that the Communist-dominated meeting was part of what compelled him to turn his back on the farmers' movement.[7]

Even as the Montana Farmer-Labor Party was coalescing, a national Farmer-Labor convention, slated for the summer of 1924, was also being organized, and Charles Taylor, with the financial backing of William Dunne, traveled to St. Paul in November 1923 to represent the Montana Farmer-Labor Party at a call committee meeting to plan the national convention. Also present at the meeting was John Fitzpatrick, whom the Communists had angered just months before at the Chicago conference. At issue was the question of whether the Communists would be included in the 1924 convention, a move that Fitzpatrick opposed. Years later, Taylor described himself as the Communists' point man at the call committee meeting, selected because he was seen not as openly Communist but as a Nonpartisan League state senator elected as a Republican. As the floor leader for the Communists, he "battled to the finish...against Fitzpatrick" and won.[8]

William Mahoney, a Twin Cities union organizer and member of the Minnesota Farmer-Labor Party, handled the arrangements for the national F-LP convention slated for June 1924. According to Mahoney, the prospects looked bright in the months leading up to the event. Thousands of delegates were expected, and it seemed possible that the convention would nominate Robert M. La Follette, the well-known and respected senator from Wisconsin for president. However, a little more than two weeks before it convened, the St. Paul convention was repudiated by La Follette, who predicted that the meeting would be dominated by Communists, to whom he was bitterly opposed. He refused to attend or to accept the Farmer-Labor Party's nomination.

Following La Follette's public censure, cancellations flooded into Mahoney's office.[9]

La Follette's concerns were borne out. The Communists at the convention did indeed use strong-arm tactics to influence the party's direction, and their activities were widely reported in the press. One maneuver was to offer their own candidate to challenge Mahoney for the permanent chairmanship position of the Farmer-Labor Party. The Communists' nominee for the post: Charles Taylor. In selecting the Montanan to oppose Mahoney, the Communists were especially cunning. Taylor was nominated precisely because he was perceived (incorrectly) to be a true Farmer-Laborer, and not a Communist. Taylor said later that he had at first resisted the nomination; ultimately, though, Taylor routed his opponent, even capturing seventy votes among Mahoney's own Minnesota delegation.[10]

In addition to finding a chairman, the F-LP also selected its nominees for president and vice president: Duncan MacDonald and Washington State's William Bouck of the Western Progressive Farmers—who were nominated with the understanding that they would step aside if La Follette changed his mind. But this understanding was nothing but a ploy, merely part of William Z. Foster's plan. In fact, Foster, the general secretary of the Communist Party, and two other American Communists had just returned from Moscow, where they had been instructed to disavow La Follette.[11]

Wisconsin senator Robert La Follette, December 29, 1923. [Library of Congress, LC-USZ62-14109]

Charles Taylor, too, was receiving instructions from higher-ups in the Communist Party. On the evening of his election, Taylor wrote out in longhand the acceptance speech he would deliver the following day, and he gave it to the Associated Press and the United Press International. An undercover FBI agent, A. A. Hopkins, later claimed to have been near William Z. Foster in the lobby of the auditorium the morning Taylor was to speak. Agent Hopkins reported that Taylor had a handwritten speech but that Foster gave him a "typewritten sheet of instructions,

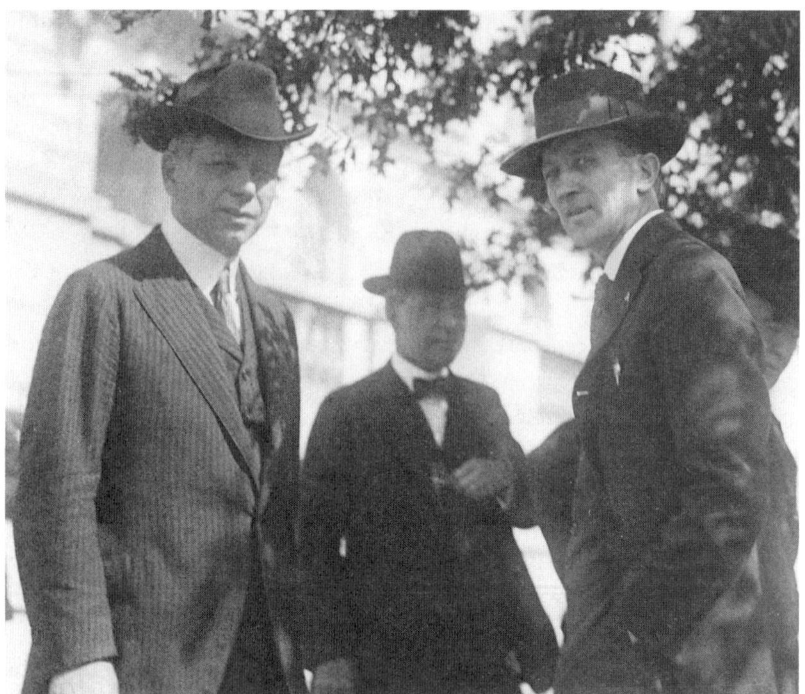

Federated Farmer-Labor Party chairman and Communist William Z. Foster (far right), October 3, 1919. [Library of Congress, LC-DIG-npcc-00400]

which he read to the convention, as his own, after reading his own speech." Agent Hopkins also noted that, in his speech, Taylor "stated that he had not talked with nor had been given any tips for his opening speech by any member of the Communist Party."[12]

Another undercover FBI agent, John Keith, noted as an aside in his report that he had seen Taylor at a Minneapolis picnic a few days before "in the continuous company of [William Z.] Foster, [Charles] Ruthenberg," and other known Communists. At the picnic, Taylor was said to have given a brief speech in which he referred to himself as "Red Flag Taylor." He said that he was willing to join any group that would liberate the masses and "did not give a damn how red they were." However, for the purposes of his acceptance speech, Taylor sang a different tune. The FBI agent reported that Taylor "stated that he is not a Communist; that he is not a member of the Workers Party"; and that, "prior to this date, June 18th, he had never talked with William Z. Foster, the Communist leader."[13]

Taylor succeeded in deceiving delegates about the true nature of his beliefs, which he may have viewed as a necessary evil in what he later said was his "battle to save the day for the Communists" at the Farmer-Labor convention.[14] After all, by that time, Communism had been under attack for several years in the United States, and many Communists thought the campaign had poisoned Americans' minds to the virtues of Communism—economic equality and social justice. Believing he and his fellow travelers were simply ahead of their time, Taylor may have felt justified in misleading his audience, especially if it was for what he saw as their own good. In the broader sphere of the American Communist movement, however, deceiving followers for the purpose of serving the party's greater good would eventually prove troublesome, and that ploy would play a prominent role in killing the radical farm movement in northeastern Montana.

Charles Taylor may have embraced deception for the sake of the cause at the Minnesota convention, but he was soon to learn it was a sword that cut both ways. Just one month later, in July, the 1924 Montana Farmer-Labor Party convention began in Great Falls. On the first day of the convention it was revealed that the national Farmer-Labor Party had withdrawn its endorsement of Duncan MacDonald and William Bouck and had replaced them on the ticket with William Z. Foster himself and Benjamin Gitlow. By no coincidence, Foster and Gitlow were also heading the Communist Party ticket in the general election.

The plot continued to thicken. Although he was the Farmer-Labor Party's national chair, Charles Taylor was stunned to learn about this last-minute switch of nominees from a local newsman who had just read about it on the wire service. The decision to pull MacDonald and Bouck's endorsement had not been made by the F-LP national committee, of which Taylor was a member, but rather by five of the seven members of the executive committee, three of whom were Communists. Taylor got his dander up: the Montanans rebelled against the selection of Foster and company, pledging to support Robert La Follette, who was running as an Independent. La Follette, however, refused to accept the Farmer-Labor electors in Montana and demanded an Independent slate. In response, Taylor insisted on keeping the F-LP ticket on the ballot. Thus, in Montana, electors' choices in 1924 included Democratic, Republican, Independent (La Follette and his running mate, Burton K. Wheeler of Montana), Farmer-Labor (the candidates' names were not listed on the ballot), Socialist (also La Follette and Wheeler), and Workers Party (Foster and Gitlow) candidates. The net effect was that La Follette's vote in Montana was split, although even if it had not been, the incumbent president, Calvin Coolidge, would still have carried the state.[15]

THE POLLS ARE OPEN FROM 12:00 NOON TILL 7:00 IN THE AFTERNOON. MAKE IT A POINT TO VOTE BEFORE THEY CLOSE.

Farmer-Labor Ticket

A VOTE FOR THE FARMER-LABOR TICKET IS A VOTE FOR LA FOLLETTE

Farmer-Labor Electors
These electors are pledged to LaFollette and Wheeler
EMMA SALISBURY
JOHN M. JOHNSON
W. R. DUNCAN
ELLA LORD
United States Senator
J. W. ANDERSON of Sidney
Congress, 2nd District
CHARLES E. TAYLOR, Plentywood
Associate Justice Supreme Court
HARLOW PEASE
Governor
FRANK J. EDWARDS, Helena
Lieut. Governor

Secretary of State
J. A. McGLYNN, Billings
Attorney-General
LINDAHL JOHNSON
State Auditor
LILLIAN MEINECKE
State Treasurer
HERMAN STRASBURGER
Public Service Commissioner
O. F. CLARK, Missoula
Superintendent of Public Instruction
BESS CREWS POTTS
Clerk of the Supreme Court

Judge of District Court
S. E. PAUL, Plentywood
For Legislature
ROBERT LARSON, Quitmeyer
A. Th. LARSEN, Plentywood
County Commissioner
ED. IVERSON, Antelope
County Treasurer
E. TORSTENSON, Raymond
Sheriff
RODNEY SALISBURY, Raymond
Clerk & Recorder
NEILS MADSEN, Coalridge
Clerk of District Court
DAN J. OLSON, Plentywood
County Attorney
ARTHUR C. ERICKSON, Plentywood
County Assessor
OLE ASPELUND, Dooley
County Surveyor
HANS RASMUSSEN, Dagmar
Superintendent of Schools
EMMA CRONE, Raymond
Coroner
MARTIN NELSON, Plentywood
Public Administrator
ODIN LUTNES, McElroy
Justice of Peace
L. S. OLSON, Plentywood
GEORGE WHEELER, Plentywood

The Producers News *"Farmer-Labor Ticket" published on August 22, 1924.*

Historians Harvey Klehr and John Earl Haynes have written that by the autumn of 1924 the national Farmer-Labor Party "was dead." This would have come as news to many in northeastern Montana, where radicalism was proceeding apace under the party's mantle. The takeover of the party by William Z. Foster, while significant to party activists, was probably of little concern to Sheridan County farmers, who were struggling through difficulties that continued to catalyze the farmers' movement. The yield per acre of wheat in Montana remained stagnant during the early 1920s, averaging a dismal twelve to sixteen bushels per acre. The local market price for dark northern wheat in March 1922 was $1.33 per bushel, and durum fetched $1.01. While it was true that economic conditions were not favorable, things were certainly not as bad as they had been in 1919, when only about half of the acres that had been planted actually produced enough to warrant harvesting, and yields averaged five bushels per acre. However, the wheat crisis of 1923, during which prices declined significantly just as U.S. wheat exports to Europe decreased, hit home in northeastern Montana. Of the twenty banks chartered in Sheridan County between 1910 and 1920, few survived the 1920s; seven banks closed between 1923 and early 1924 alone. Nonetheless, the county's population remained steady at around ten thousand people through the 1920s.[16]

It was in this context that the *Producers News* shepherded the Farmer-Labor Party into northeastern Montana. In the issue announcing a call for the formation of a national Farmer-Labor Party in October 1923,

The Producers News *promoted the Farmer-Labor Party in various ways. The large man behind the cab is probably Charles Taylor.* [Courtesy Bernice Whitney Van Curen]

a *News* editorial described a groundswell of support for the party in the neighboring Dakotas as well as in Washington and Nebraska. That "leaves no alternative in Montana," the paper claimed. Those who failed to support the F-LP would find themselves "behind the parade—for the mass of people of the state of Montana are practically unanimous for a Farmer-Labor Party."[17]

Such exaggerated statements continued to characterize the paper's coverage of the F-LP. The party was portrayed as an object of interest and excitement in Montana and beyond. Readers were cautioned not to miss out on something that was "the all pervading subject of political discussion in the state" and "the sole subject of political conversation in the corridors of the Capital [*sic*] at Helena, in the lobby of the Placer and on the Sixth floor of the Hennessy building of Butte, at a few places at Washington, D.C., and wherever else a couple of politicians happen to meet in Montana."[18] The *News* didn't specify whether the political conversations were mainly in favor of or against the Farmer-Laborers.

Run by a capable staff who were often responsible for putting out the newspaper when Charles Taylor was on the road, the *Producers News* had grown adept at the art of marketing, a skill that Taylor had honed while promoting his editorship during the paper's early years. In the early 1920s, the *News* continued to chronicle Taylor's exploits on behalf of the farmers and workers and continued to use the rhetorical strategy of contrasting bravery and cowardice, with Taylor, of course, cast as a courageous crusader. The editorial page said of him, "Probably no other man possessed the courage and ability to undertake the gigantic task of bringing this county back to the people. No other man would withstand the insults, offers of bribes and even threats of death than Senator Taylor." When Taylor "had to fight with his fists to defend himself, he did it. When the old gang brought charges in court he went into court and defended himself and every time he gave his assailants a good sound thrashing." The *News* asserted that some of the old gang had "never gotten over the day when Charles E. Taylor came to Plentywood . . . and spoiled their little game of looting the county. . . . Taylor . . . got their goat and . . . will stay on their trail until Sheridan county is rid of them all. And they are going one by one."[19]

Taylor's opponents, on the other hand, were typically portrayed as corrupt and cowardly. Although Taylor had not served in the military himself, he repeatedly claimed that Burley Bowler, his rival editor in the next county, had immigrated to the United States in order to avoid serving in the Canadian military during World War I. Referring to the anonymous editor of a competing Plentywood newspaper, Taylor lambasted the "spineless wonder" and "jelly-fish," whom he branded "A Yellow Cur" and challenged to "put up, or shut up."[20]

Certainly not all content in the *Producers News* was so confrontational, but it was consistent in its unabashed celebration of Taylor's celebrity, in particular following his election as chairman of the national Farmer-Labor Party in June 1924. Undoubtedly, most citizens of Sheridan County found it quite remarkable that one of their own had achieved such distinction, and the staff of the *Producers News* served up the story with suitably grandiose language: "[It is] indeed a great honor for Sheridan County to have its leading citizen elected Chairman of a great national party and by almost unanimous vote. Senator Taylor is now destined to be the leading figure in the new National Farmer Labor Party and as such will be one of the great national leaders."[21]

On the editorial page, readers were informed that it was their good fortune to have among them a man of such sterling qualities as Charles Taylor. Recounting Taylor's work in Sheridan County, the editorialist claimed that the senator's "perseverance and oratorical efforts" had helped save the county from ruin and that "no other man in the United States has accomplished more for his county and his community than has Senator Taylor of Sheridan County." In a turn of conceit, Taylor was shamelessly likened to the forefathers—Washington, Jefferson, and Lincoln—all of them "rebels against the present order of things" who were "denounced [in their day] as rebels and radicals. . . . So also is Senator Taylor denounced," the editorial continued, "as a radical and a disturber by every crook and thief in Sheridan County and the State of Montana."[22]

Although Charles Taylor was the focus of much of the *Producers News*'s hagiography, it also engaged in the minor idolatry of other radical leaders, including sheriff Rodney Salisbury, who was painted as something of a crusading hero and sometime-martyr in the newspaper's pages. Like Taylor, he was often portrayed as the object of fear mongering and hate campaigns and as a brave hero in an epic struggle. Still, even though it may have served the radical cause to defend men like Salisbury out of party loyalty, Taylor's readiness to come to their defense would eventually begin to taint him and his newspaper and galvanize local opposition to the Communists.

CHAPTER 8

Bootleggers and Boycotts

Liquor, the Law, and Radical Politics

As elsewhere in the United States, the 1920s were roaring along in Sheridan County. Prohibition had been in place in Montana since 1916, two years before the rest of the nation went dry, and Sheridan County had plenty of bootleggers, some of whom brought Canadian liquor over the border with Saskatchewan. Others ran stills in the countryside.

Among Sheridan County residents there was considerable tolerance for bending the rules when it came to Prohibition. Local histories note that in a coulee west of Antelope, a big still equipped with three 1,100-gallon vats did a booming business until federal authorities discovered it. According to one report, "It seems officials got suspicious because too much sugar was being shipped to the little town of Antelope. They seemed to think those few people in that area could not have that great a 'sweet tooth.'" Despite the fact that federal agents confiscated materials and destroyed the still, it was said to have been back in business in no time.[1]

Locals also took apparent delight in the exploits of their bootlegging neighbors, even helping them elude federal agents on occasion. In one case, the well-known bootlegger Ed "Fox" Estes engaged the services of a local threshing crew. Estes was carrying a load of whiskey from Canada with federal authorities in distant pursuit when he came upon a crew that was about to begin a new straw stack. Driving up under the thresher's straw blower, he implored the crew to "Turn the blower

Sheridan County's proximity to the border made it attractive to bootleggers who smuggled liquor from Canada. [*Plentywood Portrait: Toil, Soil, Oil* (Aberdeen, S. Dak., 1987), 30]

on!" Within minutes, his vehicle was hidden from the law enforcement officers who arrived to ask the crew whether they had seen a car pass by. They truthfully reported that they had seen a car, no more than ten or fifteen minutes before. The officers were baffled; "[H]e must be a fox," one of them reportedly said. "We were right on his trail and he just disappeared."[2]

Tolerant of illegal whiskey or not, many locals had a decided grudge against the man at the helm of law enforcement in Sheridan County: Sheriff Rodney Salisbury, who had been elected as part of the radicals' sweep in the polls in 1922 and was one of the county's "old time Socialists" and a friend of Charles Taylor. According to opposing newspapers, as well as rumors spread by his detractors, the sheriff accepted hush money from bootleggers, car thieves, and operators of Prohibition-outlawed bars known as "blind pigs." Of course, the *Producers News* defended the sheriff vehemently. In the summer of 1924, in a campaign to establish the sheriff's dedication to crime fighting, for example, the *Producers News* began to chronicle his raids and arrests as well as the county attorney A. C. Erickson's prosecution of these cases. Week after week, readers were informed about pool-hall busts, the volume of moonshine and Canadian beer seized, and Salisbury's

FOR PRESIDENT, ROBERT M. La FOLLETTE, ON FARMER-LABOR TICKET

THE PRODUCERS NEWS

LIBERTY IS NOT HANDED DOWN FROM ABOVE

THE PRODUCERS NEWS GOES INTO EVERY HOME IN THE COUNTY.

Official Paper of the City of Plentywood — A PAPER OF THE PEOPLE, FOR THE PEOPLE, BY THE PEOPLE — Continuing Plentywood Pioneer Press, Vol. 10, No. 4

VOL. VII No. 24 — PLENTYWOOD, SHERIDAN COUNTY, MONTANA, FRIDAY, SEPTEMBER 19, 1924 — Continuing the Outlook Promoter, Sheridan County News & Dooley Sun

Anderson Warns Against Signing Petitions

SHERIFF RODNEY SALISBURY RAIDS MOON JOINTS

Four Pool Hall Proprietors in Plentywood and One in Dooley Arrested on Charge of Dispensing Intoxicating Liquors —Two Firms Get Under Cover and No Liquor Was Found.

ALL ARE BOUND OVER TO DISTRICT COURT

Sleuths Make Investigations and Raids Follow—Only County In Northeastern Montana That Arrests Law Breakers In Connection With Volstead Act By Well Organized Raids —County Attorney Erickson and Sheriff Salisbury Receive Congratulations from All Parts of County in Their Efforts to Enforce the Law.

MUCH MOON IS FOUND BY SHERIFF'S RAIDERS

GEO. MUNSON GETS INSTRUCTIONS FROM FAMOUS JUD MATKIN

AGREES THAT COUNTY MONEY SHOULD BE PLACED IN BANKS INSTEAD OF PAYING OFF INDEBTEDNESS—ONLY WAY TO PUT BANKS ON THEIR FEET AGAIN.

In a conversation between Geo. Munson, the usurers' candidate for County Treasurer on the Republican ticket, and Jud Matkin, the famous commissioner who ruined Sheridan county, Mr. Munson was overheard to meekly agree with Jud that all moneys belonging to the county

Dolin and His Gang Meet With Bad Luck At Red Lodge, Mont.

Green Ink Rodgers and Numie Scott Have Floated All Over State of Montana, But Can Find Nobody Who Will Listen to the Kind of Bunk They Peddle Except the Plentywood Grafters—Hoped to Find Green Fields at Red

Dixon, Walsh and Combination Fire Long the Line on Both Tickets Is the Aim of the Forces Trying to Split the La Follette Forces By Putting Up Another Set of Electors When the Farmer-Labor Electors are Already Pledged to LaFollette and Wheeler.

CONSPIRCY HEADED BY DIXON AND WALSH

La Follette's Friends Should Refuse to Sign Petitions and Should Get Out and Wage An Active Campaign and Demand That Circulators Show How Two Sets of La Follette Electors Can Do Other Than Defeat Him in the Fall.

FRIENDS SHOULD UNITE TO PREVENT DEFEAT

Great Falls Leader, Sept. 9, 1924.—

"Much Moon Is Found by Sheriff's Raiders" touted a Producers News *heading on September 19, 1924; the article was an effort on the part of Charles Taylor to demonstrate that Sheriff Rodney Salisbury did not always "look the other way" during Prohibition.*

"pinching" of bootleggers and "nabbing" of car thieves. The *News* also published on page 1 Salisbury's call for drivers to register their vehicles and for "any information . . . regarding owners of automobiles who have failed to procure license[s]." The sheriff and county attorney were said to have received congratulations from all parts of Sheridan County for their efforts to enforce the law.[3]

Of course, from the perspective of the *Producers News,* no righteous crusade went unpunished, and the paper dutifully reported attacks on Salisbury by the powerful "old gang" of Sheridan County. When Salisbury was running for reelection in 1924, for example, the *News* deflected accusations of his misconduct by turning the matter into an issue of economic justice and masculinity: "Yes, the gang is out to get Salisbury. . . . Why do the bankers hate Salisbury? It is because Salisbury is a man. The cringing banker doesn't want a man for sheriff. A real man will not help them to rob women and children." According to the *Producers News,* the sheriff's reelection was not simply being challenged, he was being stalked and assailed. It reported that a "terrible fight" was being waged against Salisbury and that the newspapers "under the control of the Bankers and Usurers in the county are making weekly assaults upon him." The *News* printed an open letter from Salisbury in which he asserted that the "organized bankers of Sheridan County, who do not believe in organization of any other class besides themselves, are out to get my scalp." Using farm metaphors, a *News* reporter claimed that, although he was the best sheriff in the county's history and, indeed, in the entire state, Salisbury had "made many enemies because he will not allow his office to be used to hijack the farmers in behalf of a lot of rough collectors. He refuses to seize a red heifer on a mortgage foreclosure when the mortgage calls for a black steer. He refuses to seize and sell a hayrake when the mortgage calls for a drag. . . . Rodney Salisbury protects the interests of the workers and the farmers from the ruthless and consciencless collector."[4]

Perhaps even more damaging to Salisbury's reputation than the rumors about bootlegging were whispers that the sheriff was associated with a notorious character in town, Rudolph "Nig" Collins. Collins, it was commonly known, was the proprietor of the notorious Chicken Ranch south of Plentywood. He was also accused of running an illegal casino, a fact to which Salisbury was said to have turned a blind eye until the operation was raided by policeman Oscar Collins (who was not related to Nig). Salisbury's association with figures like Nig Collins, along with some details of his personal life that would emerge later in the 1920s, would become increasingly difficult for the sheriff, his friend Charles Taylor, and other local radicals to defend.

In the meantime, when the *Producers News* was not recounting the exploits of the local sheriff, it was trumpeting its own horn. In 1918, it had been a bantamweight upstart, dogging the established political hierarchy in Sheridan County. Editor Taylor seemed to revel in the paper's status as such. But after the radicals' electoral success in 1922, and with the notable support of local advertisers who found that the *News* was the best way to reach their rural customers, it became clear that the *Producers News* was now one of the leading papers in Sheridan County, along with the *Plentywood Herald,* the county's first paper. To hear the *News* tell it, there was no contest: it was the "leading county weekly in Montana and the Northwest: it has put Plentywood on the map."[5]

The *Producers News* portrayed itself on its pages using the familiar metaphors of war. Taylor claimed that the *News* was fighting the battle for the farmers and workers and was vanquishing corruption wherever it was found. On the occasion of its anniversary, the paper proclaimed, "We are six years old today. We have fought the battle. We apologize to no man." However, at roughly the same time, a number of businesses initiated an advertising boycott of the *Producers News,* to which Taylor responded with calumny. He claimed that the business owners were attacking the paper because it was "a free press: because it tells its readers the truth about what is going on: because it exposes fakirs

One of the sensationalized stories published in the Producers News *involved county doctors J. C. Storkan (right) and Clifford Sells. The ever-pugnacious Taylor accused the doctors of being unprofessional, unethical "amateur surgeons" and of slandering one of their colleagues who practiced in Outlook.* [*Plentywood: Golden Years, 1912–1962* ([Plentywood, Mont.], [1962]), 8]

and grafters both in high and low places." But the *News* vowed to press on and to "let the people know the truth" and to "continue to hold the respect and friendship of every honest, working, producing man in Sheridan County—men who believe in truth, honesty, and decency."[6]

The foundation of the advertising boycott had been laid nearly two years before. The *Producers News* had, from the very beginning, assailed big business, eastern bankers, and their ilk. However, in 1922, new lines of attack were drawn, at least one of which seems inexplicable, though it proved titillating for readers to follow. In February of that year, Taylor began what would become a grand crusade against two of the county's doctors. First, he accused Dr. Clifford Sells, the physician at the Outlook hospital, of "what looked like an effort to sabotage" the hospital in order to eliminate it as competition for the new hospital under construction in Plentywood.[7]

Little more was heard on this subject until March 1923 when the *News* condemned Dr. Sells and Dr. J. C. Storkan, the county's health officer. At the time, Sells was being considered to fill the position of county welfare physician, or "poor doctor." The editorial concluded that, if Sells was selected by the county commissioners to serve as the poor doctor, it would be evidence of "an arrangement between a couple of County Commissioners and Dr. Storkan and Dr. Sells whereby it is agreed that these gentlemen will divide the medical exploitation of the taxpayers between themselves." The commissioners selected Sells, and the fight was on.[8]

Among the *Producers News*'s most outrageous charges was that Storkan and Sells had "murdered" a patient at the Outlook hospital by secretly transferring him, in the middle of the night, to their hospital in Plentywood. They were called unprofessional, unethical, "amateur surgeons," and slanderers of their fellow physician in Outlook. Storkan responded by filing a libel complaint against Taylor. It happened that

Taylor was out of the state at the time the charges were filed, and the next week's edition of the *News* played the story to the hilt, running an item that had all the imagery of the old Wild West. Taylor supposedly had sent a telegram to Sheriff Salisbury, which the *News* reprinted: "The Telegram: 'I am on [Train] No. 3. Will surrender at Bainville. Taylor.'" The story's subhead read, "Victim of Dr. Storkan's Wrath Gives Himself Up to Officers of the Law as Soon as He Learns of Arrest."[9] (Bainville was the first town the train entered in Montana after crossing the North Dakota border.) It is unclear whether Sheriff Salisbury drove to Bainville to arrest his friend on these minor charges or simply waited for Taylor's train to arrive in Plentywood.

It is probably not mere coincidence that during this period Dr. Storkan set up his Farmers and Merchants Mutual Publishing Company and purchased a newspaper of his own, the *Sheridan County Farmer,* which Taylor took to calling the "Farmerine" and the "Ku Klux Journal." As soon as Storkan took over the *Farmer,* the assault on Taylor was under way. Referring to Taylor as the "Bombastic One," Storkan's paper asserted that Taylor was failing to do his duty at the legislature. Indeed, the *Farmer* claimed that he had run off on "another speech making trip but this time he failed to furnish amusement for the Montana Legislature where he was supposed to be representing Sheridan County in the Senate. It is the supposition that he called at Helena to collect his mileage and to whence he went or from whence he came after that mostly supposition but some of his followers here claim that he went to 'represent' the farmers at a farmer and laborers' meeting at Denver." Taylor had indeed taken leave of the legislature to

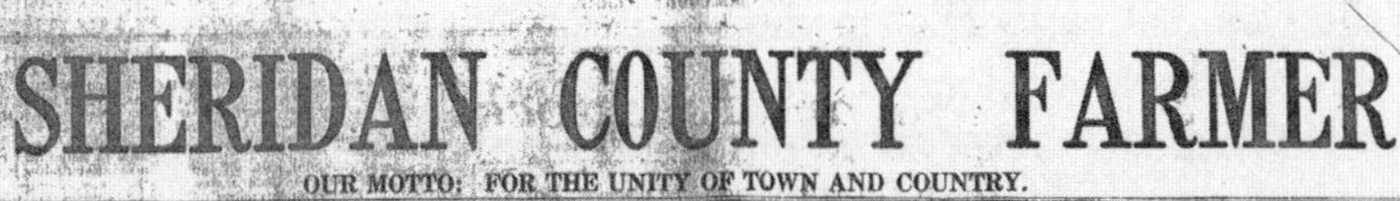

SHERIDAN COUNTY FARMER

OUR MOTTO: FOR THE UNITY OF TOWN AND COUNTRY.

Subscription $2.00 Per Year — PLENTYWOOD, SHERIDAN COUNTY, MONTANA, FRIDAY, FEBRUARY, 8, 1924. — Volume 1, No. 18.

Farmers and Merchants Organize Publishing Co.

TAYLOR IS BACK WITH TAIL FEATHERS DRAGGING

Chilly Welcome Greets The Bombastic One At Denver Meeting ; Not Recognized as Farmer Representative

Stockholders Meet Next Week to Elect Board of Directors and Engage Manager and Editor— Sentiment Chrystalizes Into Action Favoring Mutual Publishing Company; Printing Plant and Business of Sheridan County Farmer Purchased.

EX. PRESIDENT PASSES FROM STAGE OF WORLD

War President Passes Away At His Home In Washington From the Results of a Stroke of Paralysis.

Dr. Storkan purchased the Sheridan County Farmer *and used it to attack Taylor for his absences from the state senate, referring to his politics as "Taylorism" and calling him names, including "the Bombastic One," "Tubby Taylor," and "Red Flag Taylor."* [*Sheridan County Farmer*, February 8, 1924]

"FARMERINE" STOCKHOLDERS ASSEMBLE IN "BUTTER ROOM"

Directors Gather in Refrigerator Behind Closed Doors in West's Creamery to Talk Over Financial Troubles of Publication—Some Enter from Front, Others from Rear.

MARCH COMES IN LIKE A ROARING LION AND GOES OUT LIKE A GAMBOLING LAMB

Storkan "Drags Tail Feathers" Down Alley, After Emerging from the Frigid Rendezvous—Charter Members of Grafters Union in Despair.

BURLEY BOWLER CUTS NOT THE MUSTARD

There is trouble among the stockholders of the Farmerine. The great exponent of Unity of Town and Country is having the devils own time of it, if the stories told by those close to that enterprise can be cred-

Your Commercial Club meets on the Second and Fourth Tuesdays of each month; have you been attending? If not, you should, for it is only by your cooperation that results can be ac-

FARMER-LABOR PARTY SOCIAL AND DANCE AT COMERTOWN, MARCH 29

There will be a Farmer-labor dance and basket social at the hall at Comertown tomorrow, Saturday evening, March 29th. Sen. Taylor will speak and there will be a good program. There will be good music and there promises to be a good crowd. Everybody in the Comertown territory is invited to come out and have a good time. The proceeds will go to the Farmer-Labor party to help get ready to make LaFollette president of the United States and to elect a complete Farmer-Labor ticket in Montana.

SOME MORE HIJACKING!

Taylor ridiculed the Sheridan County Farmer *by calling it the "Farmerine" and met Storkan's attacks with equal ferocity.* [*Producers News,* March 21, 1924]

attend and speak at a Colorado Farmer-Labor convention, a decision he was forced to defend in a subsequent *Producers News* front-page story. Until the *Farmer* held his feet to the fire, there had been little need for Taylor to account for his comings and goings.[10]

The *Producers News,* always adept at doling out accusations, fired back, asserting that Storkan did nothing to earn his pay as a county employee and cited as evidence the case of the destitute Triplett family, who had nearly died of smallpox before the doctor arrived to care for them. The *News* also claimed that Burley Bowler, former editor of the *Scobey Sentinel* in neighboring Daniels County and new owner-editor of the *Daniels County Leader,* who had been a constant source of irritation to Charles Taylor, had been sneaking into Plentywood under cover of darkness to pen poisonous stories for the *Farmer.*[11]

In 1924, as the Sheridan County radicals were gearing up for the transition from the Nonpartisan League to the Farmer-Labor Party, the *Sheridan County Farmer* correctly predicted that the F-LP's national convention would be dominated by Communists. The *Farmer* ran the headline, "'Red Flag' Taylor, Bill Dunne and Ruthenberg, Dyed in the Wool Communists, Small but Lusty Lunged, Determined to Get Control of the Farmer-Labor Party by Boring from Within." It cited a story from the *Daily Worker,* the national newspaper of the Communist Party, in which "the Communists admit officially they expect to sabotage the Farmer-Labor Party and gain control of it." It was,

The war of words escalated to competing boycotts. "Boycott the Boycotters!" urged the Producers News, *May 16, 1924, when local businesses refused to place advertising in the newspaper.*

Boycott The Boycotters!

A number of Plentywood's so called businessmen, organized by Dr. Storkan and Dr. Sells, instituted a boycott on the Producers News last November, when this paper owned by six hundred farmers in this county, exposed the plot of the doctors to destroy a competitor and ruin the Outlook Community Hospital for obvious reasons. Just why these merchants should have made this defeated conspiracy of a couple of questionable medical practicioners a personal matter and something for them to resent, is a seven days wonder for people who believe in common decency.

It may be that these merchants were behind this conspiracy to wreck the Outlook Community Hospital: if this is true the sooner the people in the north half of the county understand the facts and take the necessary steps to show their resentment, the better.

These business men are out to destroy the Producers News by withholding advertising patronage—the directors and employes and county officers elected by the farmers and who are interested in the paper, together with many of the stockholders of the paper have agreed among themsevles and their wives and their families that they will not patronize any of the business houses who are boycotting the Producers News until these business men recognize the Producers News and the farmers who own it, and they ask all friends of fair play and the farmers and the Producers News to refrain from patronizing the merchants and business places listed below, until they renounce their boycott and demonstrate it by patronizing the columns of the Producers News as liberally as the columns of other papers who have not one-tenth of the circulation of the Producers News:

BUSINESS MEN UNFAIR TO FARMERS

MONTANA MOTOR CO.
ORPHEUM THEATRE
A. INGWALSON & CO.
WEST CABARET
HARRIS CONFECTIONERY
ZEIDLER HARWARE
KAVON GARAGE

The above firms will be announced fair as soon as they become fair: the names will be taken off or added to as the facts warrant.

incidentally, this same coverage in the *Daily Worker* that had helped Robert La Follette reach his decision to denounce the Farmer-Laborers shortly before their national convention.[12]

The war of words escalated to competing boycotts. First, the doctors reportedly organized an advertising boycott against the *Producers News,* enlisting the participation of seven local businesses. The *News* immediately began running a front-page announcement asking readers to "Boycott the Boycotters!" Readers were informed that "these business men are out to destroy the *Producers News*" and to "wreck the Outlook Community Hospital" and were asked not to patronize the seven businesses until they renounced the boycott and began advertising once more in the *News* as they did in "the columns of other papers who have not one-tenth of [our] circulation."[13]

It must have come as something of a disappointment to the staff of the *Sheridan County Farmer* when Charles Taylor became the chairman of the national Farmer-Labor Party in June. In fact, during the summer of 1924, the *Farmer* was less pugnacious, though it still issued the occasional accusation and did not hesitate to call the local radicals "Reds." As the November elections approached, the newspaper became somewhat enlivened. The *Farmer*'s headlines asked, "Do you Worship at Shrine of Taylorism? Question Confronts All Voters of Sheridan County." The newspaper acknowledged that many people had asked why the *Farmer* "devotes so much space to the activities of Charles E. 'Tubby' Taylor" and noted that some readers had grown bored with the squabble. However, the *Farmer* maintained that "Taylorism" was the key issue of the election and that voters had an important choice to make: "Independence, honesty, ability and efficiency or Taylorism, dishonesty, ignorance and inefficiency. Which shall it be?"[14]

As always, the *Producers News* made this accusation a fight for the farmers, invoking the language of class warfare. It deconstructed the epithet "Taylorism," arguing that this term was simply "a blind," a shorthand term for a "slam at the farmers' administration." Indeed, the paper continued, "It is not Taylorism the white-collared, soft-handed parasites mean—they mean the farmer's administration which is keeping them out of the county funds, where they would again help themselves and revel in fine cars and society events."[15]

Although the voters would answer with emphatic support for "Taylorism" and the *Sheridan County Farmer* would cease publication immediately after the 1924 election, the case of the fight with Dr. Storkan's paper is instructive for several reasons. First, it was a battle that Charles Taylor seemed to have invited, yet one that he did not need to wage. It is clear from the printed record that Taylor began dogging Dr. Sells in 1922 and Dr. Storkan in 1923, nearly a year before Storkan responded by investing in the *Farmer.* One possible explanation for Taylor's crusade is found in the Storkans' family biography, where the doctor's daughter wrote, "It was a rule of the political party in office, to require [anybody] on the County Payroll to subscribe a certain amount to their local newspaper, the *Producers News.* This Dr. Storkan refused to do, so a running feud was started."[16]

The Storkan episode also reveals the strength of the farmers' movement in the mid-1920s. Even the pugnacity of the *Producers News* and its relentless coverage of the Storkan-Taylor fight did not seem to offend readers or voters; if it did, there was no evidence of it in the outcome of the 1924 election. On the contrary, the feud may have captured the interest of readers who had a taste for scandal and rumor.

What is most telling about the *Sheridan County Farmer* episode is that it foreshadowed the opposition to come. True, Burley Bowler had been and would continue to be a thorn in the flesh of the Sheridan County radicals, but other newspapers, particularly in Sheridan County, had not been consistently vocal in expressing opposition to the radical regime. The *Farmer* was the first Plentywood paper to engage in vigorous and sustained opposition to the radicals, but it would not be the last.

CHAPTER 9

No Longer under Cover

Unconcealed Communism in Sheridan County

The Sheridan County supporters of the Farmer-Labor Party, apparently untroubled by accusations against their sheriff or boycotts of their newspaper, went about the business of galvanizing voters and recruiting new followers as the 1924 election season approached. However, during this heyday of radicalism in northeastern Montana, change was afoot and was most obvious in the new and unfamiliar material that began appearing in the *Producers News.*

On February 1, 1924, the *News* ran an editorial on the Teapot Dome scandal. It was written with the same vividness and belligerence of most *News* columns, but it was not authored by Charles Taylor or any northeastern Montanan. It was a reprint from the Communist Party's *Daily Worker.* This issue also carried other new features, including long editorials filling page 6, one of which was "Lenin—The Leader of the World Revolution Is Dead," written by John Pepper, a well-known Communist. A Hungarian, Pepper had served as the war commissar in the brief reign of the Hungarian Communist Republic before he was sent to the United States by Moscow. "Our greatest leader is dead," Pepper wrote about Lenin. In addition to brief discussions of Marx's historical materialism, the dictatorship of the proletariat, and the conflict between the Mensheviks and Bolsheviks, Pepper asserted that "Leninism is Marxism applied to the present, the final period of capitalism." Readers of the *Producers News* had become accustomed to a newspaper in which editorials accused the county commissioners, bankers, and certain

Vladimir Illich (Nikolai) Lenin, circa 1920. [Library of Congress, LC-USZ62-101877]

doctors and newspaper editors of favoritism, gambling, draft dodging, filching county money, and murdering the occasional patient. These new editorials in the *News* must have seemed perplexing to some readers.[1]

Similar offerings continued through the rest of the year. Along with John Pepper's editorials were more reprints from the *Daily Worker* and columns by Jay Lovestone. Both Pepper and Lovestone were part of a faction of the Communist Party aligned with its then-national secretary Charles Ruthenberg and opposed to a group led by William Z. Foster. Ruthenberg was also a featured columnist in the *Producers News.* The paper, which had not previously confirmed or denied its ties to the Communist Party, now seemed to embrace the terms "Bolshevik" and "Red," even advertising Farmer-Labor–sponsored dances as "Red Revels." Reds were said to have "put pep" in the city elections in Plentywood, although the paper noted that the "red haters were out in their autos hauling voters to the polls," with considerable success. The paper also commended wisdom and good fortune of the workers and farmers of North Dakota who had put A. C. Miller, a declared Communist, in the legislature.[2]

The *Producers News* was coming out of the closet. The reasons for this shift are not clear, although they presumably have much to do with the fact that Charles Taylor was in a period of harmony with the Communist Party, which would result in his selection as chairman of the Farmer-Labor Party at the St. Paul convention in the summer of 1924. Furthermore, he may have been experiencing some intoxication with his growing power as a state senator and rising star in the Communist Party. He may, too, have been inclined to curry favor with the Communists by being more openly ideological in his newspaper. And not to be overlooked is the fact that the radicals were firmly and comfortably ensconced in leadership positions in Sheridan County government.

For all of these reasons, Taylor may have felt safe in publishing more blatantly Communist material during 1924.

Thanks in part to the efforts of the *Producers News,* the Farmer-Labor Party enjoyed a landmark outing in the 1924 election. Voter turnout was strong despite the stormy weather on election day, and, in the words of the *Producers News,* the county was "redeemed" in spite of the opposition's best efforts. The Farmer-Labor candidates once again gained victory, with all but two of the party's nominees being elected. A Republican beat the Farmer-Labor candidate for justice of the peace by just two votes; meanwhile, in a three-man race, Charles Taylor lost his bid for a seat in the U.S. House of Representatives. He received 53 percent of the vote in Sheridan County but did not accumulate so much as a plurality in any other county in his congressional district, losing by a nine-to-one margin. He did, however, return to the state senate to complete his first term. As in the election of 1920, rural voters were more inclined than town dwellers to support Farmer-Labor candidates. The most significant margins of victory for Sheriff Rodney Salisbury were in his own rural precinct of Raymond (78 percent), in Outlook's three wards (75 percent), and in the communities of Coalridge and Dagmar (72 and 66 percent), all of which were farming communities with significant concentrations of Scandinavians. Salisbury won only

Outlook, looking northeast from the Minneapolis, St. Paul and Sault Ste. Marie Railroad (Soo Line), 1913. [Magnus Aasheim, ed., *Sheridan's Daybreak: A Story of Sheridan County and Its Pioneers,* 3 vols. (Great Falls, Mont., 1970), 1:466]

one of Plentywood's three wards, capturing 46 percent of the ballots overall.[3]

In spite of any town-country divide, the Farmer-Labor Party's victory in the 1924 election was indisputable. To celebrate, the party began immediately to organize both radical and politically uninvolved community members in the construction of a large civic auditorium. It was to be called the Farmer-Labor Temple and, according to the *News,* was intended to fill a "long felt need" in Sheridan County and "at the same time be a sort of memorial to the triumph at the polls" of the Farmer-Labor Party. The anticipated cost of the sprawling building, which would take up most of one side of a city block, was seven thousand dollars, though county residents donated a great deal of labor and materials. Contributors and builders ranged from Oscar Wagnild of the Outlook community, who had no involvement with the Farmer-Laborers or any other political organization, to the usual suspects of the radical movement such as Taylor, Salisbury, and Hans Rasmussen.

Outlook elevators and Soo Line railroad tracks, 1913. [Bell, photographer, MHS, Helena, PAc 83-33, detail]

Farmer-Labor Temple, Plentywood. [Courtesy Paula Hass Althoff]

The *Producers News* proclaimed that the Farmer-Labor Temple would be "a wonderful testimonial to the fact that after these years of strife and struggle, unity in a great measure has actually been attained. Unity, not on the basis of victor and vanquished, but on the basis of real cooperation."[4]

The sort of coalition spirit that led to the rapid construction of the Farmer-Labor Temple also characterized the relationship between the Farmer-Laborers and the new Western Progressive Farmers (WPF) organization, which was doing business in the state as the Montana Progressive Farmers. The organization had been founded by William Bouck, former Washington State Grange master and, briefly, the 1924 vice-presidential nominee of the Farmer-Labor Party. Described as "a hard-bitten old farmer," Bouck had caused friction during his tenure as a Grange master because of his opposition to World War I and his open admiration of the Russian Revolution. He had finally been expelled from the Grange in 1921. Taking many Grangers with him, he then founded the Western Progressive Farmers, which he hoped would surpass the Grange and the Farmers Union as an advocate for the farmers. According to historian Lowell Dyson, the WPF "combined drawing cards of family-oriented sociability—ceremonials, dances, and picnics—with the political and economic programs which large numbers of farmers had come to believe were necessary for their survival." For many northeastern Montanans, the organization blended ritual and radicalism in a way that was palatable. Like the Grange, Western

Progressive Farmers meetings had religious aspects: they began with a prayer or an invocation and often included the singing of hymns. As Charles Taylor later noted, "It went over good with a lot of the farmers that had a lot of religion."[5]

The *Producers News* first advertised one of Bouck's Western Progressive Farmers meetings in November 1925, noting in the headline that his arrival in Montana had caused a stir, and the paper continued to be a great supporter of the organization, especially its move to become a national organization, the Progressive Farmers of America. A January 22, 1926, article announced, "This is an age of organization. Every day we see how industry and finance are improving their organizations. . . . The Progressive Farmers of Montana is . . . directed against the head of exploitation and oppression everywhere. Join it at your first opportunity."[6]

Thus, even as the *Producers News* was becoming more openly associated with the Communist Party, it was also characterized by an openness to other organizations fighting on behalf of the farmer. This cooperation was in keeping with the Communist dogma of the moment. The fourth national convention of the Communist Party in the summer of 1925 had issued a report calling for Communists to expand their reach by working through other radical farmers' organizations. With the success of the Progressive Farmers in the region, Communist Party officials in New York City were eyeing the organization with interest. Charles Taylor was certainly doing his part to create alliances. At one point, Taylor wrote to Alfred Knutson, a Communist Party functionary in neighboring North Dakota, that the WPF was "growing to beat the band" and that, with Knutson's support, it would do well in North Dakota, too. Alfred Knutson, though, began to advise caution in dealing with such organizations, noting that William Bouck was "largely 'for us' because he thinks he can get some work out of us," but warning that the Communists should "be on our guard and not help these movements without gaining something for our own Party." Knutson also downplayed the WPF's influence in the region, claiming that it had little power outside of Sheridan County.[7]

While Charles Taylor supported the Western Progressive Farmers, the *Producers News*'s greatest effort in boosting the organization occurred during his absence. As a young man, Taylor had been quite a gadabout, but it seems that during the early years of building the Nonpartisan League in northeastern Montana, he remained close to his base of operations. Beginning in 1923, however, Taylor's duties in Helena at the state senate kept him away from the *Producers News* office during

Sheridan County delegates to the Western Progressive Farmers of America convention, Minneapolis, December 6, 1926 (left to right): Charles Lundeen, Outlook; Jens P. Olsen, Dagmar; Hans Rasmussen, Plentywood; P. J. Wallace, Plentywood; Emil Moe, Archer; Ed Hannah, Raymond; A. N. Wankel, Raymond; Niels Madsen, Plentywood. [Sheridan County Museum, Plentywood, Montana]

the biennial legislative sessions that lasted from January 1 to March 1. And in 1925, Taylor made a curious decision that took him away from Sheridan County for nearly a year. He invested in Radium Remedies Company, a partnership formed by several Montana politicians and businessmen. The company manufactured a product called Pyradium, its active ingredient being radium, which was used to treat pyorrhea and other tooth and gum diseases. An acquaintance of Taylor's would later describe it as "one of those gyp outfits that had high pressure sales men and literture [*sic*]." In June 1925, Taylor and two of his farmers' movement colleagues, Arthur Rueber and county treasurer Engebret

Thorstenson, set out for Minneapolis, Minnesota, to open the Radium Remedies's new factory and offices. At this point, the *Producers News* noted that Senator Taylor had not "changed his residence from Montana and will be able to spend much time in this state after he has placed advertising contracts for his company and got his office in running order." A month later, the front-page story of a farewell party for the Taylors reversed the previous statements, for the Taylors were now said to be departing "for their new home in Minneapolis."[8]

During Taylor's absence, P. J. Wallace took over editorial responsibilities at the *Producers News.* Like others in the farmers' movement, Wallace had a colorful past. He claimed to have been a colonel in the Irish Republican Army, a lawyer, a "cowpuncher," and a "working farmer." He had also served as editor of the progressive paper in Great Falls, *Town Topics*; secretary of the Montana Farmer-Labor Party; and a Western Progressive Farmers organizer. Wallace had also probably been a member of the Communist Party for at least some time. When the Progressive Farmers held their national convention in Minneapolis in December 1926, Montana sent more delegates (most of whom were Communists) than any other state, and P. J. Wallace was elected chair of the six-person national directorate.[9]

Wallace had served as an assistant editor at the *Producers News* for several months before Charles Taylor left for Minnesota, and he would stay on in some capacity until 1928. Taylor's opinions of his associate were mixed. In later years, he recalled that Wallace was "a smart Irishman" but also an "opportunist . . . freelancer and intriguer" who caused the northeastern Montana radicals "a lot of troubles."[10]

Wallace's "freelancing" might be evidenced by the fact that, while Taylor was away in Minnesota, his paper's support for the Western Progressive Farmers mushroomed. True, Taylor had been a WPF supporter, but starting in the summer of 1925, shortly after Taylor's departure, the *News* began to promote William Bouck and his organization with new zeal. Wallace gave Bouck a guest column in mid-September and, not long thereafter, began to publish nearly weekly accounts of the organization's doings in Montana and neighboring states.

Wallace made other changes at the *News.* Serials were popular newspaper fare of the 1920s, and Wallace published ones such as "Sallie's Temptation" as well as women's advice columns like "In Confidence by Flo" and "Etiquette by Flo." Compared with the combativeness of editorials by Charles Taylor and his staff, the opinion page during P. J. Wallace's stint at the *News*'s helm seemed quite staid. Guest writers like Bouck or reprints from other sources such as *Town Topics* filled most of the columns. Months passed with hardly a hint of scandal or a single case bordering on libel.

While the *Producers News* may have become more genial during Taylor's absence, there is also the distinct sense that the energy and community interest generated by the newspaper dissipated to some degree. What the paper gained in credibility may have come at the expense of its appealing character; some readers no doubt had followed it partly to see what outrageous thing Charles Taylor would publish next. Taylor continued to be listed as manager in the staff box, and he began contributing editorials again in September 1926, but even these entries were comparatively bland. In mid-October, for example, one of Taylor's editorials was titled "European Situation." It concerned the trade negotiations between France and Germany, a topic that probably held little interest for the average citizen of Sheridan County. Even Taylor's editorials on local topics lacked their old swagger, as when he noted the decrease in American voter participation, attributing complacency in Sheridan County to the voters' complete satisfaction with their local Farmer-Labor government.[11]

Thus it was that the *Producers News* ambled toward the election season of 1926. In most of the West, the election was a disappointment for the radical farm movement, with major defeats in North Dakota, Washington, and elsewhere. But radicalism still appeared viable in northeastern Montana, where the Farmer-Laborers won all but two county positions: county superintendent and county commissioner. There was one major upset: P. J. Wallace, who had made a bid for the state house of representatives, was defeated by a Republican. However, incumbent Farmer-Laborer Robert Larson, who occupied the other seat, won reelection. At this point, Larson remained comfortably in the fold, although he would later have a dramatic and public falling out with his former comrades. As for Charles Taylor, although he had been in Minnesota (and would, in fact, later be accused of failing to meet residency requirements), he was reelected to the state senate. Yet even as Farmer-Laborers in northeastern Montana celebrated the election of 1926, storm clouds grew on the horizon.[12]

CHAPTER 10

Big Trouble in "Little Moscow"

A Newspaper War Erupts

In November, the days are short in northeastern Montana, with twilight coming in the late afternoon. When most of the employees who worked at the Sheridan County courthouse left their offices after five o'clock on November 30, 1926, it was already dark. Consequently, none of them saw the two masked gunmen who entered the county treasurer's office a few minutes before six. November 30 was the last day for residents to pay their taxes without being assessed delinquency penalties, and the county treasurer, Engebret Thorstenson, remained at work late that evening as a courtesy to the public. His deputy, Anna Hovet, had stayed in the office as well.

The receipts for the day were sizeable. Thorstenson would later testify that, after he had counted the cash and bonds and taken them into the vault, a gunman appeared behind him and commanded, "Hands up!" Hovet, who had stepped out of the office for a few minutes, returned to find the door was locked. When she called out for Thorstenson to let her in, she was met at the door by one of the gunmen. According to a local newspaper report, the robbers forced treasurer Thorstenson to lie facedown on the floor and Hovet to get down on her hands and knees facing a wall. They were "subdued with forceful threats," and, after the robbers emptied the bonds and currency from the vault, the treasurer and his deputy were locked inside. The culprits had plenty of time to escape, since Thorstenson and Hovet were not discovered for nearly an

Sheridan County Courthouse, July 8, 1931. [Henry B. Syverud, photographer, MHS, Helena, PAc 77-94 v2 4.4]

Sheridan County Treasurer's Office, Plentywood, September 28, 1928, and (left to right) clerk Ida Newlon, county treasurer Engebret Thorstenson, and deputy county treasurer Anna D. Hovet. [MHS, Helena, PAc 74-72.7]

In 1926, the Farmer-Laborers won all Sheridan County offices but two (the county superintendent and county commissioner seats). County officers and employees included (left to right, standing) Ralph Hair, deputy clerk and recorder; Hans Rasmussen, surveyor; Pete Gallagher, undersheriff; M. Ostby, county agent; George Wheeler, justice of the peace; C. F. Christensen, assessor's office clerk; Clair Stoner, deputy sheriff; Ole Aspelund, county assessor; Nicolas Stenbak, assessor's office clerk; Dan Olsen, treasurer's office secretary; Rodney Salisbury, sheriff; E. S Koser, reporter; Niels Madsen, recorder; Engebret Thorstenson, treasurer; George Bantz, deputy jailer; (seated) Linda Hall,

hour. The robbers fled with sixty thousand dollars in bonds and forty-five thousand dollars in cash. They were never apprehended.[1]

Three days after the robbery, the *Producers News* reported that the crime was thought to have been committed by the same stickup men who had recently robbed banks in Malta, Montana, and in western North Dakota, but the *News*'s theory did little to hinder Sheridan County's rumor mill, which was running at fever pitch. The *Medicine Lake Wave* summarized the public sentiment when it stated that "the affair has all the ear marks of an 'inside job.'" One conspiracy theory held that Rodney Salisbury was involved in the robbery, an intimation which gained some credence from the fact that, as sheriff, Salisbury was in charge of the local investigation. Charles Taylor, in whose Radium

county superintendent of schools; Alice Redmond, county superintendent of schools stenographer; Lillian Paske, treasurer's office stenographer; Nora Thompson, county agent's secretary; Emma Crone, superintendent of schools; Arthur C. Erickson, county attorney; S. E. Paul, district judge; Anna D. Hovet, deputy county treasurer; Helga Hendrickson, clerk and recorder stenographer; Anne Hansen, clerk of court stenographer; Erna Timmerman, clerk and recorder clerk; Ellen Lundgren, clerk and recorder clerk. [Courtesy Glyn Deem, Deem Studios, Plentywood, Montana]

Remedies venture county treasurer Thorstenson had participated just a year earlier, also received scrutiny as a possible participant in the robbery. Many thought that the timing of the crime, just a few weeks after the election, was notable; had it occurred at the end of September or October instead, perhaps the candidacies of Taylor, Salisbury, Thorstenson, and their assorted colleagues would have been less successful.[2]

In neighboring Daniels County, Burley Bowler, a perennial foe of Sheridan County's radicals, published reports on the robbery as well. Bowler's *Leader* claimed in a headline, just two days after the heist, that the "Robbery Looks 'Queer' to Public." Bowler also editorialized, "Criminals do not work alone, or rarely do. . . . Just as certain as night follows day there was a lookout. . . . Who was that lookout? That's the job for the Sheridan officials to set themselves to if they don't already know. It is almost a cinch that the lookout or 'fixer' hangs out right in Plentywood; it is almost certain he is one of the Producers Noose pet gangsters."[3]

Indeed, when the county's insurer and its bonding agency launched an investigation—one that resulted in a three-year delay in paying the county's claim—many people became convinced that there had been local involvement in the robbery. Questions were raised about County Treasurer Thorstenson's decision to keep such large sums of money on hand and about the care with which Sheriff Salisbury conducted his investigation. The *Producers News,* of course, rose to the defense of the county officers, almost all of whom had been elected on the Farmer-Labor Party ticket. Regarding allegations that the sheriff, county attorney, and others had allowed crime to flourish, *News* editor P. J. Wallace claimed that "there is as little of these activities here in Sheridan County . . . as in any other county in this section of the state." He denied any involvement in the robbery and then issued his own accusations: those who spread rumors or published stories based on "insinuations that are baseless," he said, did so simply out of hate for the Farmer-Labor Party and its officials. He predicted that these "political enemies" of the farmers would "have a good time for some time now circulating anything their imaginations can conjure." Wallace's prediction was correct: the robbery would come back to haunt the radicals as area newspapers continued to speculate about it in the months and years to come.[4]

One of the area newspapermen who would keep the rumors alive for years as one of the most ardent critics of the *Producers News* was Burley Bowler at the *Daniels County Leader.* It is notable that although Bowler and Charles Taylor scrapped for the better part of two decades, they had more in common than perhaps even they knew. Bowler was fairly close in age to Taylor and had also spent his late teens and early twenties drifting from place to place, eventually finding his true calling in publishing. Born and raised in Ontario, Canada, Bowler moved to Saskatchewan when he was nineteen and arrived in northeastern Montana in 1913, five years before Taylor. He spent time in Scobey and Whitetail before finally setting up a jeweler's bench in a drugstore in the village of Flaxville. During this period, he became a newspaperman, working at a series of small papers in that far corner of the state—the *Flaxville Democrat,* the *Flaxville Hustler,* and the *Madoc Recorder.*[5]

By the time Charles Taylor arrived in Plentywood in the spring of 1918, Bowler was the owner, publisher, and editor of the *Antelope Independent,* and he began almost immediately to nip at Taylor's heels. There could not have been too much bad blood between Taylor and

Bowler early on, however, because after Bowler sold the *Independent,* he actually worked for a few months at the *Producers News.* He then moved forty miles to the west to work at the *Scobey Sentinel* in neighboring Daniels County. The paper was owned by the Farmers Publishing Company, an organization similar to the People's Publishing Company that backed the *Producers News.* Perhaps as a consequence, Bowler was thrust directly into the farm movement, even attending the 1923 organizational convention of the Montana Farmer-Labor Party in Great Falls. Bowler later claimed to have been disenchanted with the farmers' movement as a result of his interaction at the F-LP conference with William Dunne of the Butte Federation of Labor (who would eventually edit the Communists' *Daily Worker*). According to Bowler, Dunne expressed disdain for farmers, saying, "most of these jerks don't know what's going on." Bowler also claimed to have been disillusioned by some "private statements of intentions" (which he did not reveal) made by Nonpartisan League founder Arthur C. Townley.[6] In any case, his participation in the farmers' movement ended soon after it began.

In February 1924, Bowler left the *Sentinel* and bought the *Daniels County Leader.* It had started publication two years before and was quite typical of its genre: an eight-column, eight-page weekly focusing mainly on local news with some material reprinted from a news service.

Burley Bowler, shown here on the doorstep of the Antelope Independent, *circa 1918, was one of the most ardent critics of the* Producers News. [MHS, Helena, PAc 2007-65.1]

It featured the kind of boosterism typical of its day and extolled "community spirit" and hometown virtues.[7]

In his introduction to *Leader* readers, Bowler explained candidly that he had resigned his position at the *Scobey Sentinel* "for obvious reasons—one of which is that we might have got canned anyway." Eventually, the episode would be referred to vaguely as a "mutual disagreement over policy." For its part, the *Producers News* made clear the "mutual disagreement" was about money. The *News* reverted to its usual tactic, character assassination, noting that, when Bowler left the *Sentinel,* "it was wrecked in spite of the fact that he had taken in large sums of money, much of which was never accounted for."[8]

The issues at the heart of the conflict between Taylor and Bowler spanned county boundaries, in part because Daniels County had split off from Sheridan County only in 1920. Daniels County also had a fairly active farmers' movement, with nearly 20 percent of its electors voting in 1920 for the Farmer-Labor candidate for president (compared with 7 percent statewide).[9] But, if the *Producers News* was to be believed, the real issue in this case was Bowler, who the paper accused of freelancing for an opposition newspaper in Plentywood.

At the time Bowler took over the *Leader,* the *Producers News* was engaged in combat with Dr. Storkan's *Sheridan County Farmer,* a fight that would continue until the November 1924 elections silenced the *Farmer.* At first, Bowler escaped serious scrutiny by the *News*—save for the allegation that he had pilfered from the *Sentinel.* Charles Taylor's wrath was mainly aimed at Storkan. But as the conflict between the *Producers News* and the *Farmer* heated up, the *News* asserted that Burley Bowler "was brought into Plentywood after dark" to write anonymous news stories for the *Farmer.* Later, the *News* took to calling him "Burley Howler the Storkan tool" and accused him of having a gambling problem and of being a double-crosser. The paper predicted that the *Farmer's* readers would soon have only "disgust and loathing for the snake who dares not tell the world who he is." Eventually, the *News* would run a half-page exposé on Bowler listing all the disparagements it would use time and time again: Bowler had been something of a drifter, had left Canada to avoid military service, had been briefly employed at the *Producers News* to save him from destitution, and continued to be a "Knight of the Green Table" (a gambler). Summing up, the editorial proclaimed, "This traitor to every confidence reposed in him is defunct of honor, defunct of manhood, defunct of honesty and is defunct of a country. . . . King George could not find him, Uncle Sam does not want him, the Farmers of Daniels county would not have him."[10]

Bowler's name never appeared in the *Sheridan County Farmer's* masthead, and there is no proof that he served as a writer for the paper. However, the paper had no editor of record during February 1924, the first month after Storkan's takeover, so it is possible that Bowler provided temporary editorial assistance. Additionally, the *Farmer* and Bowler's *Leader* ran comparable exposés concerning accusations that Charles Taylor had overcharged the State of Montana for his mileage to and from the 1924 legislative session. Both newspapers published facsimile copies of the $186 expense reports that Taylor had submitted to the state auditor, and both reported that Taylor had left the special legislative session in order to travel to a Farmer-Labor meeting in Denver.[11] The duplicate news coverage seems to support Taylor's claims about Bowler's freelancing in Sheridan County.

The fight with Taylor became a regular feature in Bowler's *Leader*. Given the intensity of the scrutiny, Bowler tried to explain why he was so focused on Charles Taylor, writing, "We apologize to our readers this week for devoting some space to our arch accuser and slanderer, Editor Taylor of Plentywood." Bowler stated that he never would have concerned himself with Taylor's dealings in Sheridan County if Taylor and associates had not "launched their campaign to drive us out of business. We do not intend to devote any space in future issues on either of our maligners." Despite that pledge, Bowler went on to dedicate two full columns in that issue to Taylor and to publish front-page stories or lengthy editorials on the same subject every week in April and often thereafter during the summer and fall of 1924.[12]

The *Daniels County Leader* also shared with the *Sheridan County Farmer* the daring to call the *Producers News* Communist. True, by 1924, the *Producers News* had begun to embrace terms like "Red"; however, the *Farmer* and the *Leader* were pointing out something that the Sheridan County radicals were not yet admitting in mixed company: they were Communists. Burley Bowler wrote, "Be it understood that Mr. Taylor's doctrine is no longer the doctrine of the socialist party. They are too tame for him. He likes the up-and-coming he-man communist type. . . . That's the party of the hour now."[13]

After Bowler took over as editor, the *Leader* adopted one of the strategies often used by the *Producers News*, portraying itself as a tireless crusader, in this case against the destructive forces of the Sheridan County farmers' movement. As the 1924 elections approached, for example, Bowler claimed to have exposed Taylor and one of his associates as "deceiving frauds and fakirs" and noted that his was the only paper "that would dare undertake that job because of the abuse that those two abominable liars heap on all who call their bluffs. The *Daniels County Leader* has never wavered in this fight."[14]

Bowler pulled out all of the stops during that 1924 election season, mailing copies of the *Leader* to every registered voter in Daniels County in the weeks preceding the election, whether they held a subscription or not. Bowler acknowledged and refused to apologize for this tactic, saying that it was necessary given the threat to Daniels County. Likening the radicals to skunks in the henhouse, he wrote, "If a little animal with a stripe down its back and an odoriferous weapon invaded your chicken coop you would not wait until he had killed all the chickens and left of his own accord. Neither would you try to eject him with a bouquet of roses as your weapon. No sir. You would make it so interesting for him that he couldn't do much harm to any other than yourself."[15]

The strategy worked. Although the results of the 1924 elections were very positive for the Sheridan County radicals—Sheridan County's electors awarded nearly 46 percent of their ballots to the Farmer-Labor Party—they were less so next door, where Daniels County electors chose Robert La Follette's Independent ticket by a narrow margin over Republican Calvin Coolidge and gave only about 15 percent to the Farmer-Labor ticket.[16]

As time passed and the radicals continued to hold sway in Sheridan County, Bowler's newspaper began to employ more of the *Producers News*'s tactics. The *Leader* began to play with language, referring to the rival newspaper as the *Producers Noose* and to P. J. Wallace as "Pay Jay." It was sometimes entertainingly adept at cutting through the bluster and rhapsodizing of the *Producers News* and attacking Charles Taylor's cult of personality. One case demonstrates both Bowler's long memory and his ability to cut Taylor down to size. In 1926, Bowler called reader's attention to items in the *Producers News* that had likened Charles Taylor to Lincoln, Washington, and Jefferson, who were characterized as "rebels against the present order of things" and "denounced as rebels and radicals" in their day. Bowler rebutted the comparison of Taylor with the observation that the people of Sheridan County were beginning to come to their senses about Taylor's "organized gang," which allowed crime to flourish "under the noses of the officers who compare themselves to the martyred Lincoln and Christ on the Cross and are aided and abetted by a yellow sheet which would have the public believe it will emancipate all the peoples of the earth." Interestingly, the article comparing Taylor to Lincoln had been published nearly two years before, when he was the newly elected chairman of the national Farmer-Labor Party.[17]

DANIELS COUNTY LEADER

Volume V., Number 25 — Scobey, Montana, Thursday, July 15, 1926 — Official Newspaper for Daniels County

THUGS TRY TO BURN LEADER OFFICE

OIL SOAKED WASTE BOMBS USED; SPED IN BIG BUICK CAR

Sheriff Lawrence and Fire Chief Follow Car Tracks to Plentywood and Bring Car Back to Scobey; Thugs Disregard Lives and Property of Other Scobey Citizens in Attempt to Destroy Daniels County Leader.

QUICK WORK OF SCOBEY FIRE FIGHTERS PREVENTS TOTAL LOSS

Fire Bugs Are Well Known Dive Keepers Who, With Taylor and Wallace, Rule Sheridan County; Will Stoop to Anything; Hate Leader for Exposing Them.

At three o'clock Tuesday morning of this week a big Master Buick car drove into Scobey from Plentywood and after circling a couple of times to get directions firmly fixed in their minds for a quick getaway, glided into the alley along the rear of the main business block and swung east past the front of the Odd Fellows' hall and up to the rear of the Daniels County Leader office.

Entering the office they arranged piles of oil-soaked waste, stolen from railroad car boxings, in places where it would do the most damage when ignited. They then lifted the rear window and after going out and locking the door behind them ignited their arsenal through the window, jumped into their big car and sped out of town.

Explosion Awakens Citizens

The fumes from the gasoline and oil with which the waste was soaked acted like a bomb when ignited and the explosion smashed the printery windows, blowing the larger window in the front of the building almost across to the Battleson hardware.

The noise awakened several nearby citizens from their sleep, among them being Mrs. Sherman Irish and her little girl who live over the Leader office, and Joe Henault, the Leader linotype operator and printer.

The alarm was given by Justice L. C. Hitchcock, proprietor of the Daniels hotel who had just turned off his office lights and, very fortunately, Andrew Fadness was sitting up reading at the fire hall and he brought

AN EXPLANATION

A WORD TO OUR READERS AND PATRONS

NOTICE TO CONTESTANTS FOR PRINCESS

OBITUARY

Bowler left the Antelope Independent *to work for the* Scobey Sentinel*, then bought the* Daniels County Leader *in February 1924. Two years later, when unidentified arsonists set fire to the newspaper's office, he accused "Producers Noose" principals of being involved.* [*Daniels County Leader,* July 15, 1926]

Like Taylor, Burley Bowler sometimes played the role of martyr—the spirited fighter willing to endure any abuse dished out by his opponents. He was given a prime opportunity in the summer of 1926 when unidentified arsonists set fire to the *Leader* office. The fire occurred during the early hours of July 13 and was started by "thugs," according to the *Leader,* who had driven to Scobey from Plentywood, broken into the newspaper office, and ignited oil-soaked rags before fleeing in their Buick. The sound of the ensuing explosion brought people to their windows, and witnesses reported that the car had left town traveling east, on a road that led to Plentywood. The Daniels County sheriff and his deputies tracked the stolen car to a "dive run by one of the friends of Taylor and Wallace of the Producers Noose." Alongside the report on the fire, Bowler published a column thanking his supporters and noting, "While the loss by the fire will set us back to about the same status as when we first purchased the *Leader,* we are not the least bit discouraged and our policy has not changed one iota other than to become more vigorous." Bowler pledged to begin printing two thousand rather than his usual twelve hundred copies per week and sending them "into Sheridan county where our list of paid subscribers has grown by the dozen each week for the past few months."[18]

A few weeks later, Bowler's front page trumpeted that the *Producers News* was attempting to silence him. Bowler speculated that the paper's acting editor, P. J. Wallace, was disappointed by the failure of the fire to destroy the *Leader.* He further suggested that the *Leader*'s survival "sent shivers down the back of the *Producers News* editors and their friends." According to the article, Wallace's only remaining means of stifling Bowler was to file a criminal libel complaint, which he dismissed by proclaiming that he did not "care a continental hang about Pat and all the libel suits he can file." Bowler pledged to continue publishing the "facts."[19]

As could be guessed, the *Daniels County Leader* took great encouragement from the 1926 election results in Sheridan County. Although the Farmer-Labor radicals were still very much in control, Bowler's headlines blared, "Taylorites get setback in Sheridan County." And he delighted in the fact that P. J. Wallace had lost his bid for state representative, happily noting that the Taylorites had also lost control of the board of commissioners and the county superintendent's office. Bowler

Plentywood Herald *editor Cornelius Nelson and his wife, Anna Thorson Nelson.*
[Magnus Aasheim, ed., *Sheridan's Daybreak: A Story of Sheridan County and Its Pioneers,* 3 vols. (Great Falls, Mont., 1970), 1:669]

further predicted, "Another election will wipe them out completely in Sheridan County."[20] He was a bit optimistic, but not far off the mark.

As the *Leade*r carried on its rhetorical battle with the *Producers News* from across the county line, Plentywood's old establishment paper, the *Herald,* went about its usual business, which consisted of publishing local news and advertisements and, for the most part, staying above the political fray. Nearly as old as Plentywood itself, the *Herald* had been established by Cornelius S. "C. S." and Anna Nelson, who started out with an old press, inked and run by hand. They published the first issue in October 1908, and they soon had built a solid business and moved to a good location on Main Street.[21]

The Nelsons were great Plentywood boosters, and from the time of the town's incorporation, local residents continuously voted their paper "Official Paper of Plentywood."[22] During the first few years that the *Producers News* was rising to prominence and competing with the *Herald* for its subscriber base, the latter paper followed a hands-off policy as far as its rival was concerned. It remained politically nonpartisan to a great extent and published no significant criticism of Taylor, the Nonpartisan League, or the Farmer-Labor Party. Likewise, with very few exceptions, the *Producers News* left the *Herald* well enough alone. However, things were about to change.

In May 1926, C. S. Nelson acknowledged that, in the past, he had been "rather reticent . . . as to matter pertaining to local politics. The reason being that while we were mindful of discrepancies here and there—it was not of sufficient proportions or magnitude to warrant our attention." However, without specifying exactly what had sparked the change, the *Herald* took a political stance when it announced that Charles Taylor had returned from his entrepreneurial stint at Radium Remedies in Minnesota and noted that he was "back to town—with an ax up his sleeve." Even the "numerous faithfuls who have been toiling with him in the same vineyard and elsewhere for years" were said to be apprehensive. The article failed to clearly identify the cause of Taylor's colleagues' apprehension, simply stating that Taylor would be "swinging his baton of authority and leadership as of old" and implying that he would have a major role in selecting the F-LP candidates for election in November.[23] By the general election season of 1926, the *Herald* had completely abandoned its studied indifference. Virtually the entire front page of the October twenty-second and twenty-ninth editions of the paper were filled with stories about the Farmer-Labor candidates, the incumbents, and the *Producers News.* The *Herald* attacked the *Producers News,* asserting that it padded its claims and overcharged in its capacity as the holder of Sheridan County's printing contract. It asked why the stockholders in the People's Publishing Company, consisting of (by Charles Taylor's account) five hundred farmers, never received any dividends. The paper also attacked Taylor's legislative record, claiming that by voting for a new gas tax, he had failed to represent the farmers' interests.[24]

Other charges and insinuations published in the *Herald* ranged from the mundane to the exotic. Some of them were rumors that had been circulating in the county for years, and the *Herald* lent credence to gossip by asking why Sheriff Salisbury permitted "a house of ill fame to be operated within sight of his home," why county attorney Erickson failed to prosecute bootleggers, and why county treasurer Engebret Thorstenson had not paid the 1925 personal property tax assessed in his wife's name.[25]

In an unusual demonstration of restraint, the *Producers News* did not respond directly to the *Herald*'s charges, focusing instead on Burley Bowler's more incendiary attacks from Daniels County. The strongest response to the *Herald* came from editor P. J. Wallace, who noted that the *Herald* was a pioneering publication in northeastern Montana with an "ultra respectable" reputation but that the "anti-farmer gang now want[s] to put over their political schemes" by seeking support from the paper.[26]

Still, aside from the *Herald*'s foray into activism during the 1926 election season and the occasional volley thereafter, it was generally no particular threat to the county radicals. That is, until June 1928, when C. S. and Anna Nelson ended their twenty-year tenure at the *Herald* and sold the paper to Harry Polk, a newspaperman from Williston, North Dakota. A World War I veteran, Polk had been a schoolteacher and superintendent before being hired by Arthur Townley to edit a Nonpartisan League newspaper in Minnewaukan, North Dakota. In 1924, Polk purchased the *Williston Herald,* and four years later, he bought the *Plentywood Herald.*[27]

When Harry Polk arrived in Plentywood, he found conditions quite different from those Charles Taylor had found ten years before. Plentywood was now an established town with an array of new businesses, a hospital, an airport, and, of course, the brothels and illegal drinking establishments. In the countryside, conditions were temporarily improving. The mid-1920s had brought a series of fair and good harvests and improved commodity prices. The average size of Sheridan County farms was growing, and more cropland was being harvested. Montana wheat yields reached a twelve-year high in 1927, averaging 20.3 bushels per acre. Sheridan County recorded an especially good harvest in 1928, with the yield on continuously cropped land averaging nearly forty bushels per acre. Crops planted on previously fallow fields produced even more, reportedly as high as sixty bushels per acre. Although it still was not easy to become wealthy as a dryland farmer, times were certainly better than they had been.[28]

Aage Larsen, 1923. [MHS, Helena]

Perhaps sensing that economic conditions and the bruised reputations of some of their leaders had brought about changes in the political climate, members of the Farmer-Labor Party adopted a different approach in the 1928 election campaign. Rather than running as candidates of the Farmer-Labor Party, local radicals appeared on the ballot as Independents. The *Producers News* announced that it, too, would be independent in the upcoming elections, endorsing the best person for the job. Charles Taylor addressed this change of tactics in the *News*: "I believe the people of Sheridan County have arrived at the age of political maturity. They know the qualifications of candidates who will solicit their votes for public office. It is for them to decide who shall serve them. In the coming campaign the *Producers News* will maintain an independent attitude. . . . Let whoever wishes to enter the primaries enter. As far as this paper is concerned he will be sure of a square deal. We will not take sides."[29]

This sea change for the Farmer-Laborers may have been motivated, in part, by the defections of some members. In the previous election cycle, one such defector had been Aage Larsen, who had been elected state representative, with the Nonpartisan League endorsement, in 1922, and reelected as a Farmer-Laborer candidate in 1924. By 1926, for reasons that are unclear, Larsen bolted from the Farmer-Laborer Party and ran as a Republican for state senate against Charles Taylor. Larsen's accusations were published in the *Plentywood Herald* during the weeks leading up to the 1926 election: "If ever there were sent to the Legislature two inconsistent persons who wanted to make themselves ridiculous, you people of Sheridan County surely have them in Charles Taylor and Robert Larson. . . . It has been Charles Taylor's hobby ever since he came to Sheridan County to antagonize the bankers and work up hatred between the farmers and bankers and businessmen," he wrote.[30]

Even after his defeat by Taylor, Larsen was not silenced. In January 1927, he officially contested Charles Taylor's election on the grounds of nonresidency, alleging that Taylor had moved to Minneapolis for one year and had not returned to Plentywood until September 1926. Taylor denied the charge, claiming that he was gone for only nine months and always retained a residence in Sheridan County. According to the *Producers News*, "The complaint was regarded as somewhat of a joke by the assembled Senators and newspapermen and was not even read before it was referred to the Committee on Elections." Larsen's contestation failed.[31]

Disaffected radicals like Aage Larsen found their way into the local Republican and Democratic parties, which held an unprecedented joint nominating convention in 1928. In response, the headlines in the *Producers News* announced, "Mule Brays and Elephant Trumpets as Delegates Nominate and Elect Candidates to Run on Two Tickets. Cleaning House Ticket Sponsored by Mainstreeters and Their Lickspittles." The *News* belittled the convention: "Tuesday was a big day in Plentywood as the Elephant and the Mule sat peaceably side by side and saved the county from the horrible 'reds.' All the boys looking for fat contracts from the county were present, together with former disgruntled members of the Farmer-Labor party who could not realize their ambitions in that party and who are always a strong help to the 'old gang' when in need of candidates."[32]

Thus it was that the pivotal campaign of 1928 was already taking shape when Harry Polk arrived in town to take over the *Plentywood Herald.* He started out amiably enough. In his introductory editorial, Polk outlined his philosophy, stating that he would adopt the slogan of "one of the greatest organizations of service in this country," the Kiwanis Club: "We Build." He also offered an oblique contrast between his paper and the *Producers News* when he wrote that the *Herald* would not be "strictly a farmers' paper—nor will it be a business men's paper;

"Tuesday was a big day in Plentywood as the Elephant and the Mule sat peaceably side by side and saved the county from the horrible 'reds.'" [*Producers News,* May 16, 1924]

F-L BACKSLIDERS ARE STRONGLY IN EVIDENCE

Mule Brays and Elephant Trumpets As Delegates Nominate and Elect Candidates to Run on Two Tickets. Twenty-six Republicans and Ten Democrats Form Convention. Clean-House Ticket Sponsored by Mainstreeters and Their Lick-spittles.

but rather will it be a mouthpiece for all the people, always endeavoring to advocate those things which we know may contribute something to the growth and development of the city and country alike." Polk went on to applaud the *Producers News* and the *Daniels County Leader* for having declared the previous week that they would be independent in their 1928 election coverage. He endorsed Republican Herbert Hoover for president but stated, "In county politics, we expect to have little to say."[33]

Polk's remark about staying out of local politics surely was not the result of political naïveté. He knew full well that he had landed in a hornet's nest of radicalism. In an editorial that was an interesting mix of self-aggrandizement and flattery of the people of Sheridan County, he described an article that had run in a small-town newspaper just across the North Dakota border. According to Polk, the item had been headlined, "Polk Invades Little Russia." The article under the headline referred to Plentywood as "Little Moscow." Polk went on to comment that "anyone who talks about Plentywood in that kind of language has something decidedly wrong with their head. . . . We have found just as good people in this little county seat city of Sheridan County as are to be found anywhere we have ever lived."[34]

Initially, Polk may have been trying to emulate the *Herald*'s long-standing tradition of staying above the fray when it came to county politics. As a relative newcomer, he needed time to assess the community's sensibilities and avoid offending prospective advertisers. The *Producers News* was, after all, a popular paper. Soon enough, though, Polk had a great deal to say about local affairs. Within a month, the *Herald* and the *Producers News* were at war, with the radical newspaper accusing the *Herald* of having always fought the farmers' movement and the *Herald* responding that it supported the "Progressive Farmers movement" as long as it was "kept in control by sound thinking men who will not permit it to become a political football to be kicked about by unprincipled politicians."[35]

Earlier in the summer, the *Producers News* had reported that Rodney Salisbury remained undecided about running for reelection as sheriff. But the paper also noted that most of the farmers in the county were demanding that Salisbury put his hat in the ring and that they planned to draft him if necessary. Whether Salisbury ever seriously considered sitting out the race is unclear because he ultimately filed his papers. The *Herald* feigned surprise to learn that he would stand for reelection since "it had been generally believed that Salisbury had made himself so unpopular in the county that it would be possible to select a stronger

Progressive Farmer-Labor Rallies

• ALL EVENING MEETINGS

Come Out and Hear Them

EVERYBODY INVITED

Outlook—Friday Evening, October 26.
Redstone and Comertown—Saturday evening, Oct. 27.
Medicine Lake—Monday evening, October 29th
Reserve—Tuesday evening, October 30th.
Quitmeyer Precinct—Wednesday evening, October 31
Westby—Thursday evening, November 1st
Dagmar—Friday evening, November 2nd
Dooley—Saturday evening, November 3rd
Plentywood—Monday evening, November 5th

The Producers News *took care not to directly call attention to the Communist Party's efforts to recruit farmers through its Farmer-Labor Party, referring instead to F-LP members as "Progressive Farmer-Labor factors" in Sheridan County.* [*Producers News*, October 26, 1928]

candidate." A week later, the *Herald* extended this line of argument, marveling that the Farmer-Laborers would select Salisbury as their candidate for sheriff in spite of his "poorest kind of pretense at being an enforcement officer" and his "waning popularity."[36]

The *Producers News* fired back, placing farmers at the center of the conflict, explaining that by now the farmers should be accustomed to "having their candidates abused by the enemies of their movement." The paper assumed its typical rhetorical stance: the farmers' movement was under attack. The paper's official position—that voters should select the "best person for the job" regardless of party affiliation—was quickly discarded. While the *News* took care not to use the term "Farmer-Labor Party," referring instead to the Progressive Farmers and Farmer-Labor "factors," or "elements," in Sheridan County, it called upon the farmers to vote the straight Independent ticket. The *News* also tried to summon the specter of the "bad old times" before the Farmer-Labor Party had come to power. Identifying the *Plentywood Herald* as "a catspaw for the old gang that has always fought the farmers' movement," Taylor predicted that the voters would surely reject the *Herald* and the candidates it endorsed because they would "never go back to olden times when the selfish interest of a few people ruled this county." The *News* recalled the glorious day when "the farmers and workers rose up and with their paper" defeated the old gang. The editor implored the farmers and "workers [to] support your paper. You may be sure the opposition will support theirs."[37]

It had become a clash of the heavyweights, the two most influential newspapers in Sheridan County. Just four months after he had forecast having little to say about local politics, Harry Polk proclaimed, "There is no neutral ground in Sheridan county." The *Plentywood Herald* endorsed Herbert Hoover for the presidency and the Republicans vying for Congress but declared that in every other race it would support any candidate, Republican or Democrat, who opposed the "organized gang of corruptionists" currently in local government.[38]

The *Plentywood Herald* was turning the tables on the radicals in Sheridan County, stealing the language and symbols that had been the sole property of the farmers' movement. One of the *Producers News*'s favorite bedeviling terms, which had been employed for the previous ten years—"the old gang"—was now used in reference to the Taylor-Salisbury crew. Suddenly, the Farmer-Laborers found that they were the establishment and could no longer claim to be outsiders fighting the system. In what must have surely seemed to the radicals a bitter twist of irony, the formerly subdued *Plentywood Herald* could now embrace the role of regime buster. It played the part enthusiastically, and personal attacks flew.

As always, Charles Taylor was a tempting target. The *Herald* accused his newspaper of inconsistency, stating that the *Producers News* had formerly denounced the "dives, gambling joints and hell-holes" but that Taylor, "the man who declares himself boss of the county today draws down the profits of all the honky-tonks in the county and is to Sheridan [C]ounty and Plentywood no less than Al Capone is to Chicago." The *Herald* also suggested that Taylor was one of the worst "coffer filchers" in the county.[39]

Sheriff Rodney Salisbury, however, proved to be an even more popular target for the *Plentywood Herald.* One constant refrain was that Salisbury and his associates had either overlooked or, perhaps, overseen the activities of rumrunners and bootleggers. In this, the *Herald* was probably correct. Years later, Charles Taylor explained that, although he and Salisbury saw Prohibition as a failure, they recognized the public's expectation of enforcement. Thus, bootleggers were arrested in order to pacify "the Prohibitionists . . . and the teetotalers." When the lockup was full, suspects were allowed to leave the jail quietly and go home. Then the county judge, also a Farmer-Laborer, would fine the men and contribute the money to the school fund to satisfy the "church-going people." Naturally, Taylor admitted later, the *News* "played that in big headlines in the papers."[40]

Another of the *Herald*'s accusations was that Sheriff Salisbury selectively enforced the law by driving out into the country to personally sell auto licenses to farmers and by writing letters for his unlicensed friends "stating that the driver must not be molested" by law enforcement officials. Later, the paper claimed that Rodney Salisbury was a member of the IWW and that he charged the county for mileage he accumulated in taking Wobblies from place to place. Editor Polk reported that a visiting Wobbly had claimed that Rodney Salisbury's name was recognized among IWW members from coast to coast and that they would "do all in their power to re-elect him."[41]

Even more sensational than his alleged IWW association was Salisbury's alleged connection to prostitution in Sheridan County. The *Herald* claimed that a brothel operator "contributes her share towards the upkeep of Taylor and Salisbury or they would not let her remain in business." "There is nothing wrong with Salisbury—that is if you look at him through the eyes of a bootlegger, divekeeper or *Producers News* candidate," the paper concluded.[42]

The *Producers News* did not let the competing paper's attacks go unanswered. Taylor wrote that it was amusing to hear a man like Harry Polk "espousing the cause of public morals" since his own past read "like a story from Jim Jam Jems" (a magazine of the day that featured controversial social commentary on such topics as birth control and promiscuity). And, as the election drew near, the *Producers News* published an accusation unlike any before. In a long, front-page screed, the newspaper alleged that Polk had been forced to leave his teaching jobs in North Dakota because of "intimate relations with young and tender school girls . . . [and] low, indecent and immoral conduct in the high schools at Williston."[43]

In this ongoing war of words, one of the more potent weapons in Polk's arsenal was the robbery at the courthouse. Back in 1926, when the *Plentywood Herald* was still under C. S. Nelson's editorship, the paper had withheld judgment on the robbery. But Harry Polk was not so subdued when he resurrected the issue in time for the 1928 elections. He noted that Sheriff Salisbury had been "conspicuously absent" from his office when the county treasury was robbed, and he questioned the ethics of a county treasurer who remained open unusually late and who retained over one hundred thousand dollars on site rather than depositing it in a timely manner.[44]

Big Progressive Farmer-Labor Rally

SEN. CHARLES E. TAYLOR
Rodney Salisbury and A. C. Erickson
Will be the Principal Speakers
ALL CANDIDATES
on Independent Ticket will be there
Come Out and Meet Them

Speaking Starts
---at---
8:00 P. M. Sharp

EVERYBODY WELCOME
Ladies Are Especially Invited

FREE DANCE
After the Meeting---Given by the
Plentywood Council Prog. Farmers

Farmer-Labor Temple - PLENTYWOOD, MONTANA **Mon. Eve, Nov. 5**

[*Producers News,* November 28, 1928]

In October, a crucial moment in the 1928 election campaign, a case related to the robbery at the courthouse came before the federal court in Great Falls. County treasurer Eng Thorstenson and Sheridan County were suing the National Surety Company of New York, the insurer that had refused to pay the county's claim. A number of Sheridan County residents were subpoenaed, including Charles Taylor. Because of illness, Taylor did not appear, leading the *Plentywood Herald* to comment, "Of course we would not ask anyone to believe that Editor Chas. E. Taylor's present sickness has any connection with the subpoena served upon him this week demanding his presence as a witness at the trial at Great Falls. Many people are suffering from severe colds just now, and if Mr. Taylor is so afflicted—in the head, feet or otherwise—that should not be charged up against him."[45]

On the subject of the robbery, the *Herald* published insinuations and the *News* ran rebuttals, week after week during the fall. Finally, in the last issue before the election, county treasurer Eng Thorstenson published a front-page letter in the *Producers News.* He claimed that a local attorney had urged certain Plentywood residents to report to the National Surety Company that Thorstenson was involved in the robbery. Thorstenson wrote that he had been vilified and slandered by the attorney and the attorney's cronies at the *Plentywood Herald.*[46]

By the time the polls opened on an unusually warm November morning in 1928, it had been a contentious and exhausting election campaign. When it was over, the farmers' movement in northeastern Montana had suffered several devastating setbacks. One was the defeat of Farmer-Laborer Robert Larson, who had served two terms as state representative; Larson lost to a Republican. Thus, the delegation from Sheridan County in the Twenty-First Legislative Assembly consisted of Farmer-Laborer Charles Taylor and two Republicans. In the local elections, sheriff Rodney Salisbury lost his reelection bid, capturing only 38 percent of the county votes and winning in only seven of the county's thirty precincts. As usual, he did well in his home precinct, winning 60 percent of Raymond's ballots, but for the first time in his political career, he lost in the Dagmar and Outlook communities. The controversial county attorney, A. C. Erickson, lost his race to Grant Bakewell, who garnered 60 percent of the vote. Only two Independents were elected: one was unopposed and the other captured the position of public administrator.[47] It was a stunning outcome for the radicals, who had enjoyed a virtual lock on Sheridan County's government for nearly a decade.

CHAPTER 11

In and Out of the Fold

Sheridan County Radicals and the Communist Party USA

For any resident of Sheridan County who paid the least attention to local politics, it would have appeared in 1928 that the farmers' movement had fallen on hard times, particularly after the disappointing November elections. But what was not known to most northeastern Montanans was that Sheridan County had attracted the attention of Communist leaders in New York City and the Soviet Union.

The rural Montana county came to the attention of political leaders at the national and international levels in 1926 when the general secretary of the Communist Party, Charles Ruthenberg, requested copies of the *Producers News* to be "reported across" to Moscow. The following year, Ruthenberg's successor, Jay Lovestone, invited Charles Taylor to serve as a representative to the International Anti-Imperialist League conference in Paris. Although Taylor was unable to attend, the invitation was an indication of his status among the New York City Communist leadership. As for Taylor's home ground, it had become a coveted prize for both the North Dakota and the Kansas City units of the Communist Party. In 1927, the Kansas City office sent its subdistrict organizer, a "Comrade Sorenson," to Sheridan County, in spite of the fact that Andrew Omholt of Williston, North Dakota, had been assigned to work with the Plentywood faction. Sorenson must have liked what he saw because the Kansas City district organizer subsequently requested that Plentywood be assigned to him. Alfred Knutson, who edited the party's *United Farmer* from Bismarck, North Dakota, penned a letter to

Communist Party leaders, circa 1925, (left to right): unidentified, Jay Lovestone, William Z. Foster, Charles E. Ruthenberg, Ann Damon, unidentified, and Max Bedacht. [Hoover Institution, Stanford University, Stanford, California]

General Secretary Lovestone, in which he made several arguments for keeping Sheridan County in the North Dakota unit. He noted that the *Producers News*'s P. J. Wallace, "who is influential with our Plentywood comrades, though he is not a Party member yet, resented Comrade Sorenson's coming into the Plentywood territory at this time." New York finally sided with Knutson, and Sheridan County remained the "property" of the North Dakota unit.[1]

These intrigues played out beyond the view of ordinary people in Sheridan County, from whose perspective the farmers' movement must have seemed to be old news. Just a few years before, the radicals had virtually run Sheridan County and had placed three of their members in the State Capitol. Charles Taylor had been a rising star in the

Farmer-Labor Party, traveling regularly to conferences and meetings all the while publishing an entertaining and controversial newspaper that energized his political base. But the election of 1928 had changed everything. Suddenly, the Communists had only Taylor completing his term in the state legislature and his fellow radicals had won just two spots in the county government: the clerk and recorder and the lowly public administrator posts.

Complicating matters further was the fact that radicals could not even keep some of their leaders on the job at home in Plentywood. Charles Taylor had already been absent from the *Producers News* while he pursued his Radium Remedies venture, then worked for a lumber operation and lath mill in his former home of Koochiching County, Minnesota. The *News* made no pretense about Charles Taylor's whereabouts, even proudly announcing that there was talk of Taylor being the Farmer-Labor candidate for the Minnesota governorship in 1928. The news story did note, however, that "Taylor has refused to run stating that Montana is his adopted state, that he likes the people out there and was going to stay with them." As of the summer of 1928, Taylor was back in the editor's seat at the *Producers News,* but all was not well. He was finishing out his term as state senator but felt disillusioned by politics in the capital city. He later described feeling that the process was futile, unconstructive, and mainly involved attempts to "kill a lot of damn bills of no account."[2]

Taylor's replacement as editor, P. J. Wallace, also had a certain wanderlust, even during his tenure at the *News* from mid-1925 until mid-1927. He was often reported to be in Great Falls, Butte, or even Washington, D.C., on various lobbying trips, fact-finding missions, or "free-lance cruise[s] through the state." Burley Bowler at the *Daniels County Leader* took notice of Taylor's and Wallace's absences, writing, "When Kernel Pat is away from Plentywood Taylor tells us that Pat is the nation's saviour. Then Taylor goes away and Pat tells us that Taylor is a national leader. It is noticeable that there is always one of them absent." By 1928, Wallace had left town permanently for greener pastures in California, where he set up a "Montana Utopia Colony" in Los Angeles County. According to a notice in the *Producers News,* he was looking for interested parties to invest in his land development project and invited all to come out and see the promising acreage he had located.[3]

In his pithy criticisms, Bowler identified one problem that had begun to afflict the farmers' movement in Sheridan County—a lack of consistent and present leadership. Heightening the sense of instability was the movement's history of switching its alliances and endorsements. First, the Nonpartisan League was the organization du jour. In a matter of just five years, though, by 1924, the Farmer-Labor Party had supplanted the Nonpartisan League. At the same time, the newspaper supported William Bouck's Western Progressive Farmers and publicized the Montana Wheat Growers Association. While the initial transition from the Nonpartisan League to the Farmer-Labor Party seems to have aroused little concern, before long, radical farmers would be expected to call their organization by yet another name, the United Farmers League, an openly Communist group.

Insiders in Sheridan County were aware that many of the farmers' movement leaders were actually Communists, and as the 1920s proceeded, this awareness had begun to extend into the wider community. Yet, even this alliance was volatile. By 1928, Taylor had fallen out with the Communist Party, mainly as a result of his support for Leon Trotsky, the former war commissar in the Soviet Union, who had clashed with Stalin and been subsequently exiled. Like their Soviet counterparts, Trotskyites in the United States were expelled from the Communist Party, and Taylor stopped paying his dues in protest. Interestingly, at this time Taylor opposed the party's farm organization, the United Farmers

Leon Trotsky. [Library of Congress, LC-DIG-ggbain-35130]

Veteran Communist organizer Ella Reeve "Mother" Bloor (holding flowers) visited Plentywood in 1928. The others in the photograph are unidentified. [Sophia Smith Collection, Smith College, Northhampton, Massachusetts]

League, writing that it was "merely a caricature of a mass farmers' organization." When news of his defection reached Alfred Knutson, the editor of the Communist *United Farmer*, Taylor was denounced as an opportunist in the pages of the paper. Taylor later described this attack as "a regular program of the party. You left the party and they slandered you in every possible way, honest or dishonest." He retaliated in a *Producers News* editorial, calling Knutson incompetent and a "flunkey" who let the "party weathervane, not his conscience, [be] his guide." Referring to Communist Party headquarters as "the oracle," Taylor asserted that the editor of the paper dared not "write a few hundred words explaining the fundamentals of communism" until "somewhere in the east" (meaning New York City's Communist headquarters) the "latest thesis" had been produced.[4]

Although Taylor ended his editorial by expressing a "deep and hearty wish to see the Communist movement develop in the United States," it was not enough to keep him in good stead with party leaders in New York. Later that summer, veteran Communist organizer Ella Reeve "Mother" Bloor was dispatched to Plentywood where, according to reports in the *Plentywood Herald*, she denounced Taylor, Salisbury, and their ilk, saying that they were "opportunists, farmer baiters, and shysters." Soon, Taylor was being condemned on the front page of the CPUSA's *Daily Worker*. Calling him a renegade from the Communist Party, the *Worker* accused him of leading a "social fascist movement . . .

centered around the *Producers News* of Plentywood, Montana." Taylor was not to be confused, the *Worker* proclaimed, "with the poor farmers and workers" he was "seeking to delude."[5]

During this time, Taylor entered into a brief dalliance with the American Temperance League, the new pet project of the Nonpartisan League's founder Arthur Townley, while also working to revive the Montana Progressive Farmers. However, his falling out with the Communists was not permanent; a new farm crisis was developing, which would move him back toward the CPUSA. The good weather and commodity prices of 1928 had disappeared. The average wheat yield for the state in 1929 was half that of the previous year, and it fell even further in 1930. The following year, there was a complete crop failure in Sheridan County. Thus began the "Dirty Thirties" during which drought combined with relentless winds that carried away the precious topsoil of the region. Locals knew the dust storms as "black blizzards," when the air was sometimes so filled with soil that pedestrians in town could not see across the street; decades later some residents still recalled

feeling the grit of the land in their teeth. Legions of grasshoppers took what was left of crops. With no hay available, many farmers struggled to keep their livestock alive by feeding them Russian thistle.[6]

By this point, Charles Taylor had managed to make peace with the Communist Party leadership. In July 1931, just one year after she had denounced him, Mother Bloor shared the stage with Taylor at the annual farmers' picnic at Brush Lake in the eastern part of Sheridan County. For his part, Taylor no longer expressed any objections to the CPUSA's United Farmers League, which he had so recently opposed; in fact, he participated in the initiative to transfer the Sheridan County radicals' party of record to the United Farmers League.

The opposition press in northeastern Montana, now fully engaged, was prepared to seize the opportunities presented by this political shift to the United Farmers League. The league represented the Montanans' strongest and most direct link with the CPUSA, and the *Plentywood Herald* knew it. The paper announced, "Another quackery has now been foisted upon our people in the form of a political organization called

Wind erosion caused soil to drift and catch on fence lines during Sheridan County's drought years of the 1930s. [Henry B. Syverud, photographer, MHS Photograph Archives, PAc 77-94 v2 41.2]

Mother Bloor returned to Sheridan County in 1931 to help promote the United Farmers League. [*Producers News*, October 16, 1931]

"MOTHER" BLOOR MEETINGS

Mother Bloor, state organizer of the United Farmers League for North Dakota will speak at the following places:

Navajo School House, Saturday Oct. 17 at 8 p. m.

Valley School, east of Froid, Sunday, Oct. 18 at 8 p. m.

Alkabo, N. D. school house, Monday, Oct. 19 at 8 p. m.

Comertown school, Tuesday, day, Oct. 20 at 8 p. m.

Ophein, Auditorium, Wednesday, Oct. 21 at one p. m.

Peerless, Community Hall at 8 p. m., Wednesday, Oct. 21.

EVERYBODY WELCOME

the United Farmers League, which is merely another name for Communism. They dare not call it by its true name as there would be many who would not join, but when it bears some fancy name that appeals to the farmers, many are eager to join." The *Herald* later reprinted an official condemnation of the UFL by the Montana Farmers Union, a rival farm organization, and asserted that the UFL took its directions from Moscow. In neighboring Daniels County, UFL organizers were also at work, and editor Burley Bowler took the offensive, writing that "the name 'United Farmers' is mere camouflage for . . . communist leaders" and accused the UFL organizers in Sheridan County of "farming the farmer."[7]

This opposition was certainly not new for Charles Taylor and other Sheridan County radicals, and they remained undeterred. Taylor was appointed state organizer for the United Farmers League in Montana, Rodney Salisbury became the organization's county secretary, and Hans Rasmussen became the county organizer. The UFL held meetings in various communities, recruited numerous new members, and the *Producers News* declared that "such enthusiasm for organization never existed before in the west, it being even greater than during the militant days of the Nonpartisan League." In October 1931, Mother Bloor was once again in Plentywood for a UFL meeting and what was called a parade, although it could be more accurately described as a demonstration. If the *Producers News* is to be believed, fifteen hundred men, women, and children marched three blocks from the Farmer-Labor Temple to the courthouse, carrying banners that read, "No More Evictions," "We Want Shoes, We Want Clothes," and "Nobody Starves in Russia."[8]

During this period, Charles Taylor made a move that would be perhaps his greatest demonstration of loyalty to the Communist Party. It would also change the character of the *Producers News* and, more importantly, seal the fate of the radical movement in northeastern Montana. In 1931, he offered up the *Producers News* to be circulated nationwide as the official organ of the United Farmers League. The CPUSA's former farm paper, Alfred Knutson's *United Farmer* out of North Dakota, had ceased publication, and the party needed a replacement to aid in its agrarian organizing.

Although Taylor had not always toed the Communist line and had been something of a loose cannon over the years, his recent efforts on behalf of the United Farmers League stood him in good stead with people like Mother Bloor. She wrote to headquarters in New York in 1932 requesting that Charles Taylor be readmitted to the party. She noted that he had "stood the test of the responsible tasks given him by the Party very well."[9]

Not only was Taylor taken back into the fold, but CPUSA leaders, aware of Taylor's value to the United Farmers League, sent him on the road to serve as a UFL organizer, with his headquarters in Frederick,

THE PRODUCERS NEWS

Liberty Is Not Handed Down From Above

A PAPER OF THE PEOPLE, FOR THE PEOPLE, BY THE PEOPLE

Official Paper of the City of Plentywood

Sub. Rates: Foreign, $3.75 per year; In U. S. $2.00 per year

PLENTYWOOD, SHERIDAN COUNTY, MONTANA, FRIDAY, OCTOBER 16, 1931.

Entered as second Class Matter, October 18, 1912, at the Postoffice at Plentywood, Montana, Under the Act of March 3, 1879

United Farmers League Demonstration

13,000 CHICAGO INSTRUCTORS HAVE PAYLESS PAY DAY

Chicago, Oct. 15.—Pay day came again this week—without any pay day, for Chicago's 13,000 public school teachers.

They have received no cash for their services since last April, although some have accepte dscrip fro mtime to time, only to find it almost valueless. They were not even offered scrip in lieu of this week's $3,000,000 payroll because an injunction suit against further issuance of "Civil War Money" is pending.

The city is totally without money to pay the teachers. There is no prospect of any until the first of next year when the state legislature presumably may devise a financial scheme to ease Chicago's bankruptcy.

JASPER REUTER CROSSES DIVIDE

Jasper Reuter, 68, passed away at his home in Plentywood Sunday afternoon, October 11, 1931 at 3.30. He had been a sufferer from cancer for some time.

Besides his widow he leaves to mourn his passing four children, Nick Reuter, Mrs. Elmer Gooder Mrs. Claude Winands and Mrs. Carl West all, of Plentywood, and seven grandchildren. Three brothers and three sisters also survive. They are Nick of San Diego, Calif., Peter of Carlos, Minn., Phillip of Grand Forks and Mrs. Annie Ritter of Minneapolis, Mrs. Kate Thomas of Eureka, Montana and Mrs. Josephine Deiker of Alexandria, Minn.

Jasper Reuter was born in Carver county, Minnesota on March 26, 1868. He was married to Hel-

Mass Meeting and Parade of Agrarian Organization Draws Throng; No Untoward Events

Fifteen Hundred Farmers, their Wifes and Children from All Sections of Sheridan County Gather in Plentywood for Meeting — Big Farmer-Labor Temple Is Packed to Overflowing — Parade Extends Over Four City Blocks—Banners and Red Flags Carried by Marchers—Red Cross Representative Turns Down Invitation to Attend Because of "Lack of Time."

CONG. S. LEAVITT VISITS PLE'WOOD

On his trip thru this part of the state Congressman Scott Leavitt visited at the Producers News office for some time Tuesday morn-

G. B. SHAW LAUDS SOVIET OVER AIR

In Trans-Atlantic Radio Address Famous English Auther Asserts Russia Now Has the Laugh on Us With Huge Budget Surplus.

New York, Oct. 12.— George Bernard Shaw in a trans-Atlantic broadcast to the United States today maintained "Russia has the laugh on us."

The bearded Irish philosopher and playwright, speaking from London defended communism and the soviet government in Russia, which he recently visited. The program rebroadcast over a nationwide hookup was his first radio speech exclusively for Americans.

"Russia has us fooled, beaten, shamed, shown up, outpointed and has all but knocked us out," Shaw asserted.

"We have lectured her from the

GOVERNORS REACH COMPROMISE WITH SECRETARY HYDE

The new feed loan regulations agreed upon last week by Secretary of Agriculture Hyde and the governors of Montana, North and South Dakota followed conferences extending over several days in which the states' chief executives sought modification of agriculture department regulations.

(The maximum loan per family was reduced to $500 from $1,000.

Loans for livestock feed henceforth will be made for 20 head of cattle, six horses, 100 sheep and 10 brood sows, at the rate of $3 per head for horses and cattle, 30 cents for sheep and $1 per brood sow.

A compromise was reached on the question of mortgages, the government agreeing to accept second mortgages, except where prior

During the October 15, 1931, meeting of the United Farmers League, hundreds "listened for hours to Mother Bloor, and others, speaking" and, according to the Producers News, *the huge crowd poured into the streets carrying banners declaring "No More Sheriff's Sales; No More Evictions; We Want Cancellation of Debts; . . . Nobody Starves in Russia; We Object to Cast-off Clothes."* [*Producers News*, October 16, 1931]

South Dakota. And he was recognized with yet another leadership position. Within a few months, at the 1932 conference of the United Farmers League in Washington, D.C., Taylor, under the sponsorship of Earl Browder, the general secretary of the CPUSA, was appointed chairman of the executive board. It was noted that "Comrade Taylor can be utilized as a good speaker at mass meetings, but politically he also needs guidance because he very easily makes political mistakes. However, he is a very valuable force if properly utilized."[10]

In hindsight, it is no surprise party leaders wanted Taylor to be away from Plentywood. Given Taylor's unpredictability and the plan to take the *News* national, the party needed a dedicated bureaucrat as the newspaper's editor. This change at the helm of the paper signaled the beginning of the next era of Communism in northeastern Montana, one that would not end well.

CHAPTER 12

"Seeing Red"

Radicalism and Opposition Escalate

To understand the changes that occurred in the northeastern Montana Communist movement , it is helpful to know that, in 1928, the same year that the radicals had been beaten at the polls, major changes were under way elsewhere in the world. Communism had entered a new phase, and Sheridan County's radicals would be obliged to conform to various new prescriptions (and proscriptions).

In 1928, the Communist International (Comintern) announced the beginning of the "Third Period" of the struggle between communism and capitalism, which was intended to signal the growing instability of capitalism. The declaration of the Third Period would result in various initiatives. In the Soviet Union, there would be agricultural collectivization and "five-year plans" that were designed to rapidly industrialize the nation. Additionally, the 1928 program issued by the Comintern ordered that Communists distance themselves from non-revolutionary groups; for northeastern Montanans, these would include groups such as the Western Progressive Farmers.[1]

The Comintern program also contained communications directives, specifying, for instance, the types of slogans to be used by Communist organizations. The Comintern proclaimed that the slogans of the Communist Party "must be bent to the revolutionary aim of capturing power and of overthrowing bourgeois capitalist society." Furthermore, the program dictated that Communist organizations must profess their beliefs and goals openly: "The Communists disdain to conceal their view and aims. They openly declare that their aims can be attained only by the forcible overthrow of all the existing social conditions."[2]

In the United States, further directives were issued by the Communist Party USA. In 1930, for example, the CPUSA published a set of "theses and resolutions" that included a list of "flagrant examples of shortcomings" in some of the party's newspapers. These deficiencies included publishing advertisements of "professionals who were bourgeois candidates for office," printing Christmas greetings, and failing to print editorial condemnations of news stories that did not reflect party values. Any newspaper that made these errors was failing to follow the "Communist line."[3] In Sheridan County, the new editor of the *Producers News* would carefully toe this line.

That new editor was Erik Bert. In 1931, just as young Charles Taylor had been dispatched to Plentywood from Nonpartisan League headquarters thirteen years before, twenty-six-year-old Bert was sent from New York City to take over at the *News*. The New Yorker made it clear from the beginning, however, that he was no Charles Taylor. Born Herbert Joseph Putz in 1904, he took the name Erik Bert when he joined the Communist Party in 1929 or 1930. The son of a Bronx machinist, he was enrolled in a German Socialist Sunday school in his youth and later attended Columbia University and the University of

In 1931, after Communist Party USA sent New Yorker Erik Bert to Plentywood (above, circa 1930) to take over the editorship of the Producers News *and turn it into a national publication, the paper's content became more alienating to local readers by emphasizing Communist rhetoric and agendas.* [Mendro, photographer, MHS Photograph Archives, Helena, PAc 79-67]

Berlin. He brought with him to Plentywood his wife, Ruth, also a university graduate and a Communist.[4]

Bert was an avid reader, committed to staying abreast of issues. In a letter to the agricultural department of the CPUSA, he described his regret at falling behind in his reading since "making the change from New York to Plentywood." He subscribed to the *New Yorker* and wrote to CPUSA headquarters requesting subscriptions to the *Communist* and the *Communist International Magazine,* which he could not personally afford. Bert was also a keen correspondent. He wrote lengthy reports and letters, sometimes four single-spaced pages, to the agricultural department at the party's headquarters, to Henry Puro who was the director of the CPUSA's farm unit, and to others.[5]

On one hand, the *Producers News*'s star seemed to be rising under Bert's leadership as the plan to take the newspaper national was implemented. The United Farmers League launched a two-dollar-per-year subscription drive in early 1932 with the goal of a thousand new readers by the end of March.[6] Presumably, the backing of the national office would help keep the newspaper running in the black. Its editor was young, worldly, well educated, and dedicated, a person who should have been able to bring a new perspective to the *News.* Indeed, under Bert's leadership, the *Producers News* did become a new paper, but during his two years in Plentywood, Bert's editorial choices often either contributed to or were unable to diffuse controversies that presented significant stumbling blocks to the radical cause. The fact that Bert's decisions appeared to be the result of edicts from higher up did not lessen their negative impact on the northeastern Montana farmers' movement.

One of the controversial Communist initiatives covered in the *Producers News* was the local youth outreach program. It began with the Young Communist Training School held at the Farmer-Labor Temple, which commenced around the time Erik Bert took over the *Producers News.* During the thirty-day program, the school educated thirty-one "sons and daughters of poor and middle farmers" from Montana and the Dakotas who had "shown by their enthusiasm and activity that they will be leaders not only in the struggles of the farming youth against the misery that capitalism brings to the youth on the land but will become part of the leadership of all the oppressed masses against the present system of exploitation, hunger and brutality."[7] In more ways than one, this was not summer camp.

Just one month later, the *News* ran a convoluted and sensational story. Among its many claims were that Plentywood schoolchildren had

One of the efforts of the Sheridan County radicals was the month-long Young Communist Training School, "attended by pupils from North and South Dakota as well as Montana." [*Producers News,* November 3, 1931]

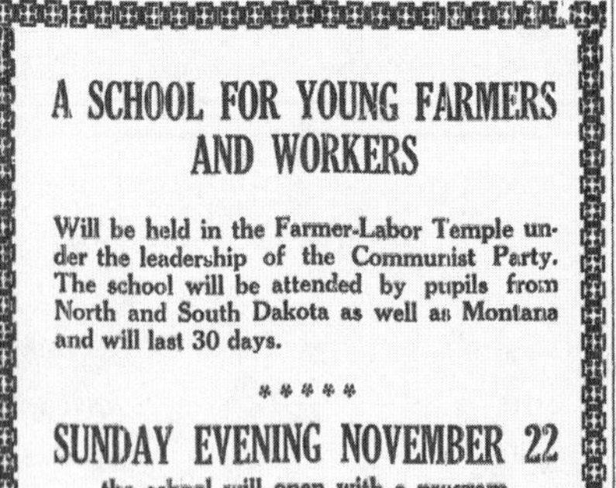

A SCHOOL FOR YOUNG FARMERS AND WORKERS

Will be held in the Farmer-Labor Temple under the leadership of the Communist Party. The school will be attended by pupils from North and South Dakota as well as Montana and will last 30 days.

* * * * *

SUNDAY EVENING NOVEMBER 22

the school will open with a program.

been forbidden by the principal of Plentywood's public school to attend the program at the Young Communist School and that some had ignored the prohibition. Former sheriff Rodney Salisbury's hired man was sent to Plentywood Elementary to bring one of Salisbury's daughters home. He allegedly assaulted a teacher in the process. A complaint was filed, and when the sheriff went to the Salisbury farm to arrest the hired man, he was confronted by Rodney's wife, Emma. Accounts varied, but it seems that she either struck the sheriff, threatened him with a sawed-off shotgun, or both.[8]

Ultimately, the hired man pled not guilty, and the case went to court quickly. Teachers, as well as children as young as ten, were called to testify in a case that captivated the entire county. One point of contention was whether the hired man had or had not told a teacher to "go to hell." It was not lost on either the *Plentywood Herald* or the *Producers News* that the trial was about much more than just what the hired man had said: it was an indictment of the Communists' youth outreach program and even a referendum on Communism itself. As Erik Bert wrote, "The United Farmers League,

Anti-War Meeting

and opening of the

YOUNG COMMUNIST TRAINING SCHOOL

will take place in the

FARMER-LABOR TEMPLE

at 7:30 o'clock

SUNDAY EVENING NOVEMBER 22

* * * * * *

MOTHER BLOOR, CHAS. E. TAYLOR AND OTHERS

will speak on

"WAR DANGER"

and other subjects of general interest.

COME EARLY and FILL THE TEMPLE

EVERYBODY IS WELCOME

The opening of the "Young Communist Training School" in 1931 was combined with an anti-war meeting. [*Producers News,* November 20, 1931] the Communist activities, the school, the demonstrations, the farmers themselves are on trial in this ridiculous, farcical prosecution, and not [Salisbury's hired man]." When the two-day spectacle ended, the hired man was found guilty but fined only ten dollars.[9]

Youth involvement in Communist activities was not deterred by the trial. One of the Salisbury girls organized a "Red Spark" club, which met on Saturdays at the Farmer-Labor Temple, and the town of Raymond had a Young Communist League branch. The *Producers News* began running a "Pioneer Corner Youth Section" that featured such festive items as the article "What Is Unemployment" and a current events quiz in which answers included "Dictatorship of the Proletariat" and "Hunger March."[10]

One of the most effective youth activities was a Young Pioneers group sponsored by the local United Farmers League for the purpose of recruitment and training. The national party also encouraged Young Pioneers groups to form elsewhere in the United States, and in the 1920s, urban units of the national Young Pioneers had been encouraged to "Smash the Boy Scouts" and to fight "For the Defense of the Soviet Union! For a Workers' and Farmers' Government!" But the party leadership finally realized that this brand of propaganda was ineffective in attracting children and proclaimed instead that "play and sport shall no longer be banned from the lives of the Pioneers." This change in tactic helped bring the national Young Pioneer enrollment from one thousand in 1930 to twelve thousand by 1934.[11]

In the summer of 1932, Erik Bert's wife, Ruth, led a Young Pioneer Camp at Brush Lake that hosted eighty-five children, who were divided into nine squads. Squad Two, "The Lenin Followers," reported to the *Producers News* that, in addition to swimming, kittenball (softball), music, and dancing, the camp featured "practice work which involves the role of trade unions" and "a study circle, one hour and fifteen minutes on the ABC[s] of Communism." Comments made by Charles Taylor indicate that the camp may have been long on dogma and short on kittenball. Taylor said later that there was an excess of "extreme . . . Communist discipline" and that he told Ruth Bert that she had "made a mess of things." Taylor claimed that Mother Bloor had "scolded [Bert] and told her that she was entirely wrong on some of the decisions she made."[12]

Still, the Sheridan County Young Pioneers attracted a large number of participants, who wore matching uniforms, memorized oaths, and attended meetings in the Farmer-Labor Temple.[13] A local resident, Louise Kavon, claimed that the Young Pioneers, with their uniform dress code,

Pioneer Corner

Youth Section

PUZZLE IN CURRENT EVENTS

Although the capitalist press tries to suppress all news about the working class, I am certain you comrades know enough about working-class activities to be able to match the answers below with the names above. We will print the names of all the Comrades who get them all correct. Send your answer to Pioneer Comrades, Box 28, Station D, N. Y. C.

Names

1. Hunger March
2. "New Russia's Primer"
3. 5 Year Plan
4. A. F. of L.
5. W. I. R.
6. Tom Mooney
7. Liebknecht
8. Dictatorship of the proletariat
9. Young Pioneers
10. Pittsburgh

Answers

1. An organization of workers all over the world which gives relief to striking workers.
2. A fake labor union which supports the capitalist government.
3. Government of, by, and for the workers.
4. A leader of the workers in Germany who was cruelly murdered by the capitalists because he opposed the war of 1914.
5. A plan by which the workers in the Soviet Union are building up the country.
6. A book about Russia's wonderful 5 year plan which everyone should read.
7. An organization of workers and farmers children which fights to better their own and their parents' conditions.
8. A worker who has been in jail for 15 years framed up by the bosses of California.
9. A march to Washington, D. C., in which over 1600 workers participated to demand unemployment insurance from Congress.
10. Place where thousands of miners went out on strike against a starvation wage.

RESOLUTIONS FOR 1932

It is customary among the pampered, well-fed and contented children of the rich to greet the new year with long and flattering list of resolutions. For these children, since their conditions are already comfortable and luxurious, nothing is necessary to improve their welfare, so they amuse themselves with such silly nonsense as "resolved not to chew gum any more," "resolved to say 'no ma'am' and "yes ma'am to elders," "resolved to give one penny a week to save heathen souls in Timbucktoo." But for us—for workers' and farmers' kids—the new year means only a continuation of the poverty and misery of the old year, UNLESS—we make our own resolutions and carry them out in the struggle against the causes of this inequality, THEREFORE, WE RESOLVE

1. To fight in the schools as workers' children in the campaign for free hot lunches, free clothes, and for free speech.
2. To help our parents in their fight against the bosses and bankers and their starvation wages
3. To bring other workers' kids into the struggle by getting them to join the YOUNG PIONEERS.
4. To read the PIONEER magazine, to sell it to other children, and to write articles for the magazine and the PIONEER CORNERS.
5. TO JOIN THE YOUNG PIONEERS.

The Producers News *published a special section for members of the Communist youth group, the Young Pioneers. The "Puzzle in Current Events" article asked "Pioneer Comrades" to match names and terms, including "Hunger March," "New Russia's Primer," "5 Year Plan," "Tom Mooney," "Liebknecht," and "Dictatorship of the proletariat" with their definitions.* [*Producers News*, January 1, 1932] became stigmatized in the community, noting that her nephew once told his mother, "Mama, I won't wear a red tie anymore because they call me a Taylor at school."[14] In spite of any stigma, local children of the 1930s absorbed the message of the United Farmers League. According to former resident Harriet Bjork, children sang an alternate version of the song "Red Wing," its lyrics having been changed to "Shall we strive and work for wages? It is outrageous, has been ages." As a child, Evedine Olson Lane attended Communist meetings in the gymnasium of the Comertown school and recalled later "their atheistic views and their songs praising Russia, not God." "I well remember," she wrote, "the fervor with which they belted out a song's last line: 'The international Soviet shall be the Human Race.'" Fay and Violet Chandler, who were both children in elementary school during this period, memorized the chants of the Young Pioneers, such as, "One, two, three, young Communists are we. Four, five, six, we're happy Bolsheviks." They noted, "We knew [Communism] was terrible because [it was] anti-religious. . . . We didn't dare tell our folks that we had anything to do with it."[15]

As the Chandlers' statement indicates, the Communist youth movement collided with an issue that had plagued northeastern Montana radicals for years: religion. From the beginning, the farmers' movement had encountered accusations about its stance on religion. In 1918, in response to questions about the beliefs of some local radicals, the *Producers News* published an editorial entitled "The Religious Issue." The writer, probably Charles Taylor, claimed that "political scoundrels" and "lackeys of big business" who were unable to confront issues honestly, would use the topic of religion "to get the people fighting about something that has no merit one way or the other, in the hopes of attracting attention away from the real issues to the bogus quarrel."[16]

Local Nonpartisan League and Farmer-Labor Party leaders argued that "the religious issue" should be separated from political matters, and yet the *Producers News* often appropriated the symbols of Christianity by acknowledging Christian holidays, claiming to strive for "Peace on earth, good will toward men," and using scriptural illustrations. In 1924, the paper even carried a series of sermons by a local pastor. One week, Pastor M. O. Sievert's sermon ran in an improbable location, alongside a column by Hal Ware, the son of Mother Bloor and a charter member of the Communist Party.[17]

Over the years, Charles Taylor had often employed religious references in attacking his opponents. In one case, he indicted a certain Fred Ibsen by comparing him to the Pharisees, "a bunch of hypocrites who made a great pretense of virtue but were as a matter of fact a cesspool of iniquity." In another editorial, Taylor played with the idea of the Holy Trinity by referring to five local men who were "consecrated to the saving of Sheridan county from Socialism" as the "Holey Quinity." But Taylor was stung with accusations of hypocrisy when the *Plentywood Herald* turned the tables and printed a gag item about talk "on the streets that Charles E. Taylor . . . will shortly resign his position and take up a course in Theology in preparation for the pulpit." He was outraged and called the *Herald*'s joke "a dastardly insult."[18]

Hans Rasmussen was a longtime Sheridan County radical and a Producers News *columnist.* [*Producers News*, November 2, 1932]

After Harry Polk took the helm at the *Plentywood Herald* in 1928, his paper could be counted on to raise the religion issue with some regularity and with increasing effectiveness. In 1929, the *Herald*'s editorial space declared that "over in Soviet Russia the government will use the radio to tell the people that Christmas is a pagan holiday, that Jesus Christ is only a myth and the Christian religion is but a superstition fostered by the Bourgois [*sic*] to overawe the masses and keep them in check." Two months later, *Herald* readers learned that "countless thousands" of Russians were forced to sign "declarations of apostacy and hatred toward God," and in March 1930 one of the *Herald*'s front-page stories, "Soviet Prepares for Great Drive on All Religions," indicated that there would be "huge anti-religious carnivals and demonstrations . . . in Moscow" on Easter. The *Herald* made it personal as well, claiming that *Producers News* employee Hans Rasmussen "does not feel at home in our churches, as he is too deeply soaked with bolshevism." Later, the *Herald* reported that the Soviet Union denied the existence of God and that Communists advocated "hatred of God [and] all forms of religion."[19]

Perhaps in response to the charges of the *Plentywood Herald,* the *Producers News* reported on the speech of a Reverend Hojbjerg, who had addressed a Lutheran congregation in Sheridan County. Columnist

Hans Rasmussen noted that the reverend and his son "spoke . . . in favor of communism and socialism" and that "the big audience applauded, which is something unusual to do in a church, but the crowd simply could not help themselves." Rasmussen then made a statement that may have unwittingly intensified fears seeded by the *Herald*, writing that it was unheard of to keep "a church-going crowd so interested in [a] subject that they throw all traditions overboard and sit there and clap to their hearts content."[20] The intention of throwing traditions overboard was exactly the accusation so often leveled at the county radicals.

With Erik Bert at the helm of *Producers News*, religious accusations continued unabated. A front-page *News* editorial during the 1932 election season was entitled "God and This Election Campaign." In it, the columnist accused *Plentywood Herald* editor Harry Polk of "dragging God into [the] election" with accusations that Communists were godless. The writer claimed that issues of religion should be left out of the campaign, emphasized that Communists were not fighting God, and maintained that the party left spiritual matters to those "who profess to be versed in such matters." Interestingly, when declaring that, if Christ were to return on election day, Harry Polk would cry "Crucify him," the *Producers News* columnist referred to "crucifiction day," perhaps a pun revealing the writer's opinion of the biblical account.[21]

During the same year, an incident occurred that sharply illustrated the conflict between religion and the Communist movement. It was the "Bolshevik funeral" for Janis Salisbury, fourteen-year-old daughter of Rodney Salisbury, who had died as a result of complications from appendicitis. The funeral, held in the Farmer-Labor Temple, was described on the front page of the *Producers News*: "Our dear young Pioneer, Janis Salisbury . . . was buried Saturday afternoon. The funeral services were those for a Bolshevik . . . the coffin was accompanied from the entrance to the front of the hall by the Young Pioneers, led by two Pioneers bearing a Red Flag. When the coffin had been placed in the front of the hall, the Pioneers arranged the flowers which had been sent by the Young Pioneers, her school mates, the United Farmers League, the *Producers News* and the Communist party, and others." The article described the Farmer-Labor Temple, its windows and stage draped in red and black with hammer and sickle emblems, as well as the involvement of the Young Pioneers, who sang revolutionary songs and recited a pledge to the "Red Flag."[22]

The *Plentywood Herald* editorialist was livid. If Communism was adopted, he wrote, "For the hope of a Hereafter, which in deepest sorrow has been the only source of comfort for those we loved, . . . would be

Bolshevik Funeral for Valiant Young Pioneer, Janis Salisbury

Our dear young Pioneer, Janis Salisbury, who died on Tuesday, March 1, following an operation for appendicitis, was buried on Saturday afternoon. The funeral services for Janis were those for a Bolshevik.

Many farmers and townspeople were forced to stand in the Farmer-Labor Temple which was crowded to capacity when the funeral started at half past two. The coffin was accompanied from the entrance to the front of the hall by the Young Pioneers, led by two Pioneers bearing a Red Flag. When the coffin had been placed in the front of the hall, the Pioneers arranged the flowers which had been sent by the Young Pioneers, her school mates, the United Farmers League, the Producers News and the Communist Party, and others.

The windows and the stage were covered with red and black drapings, decorated with hammer and sickle emblems. Over the flowers on the coffin the Pioneers draped the Red Flag.

Led by the Pioneers, the audience rose and participated in the singing of the International—the hymn of the toiling masses thruout the world. Comrade Hans Rasmussen then opened the services with a few words on the terrible loss we had suffered thru the death of our beloved comrade.

The "Red Flag" had been Janis' favorite. The Pioneers sang it with determination and verve as when Janis was with them. Karenina Petersen said the last words for the Pioneers on the death of their comrade. The services closed with the singing of the International, led by the Pioneers.

The burial took place at the Salisbury farm. While the casket rested over the grave, Janis' father, Rodney, leader of the United Farmers League in Montana, recited the following poem:

You fought a fight, a long good fight
Is all that we can say;
Sleep on, sleep on, your work is done,
Brave fighter for the day.
Kind mother earth who gave you birth
Receives you to her breast.
For us the fight, for you the night,
The night of well-earned rest.
Sleep on, sleep on your work is done.
Sleep on, sleep on, sleep on.

Pioneer Hazel Rasmussen bade farewell to Janis in a few brief words. As the casket was lowered the Pioneers sang the "Red Flag" again—Janis' song. With a few final words, Pioneer Hazel Rasmussen dropped Janis' Pioneer scarf into the grave.

Janis Salisbury's obituary in the Producers News *noted that her "coffin was accompanied from the entrance to the front of the hall by the Young Pioneers" and the "windows and the stage were covered with red and black drapings, decorated with hammer and sickle emblems."* [*Producers News*, March 3, 1932] substituted a circus ritual at the tomb and an empty 'goodbye.'" The funeral was the talk of the town, and writers for the *Producers News* became defensive. A columnist queried why it was acceptable for soldiers to be given military funerals with "one hundred percent military propaganda" but at Janis Salisbury's funeral "then it is also propaganda, but this time it is not good propaganda like the military one. Oh no, it is bad, very bad, something they must know about clear out to Los Angeles."[23]

At least one reader was persuaded by the *News*'s arguments, writing in his letter to the editor that the Communists were "closer to God Jehovah than the capitalists, whose God is money, power and greed." However, on balance, the funeral for Janis Salisbury was a catastrophe for the farm movement in northeastern Montana; it has been credited by Sheridan County historians with doing "more damage to the Communist cause in this area than any other one event."[24]

While the Bolshevik funeral was an affront to many residents of northeastern Montana, it was only one example of the tendency among the radicals to celebrate all things Soviet. There was a precedent for embracing Russian culture and political practice dating back to the early days of the *Producers News,* when, in 1919, Charles Taylor had printed the headline, "'Soviet' Means Honesty." As early as 1926, the *News* pushed for diplomatic recognition of the Soviet Union (which was not granted until 1933, during Franklin Roosevelt's first year in office), noting that "it is plain as daylight that our capitalist class is preparing itself [for] a graceful fall from its lofty mountain of Soviet Russia aloofness."[25]

Janus Salisbury Taken By Death Last Saturday

Death laid its cold hand upon Janus Salisbury, 14 year old daughter of Mr. and Mrs. Rodney Salisbury at the local hospital last Thursday following an operation for appendicitis. Janus had been ill for several days, and when she was taken to the hospital on Wednesday evening the physician was satisfied the appendix was badly ruptured and that an operation would probably prove futile. A desperate attempt was made to save the young girl's life however, but it proved in vain, and she passed away on Thursday evening.

Janus Salisbury had just passed her fourteenth birthday, having been born February 11, 1918 at Raymond. She was one of twins, and besides her parents, leaves three brothers and two isters to mourn her death.

Funeral services were conducted at the Farmer-Labor temple in Plentywood Saturday and were attended by a large crowd. The last rites were said by Eric Bert, editor of the Producers-News and Hans Rasmussen. Interment was made in the yard of the Salisbury home.

The bereaved parents have the sympathy of the entire community in the loss of their beloved daughter.

The Plentywood Herald*'s obituary, on the other hand, did not glorify Janis Salisbury's membership in the Young Pioneers.* [*Plentywood Herald,* March 10, 1932]

By the 1930s, however, radical leaders had gone beyond mere support of the Soviet Union, to celebration of nearly everything about the nation, from its collective farming to the ability of Russian workers to enjoy the "benefits of their labor." The newspaper's headlines called upon readers to "Support The UFL! Defend the Soviet Union!" Mother Bloor told her audience during a 1932 visit to Sheridan County: "I am convinced that the success of the workers and farmers of Russia in building up a new order of society is the only hope of the masses of all countries." The *Producers News* noted that Mother Bloor called Russia the only country where "daughters of the working class can be moral because they are not forced by economic conditions to sell themselves for bread and clothing."[26]

The increasing adulation of the Soviet Union in the columns of the *Producers News* drew a response from its rival. The *Plentywood Herald,* while acknowledging that farmers in northeastern Montana were enduring difficult times, noted that their suffering was small in comparison with that of Russian workers. The editorialist explained that American farmers could sell their crops when prices were highest and could organize marketing cooperatives, while "the Russian peasant has to turn over his grain when ordered to do so and accept the prices the government specifies—prices dictated by the industrialist element which has control of the government." A subsequent editorial described the "forcible stripping of agricultural ownership from all land proprietors, including their homes, cattle and implements" under way in Soviet Russia. The article ended by encouraging readers not to overlook the danger posed by Soviet propaganda published in their own hometown.[27]

The *Herald* had taken aim at one of the key impossibilities in marketing the Soviet system to American farmers: the small matter of land redistribution and collectivization. Even during the United Farmers League regime, radicals ostensibly were dedicated to helping farmers keep their land and holdings. Before the 1932 election, for example, the *Producers News* declared that the Communist candidates were the only people on the ballot who were "unitedly for the struggle of the farmers against collectors" and that, if elected, these leaders would "use the[ir] offices to protect the farmers and workers of the county, 'oaths of office' to the contrary notwithstanding." To buttress this case, the UFL brought the Communist candidate for president, William Z. Foster, to speak to Sheridan County farmers. Foster called for free emergency relief, no taxes on poor farmers, and no forced collection of rents or taxes.[28]

The United Farmers League brought William Z. Foster, the Communist candidate for president, to speak to farmers in the Dakotas and in eastern Montana in 1932. His appearances included a "monster mass meeting" at Brush Lake. [*Producers News*, June 3, 1932, p. 1]

The Communist Party USA, however, sought to have it both ways. In Erik Bert's first issue of the *News*, published in late 1931, he launched a series called "Red Villages—The Five-Year Plan in Soviet Agriculture," which appeared for several weeks. In his introduction to the series, Bert bragged that the Soviet's Five-Year program had created "huge industrialized state farms, really grain factories," and that the "multitudinous strips of land cultivated by individual peasants" had been combined into large collectives. He also compared the "stupendous achievements" in the Soviet Union with the American Industrial Revolution and claimed that the collectivization movement had reduced the number of peasant households in the Soviet Union from 25 million to a mere 12 million. (He did not mention, and perhaps did not know, that some of this reduction of the peasantry was accomplished by executing or imprisoning them.) Then, in 1932, the *News* ran a reprint from the magazine *Soviet Russia Today,* which explained the concept of collective farming in matter-of-fact terms. Later, there was a series of stories by Soviet farmers, former peasants who revealed how they had improved their lot by joining collectives. In an article entitled "What We Have Been Through: The Story of Our Collective Farm," a young farmer described the success of sowing crops "the Bolshevik way" and declared that he and his fellow farmers in the collective "believe now that the Communist Party and Soviet government can do anything." In retrospect, this focus on collectivization seems counterintuitive since any policy that would deprive them of their holdings would have been anathema to most independent landowners who had risked everything to stake their claim on Montana's prairies.[29]

Harry Polk of the *Plentywood Herald* rushed to exploit the opportunity presented by the *Producers News*'s brazen coverage of Soviet collectivization. In 1932, the *Herald* began its own series to compete with the "Red Villages" articles. The *Herald*'s articles were called "Seeing

'Red'" and offered a feisty counternarrative to the positive depiction of collectivization in the *Producers News.* The articles cut directly to the chase, asserting that all Communists, whether in Moscow, New York, or Plentywood, advocated the "destruction of private-property rights and inheritance." Another article noted, "However little you may have accumulated in life, no matter how great a sacrifice or with how costly an effort, All You Own would become the property of the 'state,' to be used for further exploitation by racketeering demagogues like the Stalins and the Trotskys."[30]

It is important to note that even the *Herald* did not tell the entire story of the collectivization movement in 1932. Press coverage of the Soviet collectivization effort was spotty at the time. Journalist Walter Duranty, writing for the *New York Times*, for example, did cover the transformations happening in the Soviet Union, but his reports failed to accurately reflect the terror and anguish caused by Stalin's actions. Other journalists took issue with Duranty's rose-colored-glasses version of the Soviet situation, most notably Gareth Jones of the *London Times,* and the press began to paint a fuller picture of Soviet totalitarianism. Eventually, it would be revealed that, when Soviet farmers resisted efforts to seize their property, they risked execution or being exiled to work camps where many would perish from starvation or exposure. At the same time, agricultural production in the Soviet Union dropped phenomenally and famine set in.[31]

The *Producers News* was unable to stem the tide let loose by the cascade of criticism regarding the Communist youth movement, the party's religious stance, and its support for collectivization; it even seemed that, at times, the newspaper inflamed rather than diffused conflict. Certainly Erik Bert made a number of crucial errors, including employing vehement rhetoric and introducing symbols that were unfamiliar and objectionable to northeastern Montanans. At the same time, the paper bore none

Joseph Stalin. [Library of Congress, LC-USW33-019081]

Under Erik Bert's editorship, the Producers News*'s motto on the masthead changed from "a paper of the people, by the people, and for the people" to the "Official organ of the United Farmers League in the Northwest."* [*Producers News*, November 27, 1931]

THE PRODUCERS NEWS

Published weekly at Plentywood, Montana by The Peoples Publishing Company, Inc.

Official Organ of the
UNITED FARMERS LEAGUE
In the Northwest

Official paper of the City of Plentywood, Mont.

Subscription Rates: National Edition — In the United States; per year $2.00; six months $1.00; three months 50 cents. Foreign, per year $2.50; six months $1.25; three months 60 cents.
County Edition—In the United States: year $3.00; six months $1.50; four months $1.00. County Edition to foreign countries, year $3.50; six months $1.75; four months $1.25.

Advertising Rates furnished upon application

ERIK BERT, Editor
HANS RASMUSSEN, Business Manager

of its original sense of humor and failed to emphasize local issues and concerns. When it was launched in 1918, the newspaper's motto had employed Abraham Lincoln's historic phrasing, proclaiming that the *News* was "a paper of the people, by the people, and for the people." Under Bert's editorship, the paper's motto was sterilized: the *News* was now "the official organ of the United Farmers League in the Northwest." This change in tone applied to the manner in which readers were addressed as well. In 1918, the paper referred to "small farmers," "the patriotic farmer," and "the people." By the early 1930s, the "patriotic farmer" was called "Comrade" and labeled a member of the "militant" or "toiling masses."[32]

Although the Communist rhetoric of the *Producers News* had, during the late 1920s, become more transparent, the paper's tone and language under Erik Bert were especially strident—and alienating. Designations ranged from the unfamiliar to the rather odious. For independent landowners to be lumped together with the "toiling masses" was patently insensitive to the unique difficulties faced by farmers. Furthermore, while the subscribers to the *Producers News* were familiar with terms like "Mainstreeters" and "money magnates," reading of themselves as "oppressed" and "exploited" surely sounded alien. Bert's radical discourse described not only struggle but exploitation, conspiracy, "capitalist terror," and brutality. *Producers News* writers invoked the language of class, referring to the capitalistic "master class" and its efforts to enslave the working class. The capitalists' "lackeys" in the mainstream press were said to be covering up the "ever great misery for the toiling farmers and the city workers."[33] It was not insignificant that this sort of language issued from an editor who was not yet thirty, a New Yorker who did not even pretend to have ever farmed in his life.

There is evidence that his comrades in Sheridan County gave Erik Bert advice about how to appeal to Montanans. He was told to use

The Producers News*'s tone and language became strident and alienating, and the humor that had helped make it popular in earlier years disappeared. For example, the paper's critique of the Anaconda Company in 1928 featured a cartoon of the "Big Ship A.C.M." and "The Copper Collar Line." By 1933, the paper's statement was doctrinaire: "[w]e are not fighting only the Anaconda Copper Company but the whole capitalist system."* [*Producers News*, July 20, 1928]

"parables" or stories that would interest farmers who were not politically astute, but Bert responded that he did not like the use of parables "one damned bit" and argued that they were "an escape from using the Soviet Union as a contrast to capitalism and using instead some idealized figment" or a "misty vision of socialism in the abstract."[34] Thus, instead of "misty visions," the *News* often featured tales of misery, terror, and struggle. By stressing militancy and revolution across the nation and around the world, the *Producers News* was virtually stripped of the humor and entertainment value that had helped make it popular a decade earlier. There were no irreverent, even lighthearted jabs at western Montana's mining companies, bankers, "town Kaisers," and "crop grabbers." Now the paper proclaimed, in full wrath, "We are not fighting only the Anaconda Copper Company but the whole capitalist system. . . . There are no good capitalists in [the] lexicon of the *Producers News.* They are all robbers." Readers were exhorted to do their part "in the struggle of the toiling farmers against the exploiter and the robber gang which oppresses them." Even the editorial section, once the most engaging and scandalous part of the paper, had grown tiresome. In Charles Taylor's absence, business manager Hans Rasmussen was the only regular columnist, and his editorials lacked the verve readers had come to expect in the *Producers News.* His offerings tended to be mainly lengthy criticisms of the county commissioners and their budgetary decisions, replete with tediously detailed statistical comparisons.[35]

The regular lambasting of the commissioners notwithstanding, the *Producers News*'s lost sense of humor might have been tolerable if the paper had still served as a reliable and interesting source for local news and commentary. However, the focus of the newspaper had also shifted, partly as a result of its national distribution. Although both local and national editions were published, it seems that little differentiated them. The *Producers News,* which in the 1920s had run engagement announcements and gossip columns alongside mainly local and some state news, now dealt with matters farther afield. There were reports on a Soviet aluminum plant, a Colorado beet workers' strike, and the conversion of a seventy-three-year-old Minnesotan to Communism. Local readers could also learn about the "bloody exploitation of Negro workers on levees," struggling Wisconsin dairy farmers, and police abuse of Ohio Reds. By 1932, there were fewer and fewer local editorials, and even the guest columns submitted by former editor Charles Taylor focused elsewhere, describing, for example, his organizing jaunt to Aitkin, Minnesota, over eight hundred miles from Sheridan County.[36]

In addition to cleansing the *News* of much of its "bourgeois influence," Bert also adhered to the Third Period contention that the answer to the problems of workers and farmers could be found only in proletarian revolution and the destruction of capitalism. Reformist or petite bourgeois organizations, it was said, misled the masses. Thus, Erik Bert denounced various farm organizations, including the Farmer-Labor Party of which Sheridan County radicals had so recently been a part. This attack on former friends and colleagues marked a significant shift. During their heyday in the 1920s, the county radicals had made businesspeople, profiteers, and the "nonproducing class" their scapegoats. Less than a year after the United Farmers League emerged from the ranks of Farmer-Laborism in northeastern Montana, the Farmer-Labor Party became just another enemy. In reporting on the 1932 Farmer-Laborer convention, the *Producers News* called the F-LP members demagogues and "agents of Wall Street" who were merely seeking "to maintain the faith of the toiling masses of the United States

The Producers News*'s new conformity to a national Communist agenda required the newspaper to denounce actions taken by farmers' groups other than the United Farmers League. For example, when a competing farm organization, the Farm Holiday Association, organized a milk blockade (above) to interfere with the flow of all commodities into Sioux City and to raise the price dairy farmers received for their milk, editor Bert denounced it for failing to address issues like foreclosures, evictions, and taxes. Such positions did not sit well with the readership in northeastern Montana.* [State Historical Society of Iowa, Des Moines, Photograph Collection]

in capitalism."[37] At best, the paper's about-face must have seemed confusing to readers; at worst, it may have appeared vicious and disloyal.

Adhering to orthodoxy was often a precarious practice. In 1932, for example, Bert denounced a milk strike in Iowa that was led by a competing organization, the Farm Holiday Association. The strike was an attempt to interfere with the flow of all commodities into Sioux City and to raise the price dairy farmers received for their milk. The *Producers News* condemned the strike for failing to address more important issues like foreclosures, evictions, and taxes. A week later, the paper reversed its stance on the strike. The reversal was ordered by Henry Puro, the farm unit director, acting at the behest of the Central Committee, which had decided that the milk strike condemnation was a mistake.[38]

While Erik Bert tried to conform to Central Committee thinking and Third Period approaches to propagandizing, things were slowly coming apart at the *Producers News.* In 1932, just months after it became the official paper of the United Farmers League, the *News* began publishing occasional pleas for subscription renewals. In September 1932, Charles Taylor wrote "An Appeal: Farmers to the Rescue of the *Producers News.*"

Although the paper was now nationally distributed and sponsored by the CPUSA, it was admittedly in a "serious financial crisis." Of course, CPUSA sponsorship, rather than being helpful, may have been part of the problem; the party's national paper, the *Daily Worker,* was itself on the brink of bankruptcy. In June 1931, for instance, the *Worker* proclaimed an "Emergency!" The party needed four thousand dollars in two days to avoid immediate suspension of the paper. Similar pleas appeared intermittently in the *Daily Worker* throughout the summer.[39]

In Sheridan County, farmers were called upon to do whatever they could, even bring in ten to twenty bushels of wheat as a means of paying their subscription, in order to save the *Producers News.* During this same period, subscribers were receiving considerably less newspaper for their ten or twenty bushels: the *News,* which had averaged eight to twelve pages an issue during the 1920s, was reduced to four pages by 1932. It was clear that most local advertisers had also abandoned the paper; among the few remaining advertisers were Radium Remedies, Charles Taylor's get-rich-quick venture in Minnesota, and attorney A. C. Erickson, who had been the radical county attorney during the 1920s. Erik Bert reported that "Charley Taylor has been drawing minimum amounts to keep his family alive while he has been away. Hans Rasmussen draws practically nothing. I have drawn $5 once."[40]

The essential problem was that the local leaders no longer had ultimate control of what appeared in their newspaper; in fact, it was no longer really *their* newspaper. The *Producers News* was now a national publication—and advertised as such—and to ignore headquarters branded one an opportunist or deviator. Thus, editorial and stylistic decisions were influenced, if not dictated, by Third Period directives from Moscow and by CPUSA orders and "corrections." And those

Pay Your

Subscription

to

The Producers News!!

It is your paper. It is up to you to support it and keep it going. Your co-operation is needed right now. If you can't pay with money bring us some wheat or chickens. We allow market price.

In 1932, just months after it became the official paper of the United Farmers League, the Producers News *was in a serious financial crisis. By August, the paper was begging readers to re-subscribe: "If you can't pay with money bring us some wheat or chickens. We allow market price."* [*Producers News*, August 19, 1932] decisions that were made abroad or in New York City and trickled down to places like Plentywood, Montana, did not often resonate with local residents.[41]

The circumstances behind the troubles of the paper were not without irony. At the height of the *News*'s popularity, Charles Taylor had maintained that the control of the paper was out of his hands—that it was the farmers' paper—although that was patently untrue.[42] Now that editorial decisions were made, by and large, with consideration of edicts from Moscow and New York City, the *Producers News* had lost its relevance among the members of its original farm audience. Moreover, while Taylor's controversial and pugnacious style served him well when he was an outsider fighting the system, the toxic residue of his attacks on opponents was about to poison the political environment for the Reds in Montana. For years, Taylor had responded to charges against the farm movement by assailing the character of the accusers. Opponents were now aligned against him and his fellow travelers, employing Taylor's own tactics to undermine the credibility of the radical leaders once and for all.

CHAPTER 13

Personnel Problems Take a Toll at the Polls

The decrees of the Third Period and the editorial blunders of Erik Bert and his comrades during the early 1930s diluted the power of the radicals' arguments and alienated readers of the *Producers News.* However, the newspaper's insensitivity was not the only problem bedeviling the farmers' movement in northeastern Montana. Other factors were at work that would have undermined even the most appealing message. The straw that broke the camel's back may very well have been the personal lives of movement leaders and members themselves. The private became public, generating a notoriety that would linger for decades. In some cases, radicals suffered guilt by association, but more often, their decisions and their lifestyles provided a rich target for the opposition press in northeastern Montana.

There was, for instance, the small matter of Charles Taylor's first family, which his campaign biographies in the 1920s had failed to mention. Secrets are hard to keep in small towns, and the *Plentywood Herald* was not above revealing Taylor's background. Asserting that Taylor had been "disowned by his own son by his first wife," the *Herald* went on to speculate that, for Taylor's son to take such an action, he must have been motivated by something more than "ordinary behavior" on his father's part.[1]

But this jab at Taylor's past was only the preface to the *Herald*'s main accusation in early 1930, which was that Taylor was dishonest to the point of thievery. The newspaper alleged that Taylor had used his ten-year-old son, Carl, to forge signatures on creditors' notes. It then resurrected a case from fifteen years before, when Charles Taylor was living in Buffalo, Wyoming, in which he allegedly failed to pay a hotel bill of $173. The man who was stuck with the bill had called Taylor "a first class swindler."[2]

Other aspects of Taylor's finances were also of interest to the *Herald,* which reported that he "is alleged to receive almost as large a salary as our District Judge." In spite of his supposed wealth, the *Herald* claimed that Taylor had an unpaid grocery bill of $300 and that he was cheating his employees, having "beat one old man, about 60 years of age, out of $1,900.00 in wages and cash." Although he was acquitted, Taylor was later charged and tried for issuing a check with intent to defraud. Burley Bowler, from neighboring Daniels County, added his two cents' worth, calling Taylor a "notorious crook."[3]

Perhaps more damaging than the revelations concerning his first family or his personal finances was Taylor's association with one of the more colorful and criminally inclined citizens of Sheridan County, Smith Rudolph "Nig" Collins. An Alabama native of about the same age as Taylor, Collins had a sixth-grade education and listed his occupation variously as rancher, professional gambler, and cardsharp. Collins operated the infamous "Chicken Ranch" brothel, but he was something of a criminal entrepreneur who also dabbled in bootlegging, sponsored gamecock fights, operated a casino, and was a suspect in the robbery of

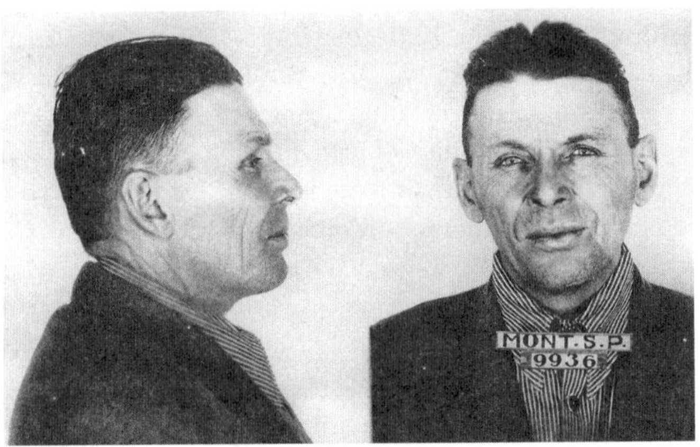

The unconventional personal lives of local radicals were perhaps more damaging to Sheridan County's Communist movement than the editorial blunders of Erik Bert and his comrades. Among Charles Taylor's transgressions was his rumored association with Smith Rudolph "Nig" Collins, whose mug shots (above) appear on his prison induction record of February 16, 1931. He was found guilty of assault on a seventeen-year-old schoolgirl at his infamous "Chicken Ranch" brothel.
[MHS Archives, Helena, RS 197]

the county treasury in 1926. The year 1930 was Collins's undoing in Sheridan County when he was charged with the attempted rape of a Plentywood high school girl. Reports vary on whether the girl and her two classmates were regular employees of the Chicken Ranch, but whatever the case, Collins was arrested for the second-degree assault of seventeen-year-old Delores Pickett. He was accused of trying to seduce the underage teens with drink, was convicted of assault, sentenced to three years in the Montana state penitentiary, and fined two thousand dollars.[4]

Accusations and threats appeared in the county's newspapers. The *Plentywood Herald* claimed that previous attempts to deter Collins's "nefarious 'business' [were] frustrated by Taylor." The *Herald* also asserted that the "henchman of the Producers Noose have been making the rounds saying that editor Taylor . . . [was] never friendly towards Nig." Taylor did himself no favors by printing a pun about a "minor charge" leveled against Collins and by referring to Collins, following his conviction, as the "sole and only victim of the recent purity hippodrome staged by [the] County Attorney . . . as an election campaign stunt." Even the *Producers News*'s threat to publish a list of Chicken Ranch patrons and its prediction that many "Mainstreeters" would be exposed for their "porniferous activities or their abortion rackets" did not faze the *Plentywood Herald*.[5]

While Charles Taylor's connection to Nig Collins was, at best, tenuous, the relationship of former Sheridan County sheriff Rodney

THE PLENTYWOOD HERALD

The Herald Solicits Advertising With the Guarantee that it Has the Largest Paid in Advance Circulation in Sheridan County.

Volume 22, No. 21 — Plentywood, Sheridan County, Montana, Thursday January 23, 1930. — $2.00 Per Year

"NIG" COLLINS ARRESTED ON FELONY

Oil Company to Resume Drilling Operations Soon

Stockholders Pledge Money To Complete Well This Spring

Charles Grant of Outlook returned home on January 17th from Fargo, North Dakota where he attended the annual meeting of the stockholders of the Sheyenne Oil & Gas Company, the company which has the acreage

SNOW BLOCKADES DELAY SOO TRAINS

Service is Stopped For a Week Despite All Efforts to Clear the Tracks

WHAT MORE EVIDENCE IS NEEDED TO CHECK CRIME?

To the people of Plentywood and vicinity the following statement of facts occasions no surprise. However, to some people in this county it may bring some enlightenment on things past and present in the administration of Sheridan county affairs. To certain blind followers of the Producers News and its editors it is a challenge to their honesty, and claims of decency for that disreputable organ.

To be brief, let us present a few well known facts first.

Who is Nig Collins?

Collins is a defendant in a criminal action preferred by the parents of three young girls, all students at the Plentywood high school, who have made affidavits charging him with taking them to his house of ill fame on the outskirts of Plentywood, giving theme liquor and attempting liberites with their person which were resisted only by force.

Collins is also self-acclaimed boss of the bootleg business in northeastern Montana. He is also known as a promoter of game cock fights.

Three High School Girls Are Complaining Witnesses

Parents of Girls Sign Complaints and Girls Make Affidavits Charging Bootleg King With Loathsome Crime; People of Plentywood Aroused over Incident and Demand Full Justice

Nig Collins, self styled king of the | in company with kindred spirits, the

The Plentywood Herald *had long held that Nig Collins, in addition to his other offenses, was a bootlegger and protected by former sheriff Rodney Salisbury. Salisbury's posting of Collins's bail reinforced the theory.* [*Plentywood Herald*, January 23, 1930]

Marie Chapman Hansen, pictured here with her groom, Andy, in their wedding photograph on September 3, 1922, took up with Rodney Salisbury in the mid-1920s. [Courtesy Ed Jensen]

Salisbury with the hoodlum was more easily established. According to the *Herald,* while Collins was out of jail on bond during the appeal phase of his assault conviction, he was arrested once more on charges of residing in a brothel, and Rodney Salisbury signed his bond for release. Later, Collins "gave a mortgage to his attorneys for fees due them, and thereafter conveyed the [Chicken Ranch] premises by deed to Rodney Salisbury."[6]

It probably would have come as no surprise to the average local citizen to see Rodney Salisbury's name associated with a character like Nig Collins. There had been accusations about Salisbury's involvement in various illegal activities throughout the 1920s, including everything from rum-running to the county treasury robbery. However, if Salisbury had engaged in those activities, he had exercised some care in hiding his involvement. Such was not the case with his long-term relationship with Marie Chapman Hansen.

Born in 1901, Marie Chapman was twelve years Salisbury's junior, and she probably met him when she worked at the *Producers News.* A family history notes that she was unconventional and "ahead of her time in many ways." As an illustration, the author of that history noted that "[a]mong other 'firsts,' she was one of the first to get her hair 'bobbed.'" Marie's daughter recalled her smoking in public, also a rather bold move in the 1920s.[7]

When she was twenty-one, Marie married Andy Hansen, ten years her senior. In their engagement story, the *Producers News* described him as a man of "sterling qualities" and congratulated Marie on her choice for a life's mate. About Marie, the *News* noted that it was "unnecessary to state the many good things one could say about this young lady as nearly all of the people in this vicinity are well acquainted with her and her popularity is numbered only by her acquaintances."[8] It is unclear whether the latter observation was intended to be as suggestive as it seems.

The Hansens had two children, born in 1924 and 1926. At some point in the mid-1920s, Marie Hansen took up with Salisbury, and he fathered three children, born in 1928, 1933, and 1935. It was only in 1933 that Marie finally left Andy Hansen; he demanded custody of his two children, forcing a painful separation of the Hansen and Salisbury children.[9]

Salisbury and Hansen's relationship was no secret in Sheridan County. The *Plentywood Herald* took to referring to her as Joan of Arc, perhaps because she had been active in the farmers' movement as an advocate for the underprivileged, and asserted that the couple had charged the *Producers News* for their personal trips to Havre and Great Falls. During that same year, 1930, the *Herald* claimed to have it on good authority that Charles Taylor had had a falling out with Salisbury over the relationship. Under the heading "Trouble Brewing in Producers N. Camp," the *Herald* reported that Taylor and Salisbury had gotten into a row because Taylor "did not want Salisbury to be so bold and brazen with his enamorita [*sic*]."[10]

Salisbury was indeed bold. As his first family continued to live in Sheridan County and participate in the farmers' movement, and as Andy Hansen managed his flour milling business, Rodney and Marie carried on their affair and had children. They were given a modest kind of approbation by the *Producers News,* which, in September 1931, listed them as the hosts of the United Farmers League's banquet. In a curious

Marie had two children with her husband and three with Salisbury, two of them before she left Hansen. The extramarital relationship exacted a toll on Salisbury's reputation and, by extension, on the northeastern Montana farmers' movement. Above, Hansen, second from left, and Rodney Salisbury, standing far right, pose with relatives circa 1934. [Toni Martinazzi, *Albert Rice Chapman, 1866–1948, and His Descendants* (Glenview, Ill.: self-published, 1993), 135]

instance of newspaper layout, a 1932 issue of the *News* featured side-by-side stories about Rodney Salisbury and Andy Hansen: Salisbury had taken over the Plentywood Bakery and was running it as a cooperative; Andy Hansen's mill was reducing its flour prices. And in spite of everything, Hansen still ran ads in the *Producers News.*[11]

Marie Hansen's family history notes that it was "public knowledge that Marie and Rodney were 'together.' . . . Most people, and the children themselves, knew Rodney was their father. The toll imposed for living this double life was great for all concerned."[12] The union also surely exacted a toll on Salisbury's already sullied reputation and, by extension, on the farmers' movement. In addition to the rift with Charles Taylor and the public's awareness of Rodney's lifestyle, his relationship with Marie may have been part of the falling out between wealthy farmer William Hass and the radicals at the *Producers News.*

William Hass, the same man who had staked a claim near Antelope in 1907 only to have it jumped and who then walked another twenty miles to claim land near Outlook, had been an early investor in the *Producers News.* During the newspaper's beginning years, its society columns regularly noted Hass's trips to Plentywood and visits at the *News* office. It was presumably during one of these visits that he met his future wife, one of the paper's employees, Margaret Helander, a University of Minnesota graduate. They married in 1928.[13]

Margaret Helander's connection to the *Producers News* was not merely employment; it was also apparently an ideological choice. In early 1927, she was the elected secretary of the Plentywood local and was referred to in a letter to Communist Party chief Jay Lovestone. Within a few months, however, in July 1927, with no explanation, she no longer held that position. On a piece of official correspondence, Margaret Helander's name had been crossed out and the new secretary's name penciled in—Marie Hansen.[14]

Although it is not clear that nepotism played any role in the replacement of Margaret Helander by Marie Hansen or that Helander or her future husband, William Hass, objected to the change, the timing of the event is noteworthy: it coincided with the beginning of Hass's conflict with the *Producers News.* The *News* itself claimed in 1930 that William Hass had been waging "relentless war" against it for three years.[15]

Even if Margaret Helander's replacement played no role in the contentious relationship that developed between Hass and the *Producers News,* the paper's eager coverage of a Hass family scandal certainly did. The *News* covered in lurid detail the story of Wanda Hass, who, in 1930, shot and killed her uncle, Hugo, one of William's brothers. In its long nley-Ridley Prohibition Debate at the Temple Sunday Afternoon

THE PRODUCERS NEWS

THE PRODUCERS NEWS GOES INTO EVERY HOME IN SHERIDAN COUNTY

A PAPER OF THE PEOPLE, FOR THE PEOPLE, BY THE PEOPLE

Sub. Rates: Foreign, $8.75 per year; In U. S., $3.00 per year — PLENTYWOOD, MONTANA, FRIDAY, APRIL 11, 1930

WANDA HASS SLAYS HER UNCLE HUGO

Farm Relief Seed Loan Protest Demonstration In Plentywood Sunday

ELEGATES FROM DANIELS, SHERIDAN AND ROOSEVELT COUNTIES TO SPEAK IN THE F.-L. TEMPLE AT 11 O'CLOCK

enator Wheeler Replies to Telegram from Producers News That His Gas Loan Resolution Has Passed Senate and Is Now Before the House. Took Matter Seed Loan Up With Department of Agriculture. Wired

Garneau, Acting For Power Company Brings Suit Against Storkan

Mr. A. J. Garneau, the eminent plumber is again on the public tongue as a result of a taxpayer's suit brought against Mayor Storkan and the city council by the Montana-North Dakota Power Co. with Garneau fronting for the company.

The action resulted from the purchase by the mayor of a Diesel engine from the Fairbanks-

DEADLINES

By United Press Special Wire to The Producers News.

London, April 10. — American delegates have little hope of completing five-power naval treaty, being unable to break the deadlock between France and Italy. The delegates are striving hard to have something to show their respective nationals as a result of the conference.

SHOOTS HIM THRU ABDOMEN ON ROAD NEAR TOBIN FARM HALF MILE NORTH OUTLOOK

The Producers News *itself generated scandal and ill will by publishing sensational stories about the murder of Hugo Hass, the brother of William Hass, who had been an early investor in the* Producers News *but who had later taken an adversarial position toward the farmers' movement.* [*Producers News*, April 11, 1930]

story on the tragedy, the *News* included behind-the-scenes quotations, such as Hugo's dying words, and Wanda's warning to her Uncle William that if she were sent to prison for life, she would "tell all."[16]

Wanda Hass was not sent to prison for life, but the *Producers News* nonetheless told all, describing Wanda's life in Sheridan County as a case of virtual white slavery. It reported that she had been brought to the Hass farm at age fourteen, was able to speak only German, and was prevented from attending school or associating with anyone but the Hass family and a few neighbors. According to the paper, "Wanda Hass knew only unremitting toil" and "never even had a friend or chum." The *News* also revealed some "ugly rumors" that it said were circulating in the county, noting that, when Wanda was sixteen, she was sexually abused, became pregnant, and her child sent away to western Montana. The paper went on to note that she became pregnant again the following year, and "Wm. and Hugo Hass were involved" when this child died of unnatural causes. The shocking assertions hardly strengthened Hass's relationship with the newspaper.[17]

After the *Producers News* ran the story, the *Plentywood Herald* weighed in, claiming that Charles Taylor had known about Wanda Hass's situation for several years but had ignored it until it suited his needs. It implied that he did nothing to help her but rather carried on his "social and business relations with Wm. Hass and the other Hass brothers." The *Herald* correctly asserted that Hass had been a financial backer of the *Producers News,* claimed that he had traveled with Taylor frequently to Great Falls and Minneapolis in the mid-1920s, and even speculated that part of a cash settlement the Hass brothers had allegedly paid Wanda Hass when she sued for back wages in 1927 had found its way to Taylor's pocket.[18]

William Hass's role with regard to the *Producers News* did not end with the coverage of his niece's trial; in 1935 he would be identified as one of two saboteurs who sought to wreck the newspaper. But Hass's initial falling out with the *News* is significant: the fact that a one-time investor in the *Producers News* and, apparently, a personal friend of Taylor's had become so completely alienated from the newspaper was just one indication of the troubles that were brewing for radicals in northeastern Montana. The Communists' inability to manage their message and to articulate a story that maintained its former persuasiveness, combined with certain political and personal choices of the movement's leaders, came together as a monumental setback for Communism in Sheridan County. The impact of these setbacks is evidenced by the election returns of 1930 and 1932.

In autumn of 1930, Charles Taylor was selected by the Farmer-Labor Party of Montana to make a bid for the U.S. Senate. In a humiliating outcome, Taylor failed to carry even Sheridan County, which cast 38 percent of its votes for Democrat Thomas Walsh and only 32 percent for Taylor. He carried a number of the precincts in farming communities, especially the old radical strongholds of Dagmar, Outlook, Raymond, and Quitmeyer, but population centers such as Plentywood went overwhelmingly for the Democratic candidate. Taylor fared terribly on the state level: the 967 votes he received in Sheridan County were more than half of his statewide total. All three seats in the state legislature went to Republicans. The only successful Farmer-Labor candidate was Carl Hansen, who narrowly edged out his two opponents to become county commissioner.[19]

By 1932, the Farmer-Labor Party in Sheridan County was a thing of the past, and the United Farmers League led an openly Communist campaign. In the June primaries, Sheridan County Democrats and Republicans performed a remarkable feat: they came together to form a "fusion" ticket called the Taxpayers Economy League. The *Plentywood Herald* proclaimed that the new league would run a "united front"

EVERY UFL MEMBER A READER OF THE PRODUCERS NEWS

THE PRODUCERS NEWS

County Edition

Published Weekly

OFFICIAL ORGAN OF THE UNITED FARMERS LEAGUE

VOLUME XV. Number 32 — PLENTYWOOD, SHERIDAN COUNTY, MONTANA, FRIDAY, NOVEMBER 2, 1932

VOTE COMMUNIST TUESD'Y, NOV. 8

Harry Polk 'Godfather' of County Liberty Party

Uses it as a Mascot for His "Economy League" Hag— Hopes it Will Deflect Enuf Votes to Defeat 'Red' Ticket—Especially Magnus Danielsen

Pat & Bob Bring Forth "Liberator"

Renegade Wobbly Pays Polk, Notorious Publisher of North Dakota, Liberty Kale Provided by Main Streeters to Print Party Paper

COUNTY RELIEF IS MIGHTY SLIM

HOW TO VOTE AND VOTE RIGHT

On election day you will be handed a ballot the size of a small bed sheet, but don't be confused, just take it cool, you can study it all day if you want to. There are six parties on the ballot, each party has a column running fro mtop to bottom. they run in rotation like this: Republican, Democrat, Socialist, Communist, Liberty, Independent.

The Republican you don't want, you had enough of that, the Democrat is the same thing with a different name, so that you don't want either. The Socialist has only a few names on it, and those who are there are no good, so just pass them up and go to column number four, the Communist Party column. When you get to there you start from the top and make a cross in each square in front of every name until you get to the bottom, when you have done that you can go home and be satisfied that you have done a good days work. The last two columns you need not pay any attention to.

RODNEY SALISBURY

Communist Candidate FOR GOVERNOR

God and this Election Campaign

(BY CHAS. E. TAYLOR)

Roosevelt's Ryder Recommends Froid's Olson for Polk's Commissioner

TURKEY POOL HAD MEETING SATURDAY

Who Is Arthur Ryder?

FEDERAL LAND BANK SELLS MONT. FARMS

Only the Communist Party Opposes War Laursen Points Out

Big Rally at Temple Monday

By 1932, the Farmer-Labor Party in Sheridan County was a thing of the past, and the United Farmers League led an openly Communist political campaign. [*Producers News*, November 2, 1932]

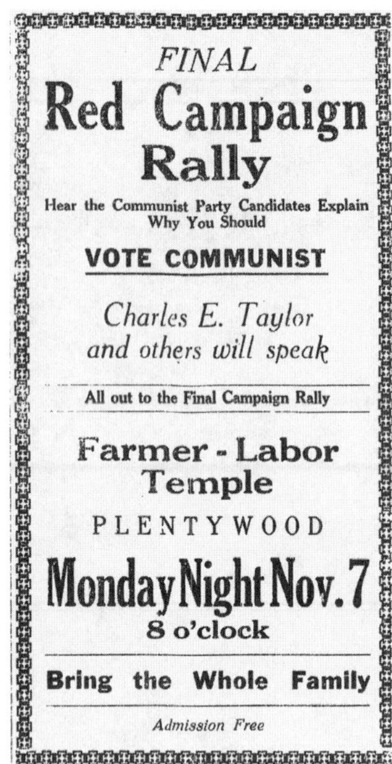

FINAL
Red Campaign
Rally
Hear the Communist Party Candidates Explain
Why You Should
VOTE COMMUNIST
Charles E. Taylor
and others will speak
All out to the Final Campaign Rally
Farmer - Labor
Temple
PLENTYWOOD
Monday Night Nov. 7
8 o'clock
Bring the Whole Family
Admission Free

Despite the Producers News*'s efforts to convince readers of "why you should vote Communist," Salisbury lost his bid for the office of governor and Taylor lost the race to become state representative to a Republican in the 1932 election.* [*Producers News*, November 2, 1932]

of candidates for local office in order to fight the "inroads of the 'Red' menace."[20] By adopting the radicals' militant campaign tactics and turning the tables on the United Farmers League, the backers of the fusion ticket indicated that they would not surrender leadership in the county as they had during the early 1920s.

The *Herald* took another page from the radicals' old playbook in using the well-worn scare tactic, a "return to the bad old days." It warned, "Communism in Sheridan County means even more than endorsement of the overthrowing of our national government. It means the return to power in this county of Charles E. Taylor and Rodney Salisbury. If any of the candidates on the Communist ticket should be elected, no one questions but they will be under the absolute control of these two men." The article implied that, of the two potential catastrophes, it would be worse for Taylor and Salisbury to be empowered than for the national government to be overthrown.[21]

When the ballots were counted, the county results stood in stark contrast to the rest of Montana. Even with its Communist organization in a diminished state, Sheridan County cast more votes for the Communist candidate for president, William Z. Foster, than did any other county in the state. Voters also distinguished themselves in their balloting for governor, giving the Communist candidate 25 percent of the total votes cast, though not enough to carry the county. However, there is more to this story: the candidate in the gubernatorial race was Rodney Salisbury, who might have been expected to have favorite-son status and thereby gain considerably more votes. Not only was Salisbury bested by both the Republican and Democratic candidates in his own county,

THE PLENTYWOOD HERALD

OFFICIAL NEWSPAPER OF SHERIDAN COUNTY, MONTANA

Vol. 25 No. 10 — Plentywood, Sheridan County, Montana, Thursday, November 10, 1932 — $2.00 Per Year

Communism Dealt Crushing Blow By Sheridan County Voters Tuesday

GOV. ERICKSON WINS CLOSE RACE

Leavitt Defeated by Ayers for Congress

NATIONAL LANDSLIDE FOR DEMOCRATS SWEEP OLD GUARDS FROM CONGRESS; SHERIDAN COUNTY GOES 2 TO 1 FOR ROOSEVELT

Running far behind his colleagues who were swept into state offices on one of the greatest Democratic landslides ever known in Montana, Governor John E. Erickson, was declared winner in the gubernatorial race over Frank Hazelbaker late Thursday by a scant margin of 3,000. Only a few precincts were left to be heard from and it was believed these would not bring any change in the final results.

As a nation turned in one of the greatest victories for a party ever recorded, sweeping Franklin D. Roosevelt into the presidency with unprecedented majorities, Scott Leavitt, veteran Republican congressman from eastern Montana, joined the ranks of the defeated, surrendering his toga to Roy E. Ayers who will have a final majority of more than 10,000.

Only five of the nation's 48 states recorded majorities for the Hoover electoral candidates. They were Maine, Deleware, Pennsylvania, New Hampshire and Vermont.

The Roosevelt landslide

Democratic House of Representatives and a Democratic United States senate. The electerate set the stage and rang up the curtain for that new deal in affairs of the country which was stressed as the major issue of the campaign.

PRESIDENT-ELECT

Franklin D. Roosevelt

Record Vote Established In Tuesday Election

EVERY CANDIDATE OF TAXPAYERS ECONOMY LEAGUE SWEPT INTO OFFICE; SET UP NEW RECORD IN COUNTY POLITICS

Going to the polls in greater numbers than in any previous election, the voters of Sheridan county dealt a crushing blow to Communism Tuesday. Every candidate on the ticket of the Taxpayers Economy League was swept into office with majorities ranging from 1000 down to 200. Many old residents of the county hailed it as one of the most significant triumphs ever won and pointed to it as a definite turning point in the county's political history.

It was a death blow to Communism. Leaders of the "Reds" had carried their candidates through one of the most intensive campaigns ever conducted. Public meetings had been held in school houses and community halls in every part of the county. The countryside had been placarded with "Vote Communist" posters until they greeted the eyes of highway travelers in every direction. Hundreds of dollars were spent in printing and advertising. The Producers News, official Communist organ had opened its columns to one of its most vituperative campaigns, hurling unmitigated attacks on the personal character and public record of opposition candidates in a desperate effort to bolster up

tical history of the county stated that this was the first time all candidates on any ticket had been successful one hundred per cent in any election.

Niels Madsen led the parade of the victors with the largest vote ever given to a candidate with two opponents in the field. Carrying all but four precincts with wide margins, he piled up a total of 1824 votes

The Plentywood Herald *celebrated the outcome of the election with this headline.* [*Plentywood Herald*, November 10, 1932]

but Charles Taylor, who had served for eight years as a state senator, was soundly defeated in his bid for state representative. Sheridan County would again be represented in Helena by an all-Republican legislative delegation. The fusion-ticket candidates in the local races trounced the Communists, winning all of their respective offices. The outcome of the election led the *Plentywood Herald* to crow in a headline, "Communism Dealt Crushing Blow by Sheridan County Voters Tuesday."[22]

Although the 1932 election was not the official end of the Communist Party in northeastern Montana, future prospects for the farmers' movement were dismal.

A post-election letter by Robert Larson, once a faithful Communist Party activist and state representative, summed up the disillusionment of many former radicals in the area. Admitting that he was an "old IWW organizer and soap-boxer, Socialist and at one time a member of the Communist party" and the "reddest of the Reds in the northwest," Larson said that the Sheridan County group turned a blind eye to the

Summing up the disillusionment of many former radicals in the area, ex–Communist Party activist and state representative Robert Larson, seen here circa 1927, was, by 1932, calling the Sheridan County Communists "traitors to the working class." [MHS Photograph Archives, Helena]

atrocities that were happening in Russia under Joseph Stalin. Calling Charles Taylor, Mother Bloor, and their ilk "traitors to the working class," he accused them of ruining the farmers' movement and the possibilities for a true Communist utopia by supporting Stalinism and backstabbing former comrades. Communism, he wrote, should have become "a paradise, and yet it is nearly the worst hell on earth."[23]

Larson's feelings would later be echoed all over the country as reports of Stalinism's atrocities began to circulate in the press. It would take decades, but the convulsions in northeastern Montana's Communist enclave were a portent of the disease that would virtually annihilate the Communist Party in America.

CHAPTER 14

Death Throes of a Movement

Even after being routed at the polls in the 1932 election, there still should have been some hope for the Communist cause in northeastern Montana. A dismal economic climate and difficult living conditions for farmers would certainly suggest the possibility. Devastating dust storms stirred up by strong winds earned for the decade the name "Dirty Thirties." "Fence lines and abandoned machinery sifted in with drifted top soil," Sheridan County historian Magnus Aasheim wrote; "housewives closed their doors and windows in a vain attempt to keep out the air-borne dust." Farmers continued to encounter low yields, rock-bottom grain prices, and declining cash receipts on both livestock and crops.[1]

The harvest of 1931 had been dreadful; there had been little rain that growing season, and many fields produced nothing. According to Sheridan County resident Curtis Stadstad, only a "few straggling stalks of wheat headed." The average wheat yield on unirrigated land in the state that year was less than six bushels per acre. The next year was better—yields doubled (to a level that still would not be considered good), but average prices hit a record-low of thirty-five cents per bushel. And in 1933, yields declined again.[2]

Since there was little grain to harvest and hay pastures were barren, farmers and ranchers in desperation mowed weeds and brush to feed their cattle. The cost of raising and shipping animals and crops often exceeded their value. Magnus Aasheim noted that "sales tickets from

The 1930s earned the nickname "Dirty Thirties" for the devastating dust storms of the time period, like this one that engulfed the town of Raymond in 1938.
[MHS Photograph Archives, PAc 77-94 v3-22.3-129]

the Hoven Grain Company in Antelope show wheat purchased for 23 cents, [and] cattle shipped to eastern markets would not sell for enough to pay the freight." Finally, the federal government intervened by buying livestock and destroying the animals. Families like the Deubners of the Homestead community sold their herd of cattle to the government for thirty-three dollars per head.[3]

Like livestock, other commodities brought in little cash. The price for a dozen eggs fell to five cents. Sheridan County resident Ray Stoner noted that "later you could not give [eggs] away. Many farmers fed them in milk to the calves. Butter was 10 cents per pound, if you could sell it. The local merchants had an oversupply and no outlet for it."[4]

As the economic situation worsened, some farmers faced repossession of their machinery, which was then resold for a fraction of its original cost. A combine that had originally cost $1,200 and been used for only a few harvests might bring $150 at auction. Many farmers found it difficult to provide the bare necessities for their families, and some looked elsewhere for opportunities. According to Ray Stoner, "Some people became discouraged and turned their land over to the bank or mortgage holders. Others sold and got out with a few dollars clear, moving west or returning to family in the East." For those who remained in Sheridan County, a fortunate few with cash on hand could often purchase acreage simply by paying the back taxes to the county.[5]

Between the dust storms, drought, low yields and prices, and high freight rates, there should have been potential for the farmers' movement to tap into significant agrarian discontent. In fact, historian Harvey Klehr has called the Depression decade the "heyday of American Communism."[6] Nonetheless, the radicals in northeastern Montana continued to lose ground. The power and appeal of their message had been eroded by Third Period edicts from Russia and New York City, and the *Producers News*'s editor Erik Bert failed to bridge the chasm between Communist doctrine and his audience.

The outlook worsened on 1933 as the *Producers News* suffered a kind of identity crisis caused by managerial instability. The year 1933 began with Erik Bert as editor and Charles Taylor as managing editor, although Taylor's duties as a United Farmers League organizer kept him out of the state for most of the time. Bert was not long for Plentywood either, probably because he found the political situation there untenable. In August 1933, the society column of the *News* noted that his wife, Ruth, had left on the train to visit with her parents in New York and that she was planning to stop over in Chicago en route to take in the World's Fair. The *News* did not list a scheduled stop in Minneapolis, but apparently Ruth spent time there too. She visited Alfred Tiala, national secretary of the UFL, bringing "a dismal tale from Plentywood" and conveying her husband's wishes to leave his post at the newspaper. Tiala

THE PRODUCERS NEWS

Liberty Is Not Handed Down From Above

A PAPER OF THE PEOPLE, FOR THE PEOPLE, BY THE PEOPLE

Official Paper of the City of Plentywood

Sub. Rates: Foreign, $3.75 per year In U. S. $3.00 per year

PLENTYWOOD, MONTANA, FRIDAY, JUNE 26, 1931

Entered as second Class Matter, October 18, 1912, at the Postoffice at Plentywood, Montana, Under the Act of March 3, 1878

Sheridan County People Face Starvation

Secretary Hyde's Representative Visits Williston, Glasgow

FARMERS OF THE NORTHWEST SAY DROUTH AID IS IMMEDIATE NEED

Tillers of the Soil Tell Secretary Hyde's Man, Brown, that Large Area in Montana and North Dakota Now Is In a Very Serious Predicament.

Williston, June 25.—Commissioners of eight North Dakota and Montana counties today told a federal department of agriculture representative that their farmers need immediate help because of drouth. Chairman Frank French of the Sheridan County board of commissioners represented Sheridan county at the meeting.

Meeting with J. G. Brown representing Secretary of Agriculture Hyde they said farmers' credit was

Banks and Bankers

by H. Lowndes Maury

Modern industrial life cannot function without banks. A man cannot live without nerves. Banks of loan and deposit were known in Nineveh and Babylon, two thousand years before Christ. There is in the British Museum an Assyrian tablet describing a prosecution for usury o fthe Eloihim Brothers. They were convicted of collecting eighteen per cent for the year 1937 (approx.) B. C. Many indulge the error that the invention of exchange, commercial drafts, the transfer of credit, without actually transporting all or much of the money

Bond Issue Four and One-Half Per Cent Gallatin County Bought by First National Bank of Butte" (an independent house.) Gallatin County's credit has always been good. The rate of interest is fair. It is a likely investment for large capital. It is a good sign of returning independence in Montana. None of the interest n this bond issue will be divided in Minnesota.

The large banks of Bozeman are in one or the other of the mergers. They did not buy it. They, for two years, have been running an institution, unadapt-

Robert Larson Calls on People of County to Form Organization for Relief

Says Farmers in Southeastern Sheridan County are Hungry Now, with no Hopes of Crops or even Feed for Cattle — Wants Farmers to See County Commissioners and Petition State and National Authorities for Relief — Prefers Organized Action to Individual Action.

CELEBRATION AT POPLAR JULY 4th

Farmers' crops failed in Sheridan County in the 1930s, and many faced bankruptcy and starvation, but despite significant discontent among farmers, which might have helped their cause, the Communists in northeastern Montana continued to lose support. [*Producers News*, June 26, 1931]

immediately wrote Erik Bert asking him not to give up his work at the *Producers News.*[7]

Apparently the editor was unmoved because two weeks later Tiala wrote Henry Puro, head of the Communist Party USA's agricultural department, that Bert "positively will not remain in Plentywood." Interestingly, in the same letter, Tiala complained bitterly about what he described as a plan formulated by Charles Taylor, Rodney Salisbury, and an associate named Pete Gallagher to start organizing in North Dakota. He claimed that "these fellows . . . have nothing to show in their home state and even in their supposedly 'red' home county in the way of UFL organization." He conceded that "Charles is sincere and well meaning, but you know that he is prone to grandiose ideas." Citing Ruth Bert's report of the terrible political conditions in Plentywood, he called for a "house cleaning in the Party" in northeastern Montana, "otherwise we're apt to hatch a nestful of rotten eggs out there that will stink our movement to the high heavens."[8]

Rather than cleaning house in Sheridan County, the CPUSA sent one of the party faithful to Plentywood as the new editor of the *Producers News*: L. M. "Abe" Lerner, who had worked on the CPUSA's *Farmers National Weekly.* Charles Taylor later said that, of all those who filled his place at the helm of the *News,* Abe Lerner did the best job, that he understood the local character and appeal of the paper. But Lerner was a dyed-in-the-wool Communist who expressed serious concern about the paper's political stance and complained that he did not have enough

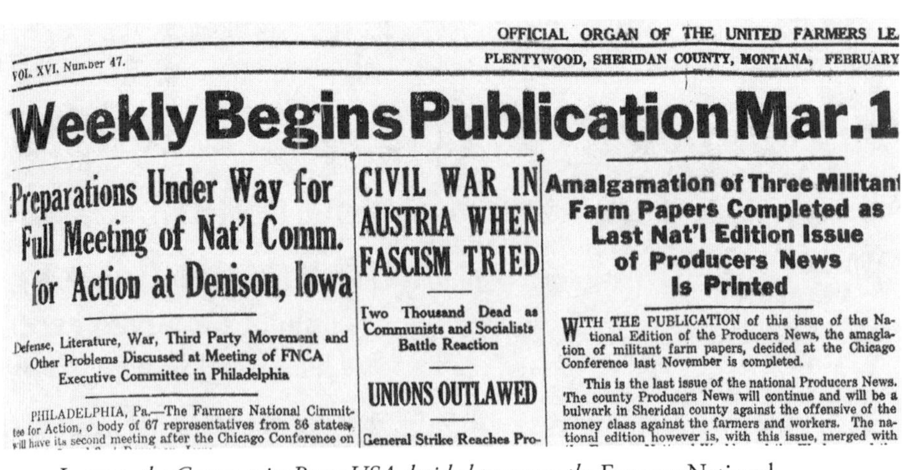

OFFICIAL ORGAN OF THE UNITED FARMERS LE

VOL. XVI. Number 47.

PLENTYWOOD, SHERIDAN COUNTY, MONTANA, FEBRUARY

Weekly Begins Publication Mar. 1

Preparations Under Way for Full Meeting of Nat'l Comm. for Action at Denison, Iowa

Defense, Literature, War, Third Party Movement and Other Problems Discussed at Meeting of FNCA Executive Committee in Philadelphia

PHILADELPHIA, Pa.—The Farmers National Cimmittee for Action, o body of 67 representatives from 86 states will have its second meeting after the Chicago Conference on

CIVIL WAR IN AUSTRIA WHEN FASCISM TRIED

Two Thousand Dead as Communists and Socialists Battle Reaction

UNIONS OUTLAWED

General Strike Reaches Pro-

Amalgamation of Three Militant Farm Papers Completed as Last Nat'l Edition Issue of Producers News Is Printed

WITH THE PUBLICATION of this issue of the National Edition of the Producers News, the amaglation of militant farm papers, decided at the Chicago Conference last November is completed.

This is the last issue of the national Producers News. The county Producers News will continue and will be a bulwark in Sheridan county against the offensive of the money class against the farmers and workers. The national edition however is, with this issue, merged with

In 1934, the Communist Party USA decided to merge the Farmers National Weekly *with the* Producers News. *Seeking to assure readers, the* News *announced that "[t]he county Producers News will continue and will be a bulwark in Sheridan county against the offensive of the money class against the farmers and workers."* [*Producers News,* February 16, 1934] time to do important background reading. He claimed that he barely had time to read the *Daily Worker.* And he lasted less than two months in Plentywood. Having been named the new editor at the end of September 1933, by November 3, he was listed in the staff box as "acting editor." With no explanation, Erik Bert was once more listed as editor and Charles Taylor as managing editor. And by the end of November, Lerner's name had disappeared from the staff box entirely.[9]

The shifting of personnel was related to a plan to consolidate the *Producers News* with the *Farmers National Weekly,* which at that time was published out of Washington, D.C. There was discussion within the leadership as to whether the headquarters of the paper should be in Plentywood and, if not, whether the printing plant should be moved elsewhere or simply left behind. During Abe Lerner's brief tenure at the *Producers News,* he was in regular correspondence with Henry Puro concerning the feasibility of moving the printing equipment. Though Charles Taylor expressed a positive opinion of Lerner in a later interview, it is possible that he was unaware that Lerner had been very critical of him. In letters to Henry Puro, Lerner accused Taylor and Rodney Salisbury of maneuvering to collect subscription fees from farmers even though they knew the future of the *Producers News* was uncertain. He also claimed that Charles Taylor was putting out the word that, if the *News* remained in Plentywood, it could not support itself financially and might be bought out by a certain "Mainstreeter," who was, in fact, Outlook farmer William Hass.[10]

Suspicions about the consolidation of the *News* with the *Farmers National Weekly* were soon being discussed in Sheridan County. Staff writer Hans Rasmussen hastened to assure readers that the *Producers News* would not abandon the farmers but would instead return to the good old days as a truly local paper that would be dependably delivered on time and have no national edition. However, many readers likely noted that the changes did not extend to the paper's editorship: the paper would still be edited by a person of the CPUSA's choosing. Certainly, the CPUSA was scrambling in the wings to find that person. When George Anderson, one potential candidate, was offered the position, he responded "emphatically 'no.'" Alfred Tiala noted that "the political situation in Plentywood is abominable, and it is possible that in such a situation Anderson might become demoralized. . . . Isn't someone available in New York?"[11]

The *Producers News* masthead reveals that the parade of editors continued: Erik Bert was still listed as the editor in January 1934, although he was no longer in residence in Sheridan County. During

THE PRODUCERS NEWS

Published Friday of each week at Plentywood, Montana, by The Peoples Publishing Company, Inc.

Entered as Second Class Matter, October 18, 1918, at the Post Office at Plentywood, Montana, Under the Act of March 9, 1879.

OUR PROGRAM

1. No evictions, no forclosures.
3. Passage of the Workers Unemployment Bill (H. R. 7598)
2. Cancellation of all secured farm debts.
4. Immediate cash relief for unemployed workers and destitute farmers.

Subscription Rates: Per year, $2; six months, $1; three months 50 cents. Foreign per year, $2.50; six months, $1.25; three months, 60 cents.

Advertising Rates furnished upon application.

ALFRED F. MILLER, Acting Editor
HANS RASMUSSEN, Business Manager

Alfred Miller replaced Erik Bert at the helm of the Producers News *in 1934. The masthead now included a heading "Our program" under which was listed objectives including "no evictions, no foreclosures, passage of the workers unemployment bill (H.R. 7598), cancellation of all secured farm debts, and immediate cash relief for unemployed workers and destitute farmers."* [*Producers News*, February 23, 1934]

that same month, Charles Taylor's name disappeared from the staff box. By early February, Rob F. Hall, an Alabama native educated at Columbia University, was listed as acting editor. In the community, there was a mounting problem: the *Producers News* was no longer seen as belonging to local residents. Yet, neither the new editor nor the staff writer and longtime business manager Rasmussen made any apologies, instead placing the responsibility for the paper in the hands of the farmers. They noted that the paper—at least the county edition—would improve "just as fast as farmers and workers write for it, criticize it, make it ACTUALLY their own." But convincing the farmers to take ownership was a challenge, as the editor's position remained in flux. At the end of February, shortly after the national edition ceased publication—and with no published introduction—Alfred Miller assumed editorial duties at the paper.[12]

Miller, a German expatriate who had changed his name from Fortmueller, had immigrated to the United States in 1929 and worked for a time as a toolmaker in New York City. Later, just before coming to Plentywood, he worked on a publication called the *Organization Farmer* in Pennsylvania. Predictably, in spite of the fact that there was no longer a national edition, the *Producers News* was not magically transformed into a local paper under Miller's editorship. The paper still covered national stories such as the exploitation of New York City newsboys and California pea pickers. The paper also featured an attack on Charles Taylor authored by A. H. Anderson, chairman of the board of the People's Publishing Company. Under the headline "Lie of a 'Sell-Out' Is Exposed by Board," Anderson accused Taylor of a "consistent campaign of slander" against the board, including the assertion that the board had sold out to farmer William Hass. Anderson also quoted Taylor as having said that he would retake control of the newspaper "whether the Board likes it or not."[13]

Miller sprinkled more local stories and tidbits throughout the paper, rather than confining them mainly to one inside page, as had been the recent practice. As time passed, he began to recapture the local focus that had characterized the *Producers News* in the 1920s. There were fewer press service editorials and more columns about local issues and controversies. The tone of the news writing was not as angst-filled and tended to focus on topics about which readers might care and on problems that could conceivably be solved. Miller also seemed to recognize the need to create a sense of empowerment among his readers. For example, after he had been in Plentywood for a short time, he published fewer stories on California pea pickers and more on local actions, such as the attempted eviction of a widow and her five children from a Sheridan County farm. The eviction was halted by a group of fellow farmers.

Alfred Miller was not a skilled writer. Perhaps because English was his second language, his sentences could be tortured, and under his watch, the *News* would have benefited from much closer proofreading. But he brought more vitality to the paper than it had had under some of the previous editors. He renewed the offensives Charles Taylor had made against the competing *Plentywood Herald,* assailing editor Harry Polk, though generally with less severity than had Taylor. There were no accusations of involvement with schoolgirls, but only the assertion that Polk was the boss of a "Mainstreeter" conspiracy against the farmers and their party. At one point, a *Producers News* editorial even congratulated the *Herald* for "becoming more intelligent in its attacks on the Communist Party" and noted that "there are less slanderous remarks in Mr. Polk's editorials, fewer misrepresentations and more facts." Of course, Miller went on to offer a point-by-point refutation of a recent *Herald* editorial and challenged Polk to a public debate.[14]

As in the days of old, controversy dogged the *Producers News,* which may have restored a certain sense of intrigue to the paper. One imbroglio involved Outlook farmer William Hass, the former *News* investor who had fallen out with the paper in the late 1920s. In nearly two decades in Sheridan County, Hass and his brothers had established themselves as prosperous farmers. By the 1930s, William Hass was a major stockholder in Plentywood's Security State Bank and served as its president. In late 1933, he filed suit against the *Producers News* for a $650 note owed to him. A court appearance was avoided only when the board of directors of the People's Publishing Company took a second mortgage on the printing plant in order to repay the loan.[15]

In the same issue of the *News* that reported on the withdrawal of Hass's suit, a front-page story accused him of serving an eviction notice on a certain Carl Hovdey, whose thirty-five-hundred-dollar mortgage Hass held. The newspaper described Hovdey as a "pioneer of Sheridan county," a "hard worker [who] dug the rock, put up the building, dug the well and broke the virgin soil" on his property. The article contrasted Hovdey with the affluent Hass, listed all of the neighbors' property that Hass had bought up, and called upon the members of the United Farmers League to help keep Hovdey on his farm.[16]

By May 1934, things had begun to heat up and a twelve-page mimeographed pamphlet, purportedly written by James Ostby, vice president of the People's Publishing Company board and president of what the pamphlet referred to as the "Save the Producers News Club," began circulating. The pamphlet excoriated William Hass and longtime *News* employee Hans Rasmussen and sang the praises of Charles Taylor and Rodney Salisbury. The purpose of the publication, which was apparently mailed to all People's Publishing Company stockholders, was to warn of an imminent sale of the *Producers News* to William Hass.[17]

Alfred Miller immediately repudiated the information in the pamphlet, reminding Jim Ostby "that the attack on the *Producers News* is also an attack on the working class movement and on the Communist Party in particular." The *News* blamed the whole affair on a group of "renegades" who had been expelled from the Communist Party in recent months because they had formed a joint electoral ticket with a competing farm organization. This accusation was indicative of a tendency in the *Producers News* that had been true of the larger American Communist movement for its entire history: factionalism, disloyalty, and a willingness to quickly turn on longtime supporters when they disagreed with the party line.[18]

Among those who had recently been expelled from the CPUSA were Rodney Salisbury, John Boulds, and two other comrades from the Red heyday in Sheridan County. By the summer of 1934, they were classified with all other traitors to the Communist cause because of their association with the National Farm Holiday Association, a direct-action organization that encouraged farmers to withhold their crops until cost-of-production prices were reached. (During the Third Period of Communism, which lasted until 1935, the CPUSA opposed the Farm Holiday as well as the Farmers Union as agents of Wall Street.) According to the *Producers News,* Salisbury, Boulds, and their colleagues were the "worst reactionaries" and had turned against the party and the entire working class.[19]

Even Charles Taylor was enlisted to condemn his former comrades. He wrote a guest editorial for the *News* from Nebraska, where he was engaged in organizing, reporting that his "life long friend" Rodney Salisbury had failed the revolution, had begun an "anti-party" organization that was undermining the Communist Party in Sheridan County, and was therefore another "enemy of the working class." Former *Producers News* editor P. J. Wallace was back in the area, working with Salisbury on a newssheet they called the *Militant Farmer.* Wallace, too, was now branded an enemy who was helping the Mainstreeters by potentially splitting the radical vote.[20]

Charles Taylor, though currently in good standing with CPUSA headquarters, had himself recently been put through the mill. Back in 1932, he had been appointed national chairman of the United Farmers League by Earl Browder, the general secretary of the CPUSA. In 1934, the UFL secretary under Taylor was Alfred Tiala, a protégé of Henry Puro, the party's agrarian secretary and a Third Period hardliner. Tiala and Taylor were at odds: Tiala wrote to Puro about their differences of opinion and noted that Taylor "has called me all the names he can think of. I don't care so much about that, but it's certainly beginning to seem to me that he's an incorrigible Townley [Nonpartisan League] politician and that he'll never be anything else." Puro engaged Erik and Ruth Bert to join him in assailing Taylor in the pages of the *Farmers National Weekly.* In the late winter of 1933, in spite of the fact that he was still chairman, Taylor was not invited to the United Farmers League's executive council meeting. Then, in March 1934, the UFL unceremoniously removed Taylor from the chairmanship; his replacement was Alfred Tiala.[21]

In retrospect, Taylor said that his removal surely came at the behest of "Puro and his bunch," but he recognized that this would have required the concurrence of the party leadership. The following month, Taylor was refused seating and criticized by Henry Puro at the Eighth Convention of the Communist Party in Cleveland; the *Daily Worker* published Puro's remarks. Subsequently, General Secretary Earl Browder took Taylor to dinner and then summoned him to New York City for two weeks. Ultimately, Taylor appeared before the executive council of the CPUSA and was fully exonerated, although he was given no opportunity to place a rejoinder in the *Daily Worker.*[22]

Following his reinstatement, Taylor was sent to Nebraska for roughly nine months to do organizing work for the Farm Holiday Association.

The construction of the new courthouse in Plentywood, pictured here at the end of Main Street in the late 1930s, was one of several New Deal projects that seemed to belie the Communists' argument that the capitalist system was deteriorating. [*Plentywood Portrait: Toil, Soil, and Oil* (Aberdeen, S. Dak., 1987), 174]

The CPUSA, again in a head-spinning change of direction, had reversed its position on the Farm Holiday organization. The move signaled the beginning of the Communists' Popular Front in agriculture. Among his other activities in Nebraska, Taylor was in charge of organizing a conference in Loup City that culminated in a violent clash between a local vigilante group and radicals, among them Mother Bloor, who were attempting to organize women employed as chicken pickers. Six demonstrators, including Bloor, were arrested, and Taylor had to find a prosperous local farmer to bail them out. Despite all his troubles with the party, Charles Taylor remained dedicated to the cause.[23]

While Taylor was still in Nebraska, the 1934 election season was warming up in Sheridan County. Once again, the conditions in the county would have seemed to offer plenty of potential for a Communist victory. Sheridan County was in its sixth year of drought, teachers' salaries had been cut, and the *Producers News* reported that nearly three hundred children in the county were suffering from malnutrition. There was a dire shortage of animal feed. To make matters worse, there was a damaging frost on July 6.[24]

By August, however, the effects of New Deal reforms began to be felt. The *Plentywood Herald* reported that the federal government had purchased ten thousand cattle in Sheridan County—either to be sent to lands that could support them or to be slaughtered. The next month, the county received its first shipment of fresh meat from the Federal

Emergency Relief Administration; in the coming months, six thousand pounds would be delivered once every two weeks to points all over the county. And in October, Sheridan County's relief administrator announced that ninety-two men would be hired to extend Plentywood's sewer and water lines. Before long, work began on a grand new county courthouse, a Works Progress Administration (WPA) project costing the county approximately eighty thousand dollars, funds that were matched by the federal government. Not long after that, the WPA built a golf course in Plentywood. Workers in Sheridan County could expect to make roughly forty dollars a month on these WPA jobs. Consumer confidence seemed to be rising to the point that, by December, the *Herald* reported the most robust Christmas shopping season in six years with "clothing and household goods . . . much in demand."[25] These gradual improvements made it more difficult for Communists to argue that the present system was deteriorating. And this was not the only new challenge the

CCC Camp Gets 30 Sheridan Boys

First Contingent Leaves Plentywood Friday to Get Training as Strikebreakers and to Be Taught How to Behave as Wall Street's Cannon Fodder

PLENTYWOOD, July 25.—Thirty Sheridan county boys are going to be sent to a Civil Conservation Corps camp this week, it was announced by the county relief administration today.

The boys are to leave town Friday noon by train. Their destination was unknown to the officials. Other sources

it is pointed out to them that it would be far more logical to put the camps under the administra-

The Producers News *questioned the War Department's jurisdiction over CCC camps, fearing that the main purpose of the camps was "to get boys ready for another world slaughter."* [*Producers News,* July 26, 1934]

The Civilian Conservation Corps (CCC), another New Deal program of the Works Progress Administration (WPA), put many Sheridan County residents, including these men from Outlook and Daleview, to work. [Outlook, Montana, Community and School Club, *The Outlook-Daleview Community Diamond Jubilee Book* (Aberdeen, S. Dak., 1985), 105]

Communists faced: in the 1934 elections they were aligned against not only Republicans and Democrats but another radical ticket as well, the United Front, led by their old comrade Robert Larson. Larson was the former Farmer-Labor Party legislator who had denounced his colleagues in print after the 1932 election, accusing them of abiding Stalinism. Now he, Rodney Salisbury, and other former Communists, some of whom had been purged by the CPUSA, appeared on the ballot, hopelessly splitting the Sheridan County radical vote. Editor Miller claimed in the *Producers News* that the United Front was a tool of Harry Polk of the *Plentywood Herald* and other "Mainstreeters."[26]

As it turned out, even if the United Front had not siphoned away any of the radical vote, the Communists still would have been thrashed in the general election. The closest race was for county surveyor, and it was won by Robert Wheeler, who, the *Plentywood Herald* conceded, was given a "real scare from Hans Rasmussen, the only Communist candidate to show any material strength." It wasn't much of a scare really: Rasmussen garnered only 37 percent of the votes. In each race, the Communists were defeated, typically capturing no more than about 15 percent of the total ballots cast. A few precincts, including Raymond and Dagmar, were still fairly radical, but even voters in those communities could not be counted on to vote the straight Communist ticket. In the state senate contest, for instance, both communities gave

the Communist candidate the most votes, but the margins were much narrower than in previous years. The *Producers News* found itself in the discouraging position of conceding that "the election is over and the Mainstreet politicians are again triumphant. Again hundreds and hundreds of farmers and workers in the county have been tricked into voting for their enemies, the class that squeezes the blood out of them to the last drop and then throws them upon the scrap heap of humanity."[27]

As bleak as the election results were, the situation was about to become even more desperate for Alfred Miller at the *Producers News.* In March 1935, he was questioned by a U.S. Immigration inspector in Plentywood and subsequently charged with violating the Immigration Act of 1918 in that he was "an alien who believes in, advises, advocates, and teaches the overthrow by force and violence of the government of the United States." Deportation proceedings began. In April, the Farmers Emergency Relief Conference at Sioux Falls formally protested Miller's possible deportation, but he was nonetheless arrested, and a legal defense fund was established in Sheridan County.[28]

Just as Miller's troubles were escalating, Charles Taylor returned to Plentywood and staged a coup at the *Producers News,* engaging in a brief and successful fight for the paper's leadership at the July 1935 stockholders' meeting. Alfred Miller and his business manager walked out of the meeting; after their departure, a new board of directors was

Even the communities of Dagmar and Raymond, though still fairly radical, did not vote the straight Communist ticket in 1934. The Producers News *opined, "Farmers and workers in the county have been tricked into voting for their enemies, the class that squeezes the blood out of them to the last drop and then throws them upon the scrap heap of humanity." Dagmar appears here during its Community Fair, October 5, 1929.* [Henry B. Syverud, photographer, MHS Photograph Archives, Helena, PAc 77-94 v2-7.1]

selected. The board wasted no time in appointing Taylor to his former position as editor. In his later years, Taylor claimed to have left the Communist Party at about this time.[29]

In Taylor's view, his newspaper had gone downhill in the roughly five years he had been away. After the Communist faithful took over at the helm, he said, it had "not only lost kick and zest but had lost local interest." Taylor's first editorial after his return was titled "Again, the Farmers' Paper." He announced that the paper would still support a "mass labor party built upon the immediate needs of the farmers and workers," but that it would serve the farmers "in a better and more realistic way, in a more tolerant and less sectarian way." Furthermore, the editor pledged to "let by gones be by gones [*sic*]" and nostalgically invited readers to make "the paper your headquarters as you did in the days gone by."[30]

After his editorship was restored, Taylor maneuvered to align the *Producers News* more closely with the Farm Holiday Association. In September 1935, the board of directors of the Montana Holiday Association selected the *News* as its official newspaper. In March 1936, the paper announced that plans were under way by the association to "refinance and build the *Producers News,*" which Charles Taylor had described as being in "desperate financial circumstances right now." But Taylor's newspaper was on no more solid financial ground with the Montana Holiday Association than it had been with the Communists. Moreover, community support had been so seriously eroded over the years of Taylor's absence that there was nothing but rough road ahead.[31]

In spite of Taylor's passionate plea to the Montana Holiday Association conference, the paper spiraled into financial ruin. Advertisers had all but abandoned the *Producers News* in favor of the *Plentywood Herald,* and without advertising revenue, Taylor was unable to pay his employees. On the occasion of the newspaper's eighteenth anniversary, Charles Taylor wrote that although the past winter had been the hardest in the paper's history, "we are still here, sustained by the faith in the farmers and workers, and still hewing to the line." He ended his column with the question, "Can't the *Producers News* have this little birthday offering today?" by way of pleading that readers pay up their subscriptions.[32]

In 1936, the *News* cut its pages in half, made occasional pleas to subscribers for funds, and published very few local editorials. Even Taylor's jabs at the *Plentywood Herald*'s Harry Polk seemed to lack their former zing. As the general election approached, the *Producers News* was uncharacteristically quiet. Charles Taylor's home burned in the fall (no

Stormy Career For Newspapers In Sheridan County Is Recalled

Sheridan county, which at one time boasted as many as seven newspapers, this week saw its news mediums dwindle to two.

Friday of last week, the Redstone Review went to press for the last time, the publisher, Blanche Sherry, at the helm since the death of her fater, announcing the Review would discontinue publication.

The Review is the second newspaper in Sheridan county to cease publication within six weeks.

Twenty-four years of publishing came to an end when the key was turned in the Review door after the paper had been put to bed and placed in the mails Friday.

Founded in the boom days of this section when land-seeking homesteaders swarmed to a new Utopia, the Review each week was a regular "comer" to homes in that community. It was an important part of the community. Frank Sherry became its editor in 1918.

Dwindling patronage resulting from hard times caused the suspension of the Redstone paper.

The paper's suspension brings to mind the coming and going of "the press' in Sheridan county in twenty-some-odd years.

Twenty years ago practically every community boasted a newspaper. Frank Sherry's publication stuck for 24 years, but the majority of the early founded newspapers floundered.

Possibly no section of the northwest has seen journalism flourish and fall as in Sheridan county, where the most bitter campaigns of caustic journalism undoubtedly on record have been waged.

At one time three newspapers were published in Plentywood. In Outlook, Dooley, Westby, Antelope and Medicine Lake the press flourished—but not for long, with the exception of Medicine Lake.

Chief among the county newspapers at that time was the Producers News, which gradually absorbed the smaller publications and for many years carried their names in its masthead.

Six weeks ago the key in the door of the Producers News was turned and publication ceased.

The discontinuation of the Producers News closed an eventful career of many years.

Founded as a newspaper for farmers, it road the crest of prosperity. Followers of the paper's doctrinal teachings were by the hundreds. It rose to great heights, then fell. It was revived several times and of late years dwindled to its final passing a little more than a month ago.

Producers News editors poured forth volumes of stormy journalism, critical constructive and abusive. Of all the newspapers started in Sheridan county, and now suspended, the Producers News had the most colorful career.

Dusty, old and time-worn files some day will reveal interesting facts of the journalistic profession here. The newspaper history of Sheridan county is destined to be long-lived.

Ironically, news of the ultimate demise of the Producers News *came on the front page of the* Plentywood Herald *in this article that recounted its history as well as those of several other defunct Sheridan County newspapers.* [*Plentywood Herald*, April 29, 1937]

foul play was suspected), and the newspaper began to appear late or not at all. In November, only 1 percent of the total county vote was cast for the Communist candidate for president.[33] Taylor managed to put out only three issues of the paper in 1937, the March edition being the last.

Ironically, the obituary for the *News* was published in none other than the *Plentywood Herald*. "Six weeks ago the key in the door of the *Producers News* was turned and publication ceased," the *Herald* reported on its front page in late April of 1937. "The discontinuation of the *Producers News* closed an eventful career of many years. Founded as a newspaper for farmers, it road [*sic*] the crest of prosperity. Followers of the paper's doctrinal teaching were by the hundreds. It rose to great heights, then fell. . . . Of all the newspapers started in Sheridan county, and now suspended, the *Producers News* had the most colorful career."[34]

The *Producers News* had helped put Sheridan County on the map, for better or worse, with Communist leadership in the United States and Russia and with Montanans from all corners of the state. It had risen from a being a radical start-up paper to being nationally distributed by the Communist Party USA. It had then suffered a precipitous decline. At least part of the reason for the waning of the *News* was that it failed to maintain the appealing and powerful narrative that had characterized it during the early years. In this failing, the newspaper was not alone: some members of the American left would recognize that Communists across the nation were making the same kind of rhetorical errors and would lobby for a greater sensitivity in propagandizing. By then, however, it was too late for the farmers' movement in northeastern Montana, whose members and leaders had scattered with the wind. For years to come in Sheridan County, the Communist period would be only a memory, rarely discussed in public. The once-proud crusade had been reduced to a blemish that many families preferred to conceal.

CHAPTER 15

The Demise of Communism in Sheridan County

When northeastern Montana's radical drama finally played out, the main actors went their separate ways. Some left the county while others carried on in the place they called home. The FBI monitored some of them for years, reporting on their activities, political involvement, and families.

Throughout his life, Taylor remained dedicated to radical causes, though he recognized the price his own family paid for his activism, later admitting that his wife had often been left alone with the children, Ellen, Carl, Doris, and Lorraine, in Plentywood while he was "sometimes gone for five or six months at a time." After shutting down the *Producers News* in 1937, Taylor moved with Agda and the children to Seattle, where he continued to work in the printing trade and remained politically active, joining the Socialist Workers Party. He helped organize independent fuel dealers to fight a city ordinance that would tax their trucks. When he benefited financially from an out-of-court settlement won by the fuel dealers, he used that money to move the *Producers News* printing equipment to

Charles Taylor, circa 1940. [Courtesy Carl Taylor]

The Taylor family, 1960s (left to right): Charles, Lorraine, Carl, Doris, and Ellen . [Courtesy Carl Taylor]

Seattle. For a time, he operated a commercial print shop that published a radio guide and an Italian language newspaper. During World War II, he worked in the shipyards and joined the boilermakers' union, eventually taking a job as a proofreader for the *Seattle Post-Intelligencer.* After Agda's death, he joined the People's Church. According to his son Carl, "It wasn't that he was such a believer in God, it was just a church organization that was very liberal and that's why he got mixed up in that. Mother was dead and he was alone; that's why he joined."[1]

Charles Taylor, of course, was one of Sheridan County's radicals who remained under the scrutiny of the FBI for years. As late as 1961, a report noted his address and occupation and quoted three informants who recalled Taylor's attendance at a Communist Party convention and his recruiting work for the Seattle branch of the Socialist Workers Party in the late 1930s. Eventually, Taylor returned to Minnesota, the state of his birth. In 1963, the FBI's Minneapolis Division was notified of Taylor's new address in Aitkin, Minnesota, and the appropriate files were forwarded from Seattle; this notification was the last FBI document on Taylor, who was, at the time, seventy-nine years old. He died just four years later in Little Falls, Minnesota.[2]

As for the county's other newspapermen, Erik Bert went to Chicago to edit the *Farmers National Weekly,* which had taken up where the *Producers News* left off as the CPUSA's agrarian paper. He later was employed at the Communist Party USA's *Daily Worker* in New York

City as a news writer and columnist. He remained at the newspaper and under FBI surveillance through the 1970s. Not until 1978 did the FBI conclude that he posed so little threat that his case could be closed. His wife, Ruth Bert, was employed for a time as a secretary in the offices of Minnesota governor Floyd Olson, who was a friend of the Communist Party. The Berts had one son, Herbert, in 1936.[3]

The *Daniels County Leader* and the *Plentywood Herald* carried on as before, although the papers never again had such a compelling mission as during their anti-Communist era. Burley Bowler remained in journalism for the rest of his life. In his prime, he served on the staff of Montana's senator Zales Ecton and, during this stint in Washington, D.C., became a member of the National Press Club. He was a staunch Republican and a delegate to the Republican National Convention of 1948. Later, Bowler was installed as president of the Montana Press Association. It was during his term as president, in 1959, that he invited FBI director J. Edgar Hoover to address the organization's seventy-fourth annual convention, an invitation Hoover politely declined. The FBI noted on its copy of the correspondence that their files contained "no derogatory information concerning Bowler." He continued writing a column for the *Daniels County Leader,* published by his son and later his grandson, until just weeks before his death. Bowler died of cancer at the age of seventy-seven in late 1967, just eight months after the death of his longtime rival, Charles Taylor.[4]

Harry Polk, too, stayed at the helm of the *Plentywood Herald* long after the radical days had passed. In 1961, his son Stuart assumed the roles of editor and publisher. In contrast to the contentious material

Burley Bowler. [University of Montana School of Journalism, Missoula]

Harry Polk. [*Sheridan County News*]

that appeared in the paper during the late 1920s and 1930s, the latter-day *Herald* tended to cover the usual small-town fare of city council and school board meetings, crop reports, and other local news. (There was one exception: in 1966 an angry assailant killed the mayor of Plentywood and wounded the city judge and police chief in a shooting at city hall, and Plentywood again made national headlines.) Polk outlived his fellow Red-era editors by a few years, dying in Williston, North Dakota, in 1971. The *Herald* closed its doors in 1995, though several of its staff started the *Sheridan County News,* which, as of this writing, is published by Harry Polk's grandson.[5]

As for the leaders in the farm movement, most went their separate ways. In the mid-1930s, former sheriff Rodney Salisbury left Sheridan County with his lover, Marie Hansen, and moved with her and their three children to Billings. There he served as the president of the Montana Farm Holiday Association. He later relocated with Marie to the Missoula area, where he continued his militant activities in the western part of the state.[6]

In death as in life, Salisbury was surrounded by controversy. When he died during a visit to Plentywood in the summer of 1938, the *Plentywood Herald* reported that he had succumbed at the local hospital following a three-day illness, before which he had been in good health. The cause of death listed on the death certificate was cerebral hemorrhage, but his unexpected demise at the age of fifty led to rampant speculation. A rumor that circulated through the county found its way into an FBI general intelligence report, which noted that Salisbury died "under suspicious circumstances. The belief is prevalent that he was poisoned by Marie Hanson [*sic*]." One member of Salisbury's extended family offered another explanation: that his brain hemorrhage was the result of an injury sustained in a barroom fight. His daughter, however, attributed the hemorrhage to a stroke.[7]

After his death, Salisbury's two families had to provide for themselves. Emma Salisbury, whom Rodney never divorced, took a job with the WPA, and all of her children went to work to support the family. Marie Hansen was left with three children to whom she was, by one account, "violently abusive . . . after Rodney died." She lived in western Montana and Oregon before moving to California in 1967, where she died at the age of seventy-seven in 1976.[8]

Arthur Rueber, another of the county's "old time Socialists," had invested in the Radium Remedies Company with Charles Taylor in 1925. According to the *Producers News,* Rueber planned to serve as the company's director and sales manager. When the paper published a

The Stoner family, circa 1920 (left to right): Clair, Lucile, Helen, Alice, and Doshia. [Courtesy Lucile Ransdell]

report on the company in 1928, however, Rueber was not mentioned, nor was he involved in Sheridan County politics after that point. He eventually bought a farm on the outskirts of Littlefork, Minnesota, where he was known to locals as a Socialist. He died in 1968.[9]

Hans Rasmussen stayed in the movement from start to finish. The longtime business manager and sometime columnist at the *Producers News* eventually returned to his former profession as a mason, working on a number of buildings in Sheridan County, including the new courthouse and the Plentywood school. Like Salisbury and Taylor, he was described in the FBI's 1941 general intelligence report, but he was assessed as no great threat. A confidential informant reportedly stated that Rasmussen "used to be a 'Red' when the *Producers News* was in existence, but since it ceased publication, he has quieted down." In 1942, his family moved to Seattle. He passed away within two years of that move, at the age of seventy-three.[10]

Clair Stoner, one of the early Nonpartisan League boosters and a state representative, struggled along on his farm until 1925 when he turned his land over to the bank, explaining that the government's free land "did not turn out to be so free after all. . . . We fought the battle and lost.'" From Sheridan County, the Stoner family moved to Great Falls, where Clair was employed by the Montana Wheat Growers Association, relocating in 1929 to California. Stoner's daughter recalls that, while he was "pretty radical" in the early days, his interest in political matters waned over the years.[11]

The same could not be said about John Boulds. Although he was not a central figure during the farm movement's heyday, Boulds came into his own as a radical in later years. After his expulsion, along with Rodney Salisbury, from the CPUSA in 1934, Boulds eventually found a home in the Socialist Workers Party. According to the FBI, he became the leader of northeastern Montana's remaining leftists, although "by the national group he [was] considered a small functionary." One FBI agent perceived Boulds as rather inconsistent on doctrine, noting, "At a meeting of farmers he may take the platform and declare for an immediate revolution. At the next meeting he may declare for absolute defense of the nation and the constitution of the United States. Both speeches will be highly applauded and both mean exactly nothing. This is the temperament of Plentywood."[12]

Boulds seemed to make up for in loyalty what he lacked in doctrinal consistency. Twice in 1939, the *New International,* the magazine of the Socialist Workers Party, included Boulds among those workers deserving "special mention" and commendation for their work. Two years later, he coordinated a visit and public lecture in Plentywood by Grace Carlson, a well-known party member and political contender from Minnesota. And in 1943, notes on the Sheridan County Socialist Workers Party were found in the possession of a functionary who had been detained by police in San Antonio, Texas. He had apparently visited various locals, recording his observations. About his observations in Plentywood, he noted that only five members were present at the local meeting and the "entire setup" was poor, but that the SWP "cannot waste a man as good as Boulds." Even in 1948, Boulds was still involved in the group, arranging for a lecture in Plentywood by Farrell Dobbs, the party's presidential candidate. After Dobbs's visit in August, however, it seems that Boulds and the remaining Socialists disbanded; the FBI concluded that there was no further Socialist Workers Party activity in Sheridan County. Boulds remained in Plentywood until his death in 1968.[13]

The Hass family maintained their successful farming business in the Outlook community. The operation was turned over to William and Margaret's son, Harlow. Margaret, who had worked at the *Producers News* and served briefly as the Communist local's secretary, eventually came to support Roosevelt and his New Deal. However, when entries for Sheridan County's history book were being collected in 1970, she wrote at the beginning of her family's biography, "I am a red Red." The Outlook section editor persuaded her to reconsider the statement, and the Hass biography was published without any reference to her political orientation. The section editor's advice to Margaret Hass to keep that part of her history in the closet was representative of the feelings of most residents of Sheridan County about their region's radical past. It was better left alone.[14]

Indeed, most of the former radicals tried to distance themselves from the cause. Men like Selmer Espeland, who had been the Communist candidate for county treasurer in 1932, resumed a quiet life of farming in the Westby community after the Red heyday was over. Espeland was not included in the comprehensive 1941 FBI report on Sheridan County Communists. A. C. Erickson, who had been elected on the Farmer-Labor Party ticket as county attorney in 1924, went on to serve several terms in that office and as Plentywood's city attorney until the 1940s, in spite of his previous associations. FBI informants tended toward the opinion that Erickson was more an opportunist than a true Communist, always allying himself with the "winning side." Erickson seemed to recover well from his dalliance with the Reds, serving as the county's Red Cross chairman for twenty-five years and actively participating in the Lutheran Church. The 1941 FBI report on Erickson concluded that no further investigation of him was warranted.[15]

Particular individuals may have been able to put their radical pasts behind them, but the county itself was stigmatized for years to come, a burden that residents bore with a kind of stoic silence. Northeastern Montana, which novelist Ivan Doig has called "the Red Corner," earned that reputation in reality as well as fiction. Plentywood resident Harold DeSilva remembered being embarrassed about Sheridan County's Communist bent, recalling that, even as a child, he was "ashamed to think that our little community was known as . . . Red-oriented." Local historian Magnus Aasheim reported that, when he attended college in western Montana during the late 1920s and early 1930s, it was common knowledge that Sheridan County was Red. He claimed that, even as late as the 1970s, the county still bore

County attorney Arthur C. Erickson. [*Producers News*, August 16, 1929]

"the stigmatic 'Red' label." Indeed, local resident Clifford Peterson, in a 1985 interview, described the county's "little black eye that's kind of fading out."[16]

To deal with this legacy, in particular with pervasive Cold War anti-Communist sentiment that was rampant in the United States, it seems that the people of Sheridan County, by unspoken pact, became mute on the subject of their radical past. Until the 1990s, any content pertaining to the county's remarkable role in state and even national politics was conspicuously missing from the history taught in Plentywood schools. Only after the demise of Soviet Communism did schoolchildren begin to learn about this chapter of northeastern Montana's past, and more publications began to document Sheridan County's Red period.[17]

In the years since the radical era, Sheridan County has slowly depopulated, following the pattern of so many Great Plains communities. The exodus began during the Great Depression when, between 1930 and 1940, the county lost over 20 percent of its population. This loss was just the beginning of a trend: with each decennial census, the county's population dwindled. By 1960, the population stood at 6,458, down from nearly 9,900 in 1930. In the 1990s, while Montana's total population increased by 13 percent, Sheridan County's decreased by the same percentage, and between 2000 and 2008, it fell another 20 percent, to 3,283. Today, there are more deaths than births in the county, and there are too few job opportunities to lure former residents back after college or work experience elsewhere.[18]

Politically, Sheridan County has gone through changes as well. In 1932, when the county's voters awarded the majority of their votes to Democrat Franklin D. Roosevelt and approximately 18 percent to Communist William Z. Foster, they compensated by electing Republicans to the governor's seat and sending a Republican to Congress, as well as sending three to the state legislature, perhaps as a kind of backlash against radicalism. By 1934, with New Deal programs being implemented, the backlash subsided, and the county awarded two of its three seats in the state legislature to Democrats and chose two Democrats for the U.S. Senate. The tendency toward Democratic voting continued, with Sheridan County supporting Roosevelt twice more, Harry Truman twice, Adlai Stevenson twice (by a very narrow margin in 1952 and a larger one in 1956), John F. Kennedy, Hubert Humphrey, and Jimmy Carter, as well as mainly Democratic congressional and legislative candidates. However in the 1980s, Sheridan County chose Ronald Reagan twice as well as George Bush over Democrat Michael Dukakis. In 1992, the county gave Bill Clinton 40 percent of its votes, with George Bush and Independent candidate Ross Perot receiving roughly 30 percent each. Voters chose Clinton again in 1996, but gave George W. Bush roughly 25 percent more votes than Al Gore in 2000. Bush defeated John Kerry in 2004 by a narrower margin, 58 to 42 percent. The 2008 presidential contest was nearly a dead heat in Sheridan County: John McCain received 49.2 percent of the vote and Barack Obama 47.5 percent.[19]

The tendency of Sheridan County to support Democrats, with a few recent exceptions, might be explained by a number of factors. It could have been a kind of abiding faithfulness to the party that brought them relief in the form of New Deal programs. Added to this was the service of a number of Democratic senators from Montana like Thomas J. Walsh, Burton K. Wheeler, Mike Mansfield, John Melcher, and Max Baucus, all of whom were staunch advocates of farmers. A third factor, however, merits consideration: it is possible that the expectations and demands of many Sheridan County voters, particularly in the aftermath of the Red period, but even in later generations, were shaped by the radical era's rhetoric.

During its heyday, when the message of the farmers' movement appealed to so many in Sheridan County, the radicals played on and reinforced ideas associated with the traditional agrarian myth: that farming was an honorable enterprise and one that should be preserved and defended. By politicizing this ideology with calls for everything from state-owned grain elevators to a moratorium on debt collection, the radicals won converts and sowed seeds of expectation for government assistance and support. But when the radicals' message began to fail toward the end of the 1920s—and with the more strident Third Period Communist doctrine of the late 1920s and early 1930s—Roosevelt's New Deal, rather than the CPUSA, emerged to fulfill the expectations planted by the radicals.

In this sense, the radical rhetoric of northeastern Montana's farm movement did not fail. While it did not bring about a Communist revolution in America, it was influential, both during the 1920s and beyond, through the legacy it left among voters for decades thereafter. The radicals' story helped create politically active and empowered farmers, but it also contributed to a lasting sense of entitlement and a kind of calculus that could be applied by voters in electing future candidates. That is, the Communists gave farmers an idea of what leaders should do to protect them and their vital contributions to the nation's economy.

While the farmers' movement may have left northeastern Montanans with a new set of expectations for officeholders, it failed in its own mission. This failure cannot be fully understood without considering the impact of the narrative created by people like Charles Taylor and Erik Bert in the *Producers News,* as well as the manner in which individual decisions, doctrinal disputes, and directives from Moscow and New York City affected that narrative. The importance of rhetoric in creating any sort of movement, perhaps especially a revolutionary cause, cannot be overemphasized. The rhetoric, in short, helps move the movement.[20]

In its failure to maintain a viable and compelling narrative, the little Communist laboratory in northeastern Montana could have yielded important lessons for the CPUSA's national leadership had they chosen to take notice. Sheridan County was, in a sense, Communism's best chance for success in America, if only its lessons had been heeded. Carl R. Burgchardt, a communication scholar, has argued that the failure of the Communist Party to persuade is key to understanding its struggles. Focusing on the work of Communist pamphleteers, Burgchardt explains that these propagandists made "crucial rhetorical errors" that alienated the party's intended audience. For instance, they depicted a more brutal world than existed for most Americans, attacked political rivals too zealously, and stated their goals too bluntly. Burgchardt notes, however, that many of these choices were imposed upon the pamphleteers from above.[21]

Indeed, during the freewheeling days of the 1920s, when Charles Taylor and P. J. Wallace were at liberty to make the *Producers News* rhetorically appealing, they were able to persuade their readers. But just as Third Period edicts influenced the Communist pamphleteers, so had Erik Bert and other editors of the *Producers News* been constrained by the CPUSA and the Communist International, compelled to create a narrative that backfired in the former radical stronghold in northeastern Montana. As to the shifting positions and lines handed down by the CPUSA, historian Harvey Klehr notes that "the Communists could shift from the most belligerent hostility to the most abject wooing of former enemies, making up in intensity what they lacked in consistency." These "gyrations," Klehr contends, were damaging to the party's credibility and caused many members, who were unwilling to shift their tactics, friends, and enemies, to leave the party. Klehr also points out that, for American Communists, it was not enough to disagree with or refute a political opponent; they "coupled their idealistic devotion to the movement with hatred of their opponents, a hatred of such fervor that it sometimes bordered on the maniacal." In Sheridan County, as in the rest of the United States, the Communists came to be perceived as inconsistent and disloyal, employing far too harsh a rhetoric.[22]

Essentially, the narrative constructed by northeastern Montana's radicals became rhetorically insensitive to its audience, just as the American Communist message would later on a larger scale. In the 1930s, the writer and philosopher Kenneth Burke recognized this tendency among many propagandists. When he addressed the Communist-sponsored American Writers' Congress in New York City in 1935, he alerted them to the problem, encouraging the writers to consider carefully the manner in which they represented themselves and the American worker. A Communist propagandist, he proclaimed, should "encompass as many desirable features of our cultural heritage as possible." It was easy to "convince the convinced"; the challenge was to "plead with the unconvinced," which would require the Communists to use the "vocabulary . . . values [and] symbols" of ordinary people.[23] His speech met with disapproval by the Third Period zealots, who believed they had to proclaim their revolutionary message without restraint.

Although Burke was not specifically referring to the northeastern Montana Communists, he might as well have been since their manner of communicating had already done what Burke feared: it had alienated their intended audience. Sheridan County, Montana, had attracted the attention of New York City and Moscow, had merited visits by Communist luminaries, and had been one of the most class-conscious areas in the nation. Yet long before the struggles of the Communist Party USA during the Cold War and the collapse of Communism in Eastern Europe and the Soviet Union, the citizens of northeastern Montana had witnessed the demise of their own Communist regime. It followed a period that had tested friendships and families and strained the bonds of community. When all the rumors and defections ended, the people of Sheridan County began to reconstitute themselves as an ordinary farming community once again. And over time, northeastern Montana's identity as the Red Corner slowly faded.

NOTES

In referencing works in the notes, short citations have been used. Complete references can be found in the bibliography.

INTRODUCTION

1. *Producers News,* Mar. 4, 1932, 1; ibid., Mar. 11, 1932, 1.

2. Ibid., Nov. 27, 1931, 1; Dyson, *Red Harvest,* 32.

CHAPTER 1

1. *Plentywood Herald,* Apr. 22, 1910, reprinted in *Plentywood Portrait,* 18.

2. Schwantes, "Landscapes of Opportunity," 40, 38–39, 47, 51.

3. Montana Bureau of Agriculture, *Montana,* 7, 18.

4. Ibid., 1, 63.

5. Ibid., 65, 67.

6. Ibid., 285; Aasheim, *Sheridan's Daybreak,* 3.

7. Aasheim, *Sheridan's Daybreak,* 241.

8. Ibid., 237–38.

9. Ibid., 237–39. Many of the family biographies in the Dagmar section of *Sheridan's Daybreak* specifically mention the article in *Dannevirke* as the impetus for their relocation to Montana.

10. Gjerde and McCants, "Individual Life Chances," 385; Anderson, *Norwegian-Americans,* 23.

11. Stark and Christiano, "Support for the American Left," 69–70.

12. Everett, "Lutherans in Montana," 88; Aasheim, *Sheridan's Daybreak,* 239, 34.

13. Aasheim, *Sheridan's Daybreak,* 587, 34; Aasheim, *Sheridan's Daybreak II,* 24, 138, 393, 921.

14. Aasheim, *Sheridan's Daybreak,* 472, 570, 578.

CHAPTER 2

1. Segars, *One Hundred Years in Culbertson,* 59; Sandvig, "Stage on the High Line," 68.

2. Aasheim, *Sheridan's Daybreak,* 237; U.S. Department of Agriculture, Soil Conservation Service, *Soil Survey of Sheridan County,* 1.

3. Aasheim, *Sheridan's Daybreak,* 513.

4. Ibid., 921.

5. Montana Bureau of Agriculture, *Montana,* 109; Aasheim, *Sheridan's Daybreak,* 275, 530.

6. Aasheim, *Sheridan's Daybreak,* 267.

7. "Stacks o'Facts,"18; Montana Department of Agriculture, "Montana Agricultural Statistics," 2001 report, p. 7, http://www.nass.usda.gov/mt/bulletin/BulletinDist2001.pdf; U.S. Department of Agriculture, *Soil Survey of Sheridan County,* 57, 58. Incidentally, the thermometer capacity in the case of the lowest recorded temperature was –70 degrees; the actual temperature at Rogers Pass may have been lower. The temperature in Medicine Lake was provided by Brian Burleson, National Weather Service, in a letter to Helen Stoner, Feb. 14, 2003.

8. Aasheim, *Sheridan's Daybreak,* 52, 901.

9. Ibid., 4.

10. According to the U.S. Geological Survey, Nevada, the most arid state, averages 9.5 inches per year. http://www.nationalatlas.gov/printable/images/pdf/precip/pageprecip_nv3.pdf (accessed July 1, 2009).

11. Aasheim, *Sheridan's Daybreak,* 49.

12. Ibid., 11; Montana Department of Agriculture, *Montana Agricultural Statistics,* 4.

13. Montana Bureau of Agriculture, *Montana,* 107.

14. Aasheim, *Sheridan's Daybreak,* 45; Hegne, *Border Outlaws,* 16.

15. Aasheim, *Sheridan's Daybreak,* 661, 47, 61.

16. *Plentywood Portrait,* 31.

17. Ibid., 30; Stoner interview.

18. *Plentywood Portrait,* 31–32; Aasheim, *Sheridan's Daybreak,* 9, 35.

19. Montana Bureau of Agriculture, *Montana,* 285; U.S. census figures reprinted in Ellis L. Waldron, *Montana Politics,* 129, 174. It should be noted that the 1920 census included what is today Daniels County as part of Sheridan County, even though they were officially split during that year.

CHAPTER 3

1. Stone, ed., *Letters from an American Farmer,* 12, 67, 71. Historian Henry Nash Smith notes that this tendency was influenced by classical writers such as Hesiod and Virgil who had praised husbandry. Smith, *Virgin Land,* 145.

2. Thomas Jefferson, "Letter to James Madison," 682; Jefferson, "Notes on the State of Virginia," 290, 301. Franklin's quote comes from Smith, *Virgin Land,* 125.

3. Smith, *Virgin Land,* 138; Hofstadter, *Age of Reform,* 24.

4. Miller, "Farmers and Third-Party Politics," 237.

5. National Grange, "Birth of an American Treasure," National Grange, http:www.nationalgrange.org/about/history.html.

6. Buell, *Grange Master,* 75, 84, 86.

7. Ibid., 90 (emphasis in original). Buell, along with Ida Chittenden, mobilized the Grange to win woman's suffrage in Michigan, a goal they achieved in 1918. http://www.mcgi.state.mi.us/hso/sites/38395.htm (accessed June 24, 2009).

8. Buell, *Grange Master,* 17, 111; Howard, *People, Pride and Progress,* 87; Woods, *Knights of the Plow,* 172–73.

9. Woods, *Knights of the Plow,* 147–48, 152–53, 174, 177.

10. Ibid., 154.

11. Barnes, *Farmers in Rebellion,* 39.

12. Carruthers and Babb, "Color of Money," 1564; Miller, "Farmers and Third-Party Politics," http://history.missouristate.edu/WRMiller/Populism/texts/farmers_and_third_party_politics.htm. The online version of this essay includes information on the Greenbackers that is not included in the print version.

13. Crawford, "Farmer Assesses His Role," 118. The quoted passages come from Carruthers and Babb, "Color of Money," 1574; and Miller, "Farmers and Third-Party Politics."

14. Crawford, "Farmer Assesses His Role," 123.

15. McMath, *Populist Vanguard,* 5, 17. Emery is quoted in James Klumpp's unpublished lecture notes.

16. Klumpp lecture notes.

17. McMath, *Populist Vanguard,* 75.

18. Quoted in Miller, "Farmers and Third-Party Politics."

19. Goodwyn, *Democratic Promise,* xi; Ecroyd, "Populist Spellbinders," 146, 148.

20. Hofstadter, *Age of Reform,* 58, 62, 65, 73,75.

21. Calvert, *Gibraltar,* 11; Clinch, *Urban Populism,* 16, 170.

22. Dyson, *Red Harvest,* 35–36, 71; Charles Taylor interview by Dyson, 12, 13.

CHAPTER 4

1. Carlson, *Roughneck,* 50–51, 53.

2. Dubofsky, *We Shall Be All,* 58; Dubofsky, *"Big Bill" Haywood,* 20–21.

3. Dubofsky, *"Big Bill" Haywood,* 4; Kornbluh, *Rebel Voices,* 2; Carlson, *Roughneck,* 145.

4. Dubofsky, *"Big Bill" Haywood,* 24, 5, 142; Dubofsky, *We Shall Be All,* 69, 80; Wells, "Western Federation of Miners," 30. Shortly after joining the IWW, the Western Federation's leadership began to edge back from militancy and to seek closer association with the AFL, and in 1908, the WFM dismissed Haywood from office. Dubofsky, *"Big Bill" Haywood,* 50.

5. Carlson, *Roughneck,* 79; Kornbluh, *Rebel Voices,* 12.

6. McIntyre, "Rituals of Disorder," 7; Foner, *Fellow Workers and Friends,* 12–13; Carter, "Industrial Workers of the World," 368; Brazier, "Story of the IWW's 'Little Red Song Book,'" 91–92.

7. Dubofsky, *We Shall Be All,* 177–79.

8. Winters, *Soul of the Wobblies,* 134.

9. Ibid., 62–63.

10. Kraditor, *Radical Persuasion,* 100, 137.

11. Salerno, *Red November,* 151.

12. Aasheim, *Sheridan's Daybreak,* 11.

13. *Antelope Independent,* July 19, 1918: 1; Charles Taylor interview by Dyson, 103.

14. Waldron, *Montana Politics,* 80. Until 1928, Montanans voted for presidential electors rather than for candidates.

15. Waldron, *Montana Politics,* 92, 106, 120, 136; "Communist Activities,"

FBI Butte File, June 16, 1941, 81; Charles Taylor interview by Dyson, 32. The Socialists' peak years in Montana were between 1912 and 1914. Malone, Roeder, and Lang, *Montana,* 267.

16. Waldron, *Montana Politics,* 156, 158, 162.

CHAPTER 5

1. Morlan, *Political Prairie Fire,* 24, 26.

2. Calvert, *Gibraltar,* 11–12.

3. Morlan, *Political Prairie Fire,* 32, 27, 28. Dues were eventually increased, first to six, then to nine, and finally, after 1916, to sixteen dollars.

4. Ibid., 30.

5. Limerick, "Making the Most of Words," 178–79.

6. Morlan, *Political Prairie Fire,* 37, 202, 349. Morlan has estimated that no other single item contributed to the NPL's success more than did newspapers.

7. Swibold, *Copper Chorus,* 273; Calvert, *Gibralter,* 125; Vivian, "The Last Roundup," 42, 48; Morlan, *Political Prairie Fire,* 277.

8. Carl Taylor interview; Charles Taylor interview by Dyson, 33. The population estimates are based on the 1920 census summarized in Waldron, *Montana Politics,* 174.

9. Aasheim, *Sheridan's Daybreak,* 587.

10. Charles Taylor interview by Dyson, 33, 36–37.

11. *Producers News,* Aug. 18, 1922, 1; Charles Taylor interview by Dyson, 12–13.

12. Charles Taylor interview by Dyson, 9–12, 15.

13. Ibid., 10–12, 17.

14. Ibid., 19–20, 17–18; *Producers News,* Aug. 18, 1922, 1.

15. Charles Taylor interview by Dyson, 19, 21; "Francis M. Taylor," Minnesota Territorial and State Censuses, www.ancestry.com; Carl Taylor interview; *Producers News,* Aug. 18, 1922, 1. Taylor told Dyson that he had graduated from the Lincoln Jefferson Law College, and this may be the correspondence course he referred to in the *Producers News* and in his correspondence with historian Charles Vindex. Vindex, "Radical Rule in Montana," 6.

16. Charles Taylor interview by Dyson, 24, 26, 28, 29; *Minnesota Legislative Manual 1911,* 503; *Producers News,* Aug. 18, 1922, 1.

17. Charles Taylor interview by Dyson, 28, 30–31.

18. Ibid., 32; "Communist Activities in State of Montana," FBI Butte File 100-721-50.

19. *Producers News,* Nov. 2, 1932, 4; Aasheim, *Sheridan's Daybreak,* 925; "Land Patent Details," Bureau of Land Management, Bureau of Land Management, http://www.glorecords.blm.gov/PatentSearch/; Shelley Bryan, e-mail to author, July 8, 2009.

20. Aasheim, *Sheridan's Daybreak,* 921; Lynne Nyquist, e-mail to author, July 9, 2009.

21. "Communist Activities in State of Montana," FBI Butte File 100-721-50, 81; "News Notes," *Sporting Life,* Apr. 14, 1906, 11; "Beloit Scores on Purple Team," *Chicago Daily Tribune,* Oct. 15, 1905, A1; Shearer, *Moc's Football,* 15;

Soden, "One Hundred Years Later," 4; *Bison Men's Basketball,* 60; Aasheim, *Sheridan's Daybreak,* 481.

22. Charles Taylor interview by Dyson, 32, 41, 42.

23. *Producers News,* Oct. 8, 1918, 3; Aasheim, *Sheridan's Daybreak,* 481; Charles Taylor interview by Dyson, 48; *Producers News,* June 5, 1925, 1. Billy Rueber was playing near an unattended horse-drawn wagon loaded with lumber. When the horses walked forward, he was crushed by a wagon wheel.

24. Aasheim, *Sheridan's Daybreak,* 559–60. Clair Stoner was the author's great-great uncle.

25. *Producers News,* Nov. 3, 1922, 2; Ransdell interview; Ransdell to author, Nov. 10, 2002.

26. Aasheim, *Sheridan's Daybreak,* 605; "Communist Activities in State of Montana," 86; Welter interview.

27. Kelly to Pratt, Aug. 8, 1995. Although he had only a fourth-grade education, Rodney Salisbury studied *Das Kapital* avidly.

28. Ibid.

29. Ibid.; Charles Taylor interview by Dyson, 97.

30. *Producers News,* Aug. 25, 1922, 4; Kelly to Pratt, Aug. 8, 1995; *Plentywood Herald,* Nov. 5, 1931, 1; *Medicine Lake Wave,* Dec. 3, 1926, 1.

31. Charles Taylor claimed to be "the boss" of the transition to the Communist party in 1920. Charles Taylor interview by Dyson, 48.

CHAPTER 6

1. *Producers News,* June 14, 1918, 4; ibid., June 28, 1918, 4.

2. In the Dakotas and Minnesota, the NPL sponsored day-long picnics that featured live music, games, and vendors' booths, with the added attraction of political speeches. The events drew thousands of people from as far as fifty miles away and were often preceded by a parade of vehicles, which Robert Morlan refers to as "snowballing affairs, adding a car at each farm." One parade was reportedly twelve miles long, and a 1918 picnic in Wegdahl, Minnesota, drew a crowd of fourteen thousand. Morlan, *Political Prairie Fire,* 197.

3. *Producers News,* July 22, 1921, 1; ibid., June 17, 1921, 1. *Time* went on to note that among Burdick's supporters was "the Communist Daily Worker." North Dakotans would later elect Burdick to Congress where he would serve four terms. He was the father of U.S. senator Quentin Burdick. "Eighteenth Year," *Time,* June 19, 1944, 20.

4. *Producers News,* June 17, 1921, 1. The featured speaker at the 1919 NPL picnic was to be Arthur Townley, who, it seems, also failed to appear since there was no mention of him in the *Producers News* following the picnic.

5. Aasheim, *Sheridan's Daybreak,* 10.

6. Morlan, *Political Prairie Fire,* 350; *Producers News,* Apr. 26, 1918, 3; Charles Taylor interview by Dyson, 39. It is not known if, indeed, there were ever as many as a thousand stockholders in the People's Publishing Company. In 1929, the competing *Plentywood Herald* reveled in reporting that there were only 377 stockholders and that only 192 of those were Sheridan County residents. *Plentywood Herald,* Feb. 7, 1929, 2.

7. *Producers News,* May 3, 1918, 2; ibid., May 10, 1918, 1.

8. Ibid., May 3, 1918, 2; ibid., Dec. 6, 1918; Charles Taylor interview by Dyson, 39, 94. See, for example, *Producers News,* Apr. 19, 1918, 1.

9. *Producers News,* May 10, 1918, 1.

10. Ibid., 4; Charles Taylor interview by Dyson, 34.

11. *Producers News,* Apr. 19, 1918, 1; ibid., Aug. 30, 1918, 4.

12. Ibid., Aug. 18, 1922, 2.

13. *Producers News,* Nov. 17, 1923, 3; ibid., Feb. 10, 1922, 2; ibid., Oct. 25, 1918, 4; ibid., Sept. 29, 1922, 1. Historian Charles Rankin has noted that "newly founded western newspapers had more room for humor, whether in the play of the editor's personality or in the inclusion of hoaxes and spoofs, a trait that faded with the passage of time." Quoted in Limerick, "Making the Most of Words," 179.

14. *Producers News,* Mar. 5, 1926, 1; Aasheim, *Sheridan's Daybreak,* 10.

15. *Producers News,* May 10, 1918, 3.

16. See, for example, *Producers News,* Nov. 15, 1918, 4, for Taylor's commentary on Dolin; ibid., Oct. 20, 1922, 6, for Ibsen; and ibid., Nov. 23, 1923, 1, for Storkan.

17. Timmerman interview; Peterson interview; Stoner to author, March 1993; Vindex, "Radical Rule," 16, 6.

18. *Producers News,* Dec. 6, 1918, 1; ibid., Dec. 13, 1918, 1.

19. Ibid., Nov. 15, 1918, 4.

20. Ibid., July 22, 1921, 1; ibid., July 8, 1921, 1.

21. Ibid., Dec. 13, 1918, 1.

22. McMath refers to this ideology as "producerism" in *American Populism,* 51. See also Ross, *Workers on the Edge,* 57.

23. Morlan, *Political Prairie Fire,* 28; *Producers News,* Apr. 18, 1918, 1; ibid., May 3, 1918, 2.

24. *Producers News,* Sept. 13, 1918, 1; ibid., Oct.18, 1918, 4.

25. Ibid., May 17, 1918, 1.

26. Taylor claimed that at one time, the circulation of the paper was thirty-five hundred in Sheridan County, although he did not indicate exactly when that figure was reached. Charles Taylor interview by Dyson, 100; Dyson, *Red Harvest,* 32. At one point, the *Producers News* was in competition with nineteen other papers in Sheridan County.

27. *Producers News,* Nov. 8, 1918, 1. Rankin also received the plurality of votes in Richland County, which borders Sheridan County on the south, and Valley County, on the west.

28. Charles Taylor interview by Dyson, 48, 129, 45, 42; Dyson, *Red Harvest,* 8. He reportedly admitted to an FBI agent that he joined the Communist Party in 1922. "Charles Taylor," May 28, 1953, 3, FBI Minneapolis File 100-55987-38, Department of Justice, Record Information/Dissemination Section, Washington, D.C. (hereafter RIDS). However, Dyson's book indicates that Taylor joined the party in 1920. Dyson, *Red Harvest,* 11.

29. Dyson, *Red Harvest,* 8; Vivian, "The Last Roundup," 39; *Producers News,* Feb. 6, 1920, 4.

30. Waldron, *Montana Politics,* 176.

31. Aasheim, *Sheridan's Daybreak,* 11. Taylor, running on the NPL ticket as a Republican, defeated his Democratic opponent by only 124 votes, or 6 percent of the total. Others, such as Charles Lundeen, the NPL candidate for county commissioner, outpaced their opponents by up to 30 percent. *Producers News,* Nov. 10, 1922, 4.

32. *Producers News,* Nov. 17, 1922, 1.

33. Ibid., June 22, 1923, 1; ibid., July 6, 1923, 1; Dyson, *Red Harvest,* 11–12.

34. *Producers News,* Oct. 5, 1923, 1; ibid., Oct. 26, 1923, 1.

CHAPTER 7

1. Elmer Davis, "Foster's Red Group Easily Dominates St. Paul Convention," *New York Times,* June 18, 1924, A1, A3.

2. Malone, Roeder, and Lang, *Montana,* 278; Morlan, *Political Prairie Fire,* 346.

3. Dyson, *Red Harvest,* 1–6.

4. Klehr and Haynes, *American Communist Movement,* 39–40, 41; Foster quoted in Arnesen, Green, and Laurie, eds., *Labor Histories,* 322.

5. "Report of the Worker's Party of America to the Executive Committee of the Communist International," Oct. 20, 1923, delo 199, opis 1, fond 515, Russian State Archive of Socio-Political History (hereafter RGASPI), Library of Congress, Washington, D.C. (hereafter all documents cited by delo number can be found in opis 1, fond 515 of this collection); "Report on the Federated Farmer Labor Party and Our Party Situation," Oct. 3, 1923, delo 200, ibid. As a consequence of the "Red scare" and later surveillance by the FBI, the Communist Party sent its documents to Moscow for safekeeping from the early 1920s until World War II. These documents, along with materials from the Comintern, were unavailable to American researchers until 1992, when the archive opened its doors to non-Russian researchers. In 1999, the Library of Congress purchased a microfilm copy of the CPUSA documents held in the RGASPI.

6. Charles Taylor interview by Dyson, 48. Dyson, *Red Harvest,* 15. On William Dunne, see Draper, *The Roots of American Communism,* 317.

7. "Farmer-Labor Party," Nov. 15, 1923, 2, FBI Butte File 61-1624-92, RIDS; Correspondence from J. Edgar Hoover, Nov. 30, 1927, Rodney Salisbury Main File, Department of Justice File 62-15962-2, RIDS; *Daniels County Leader,* Dec. 21, 1967, 4. Bowler is listed in a 1927 letter from J. Edgar Hoover to a Butte, Montana, field agent as one of three individuals "in possession of information that would be of value to the Government." Bowler was interviewed in December and handed over a number of letters sent by Charles Taylor to an undisclosed third party.

8. Dyson, *Red Harvest,* 15; "Call for National Farmer-Labor Convention," Mar. 13, 1924, delo 248 and delo 373, RGASPI; Charles Taylor interview, 60, 57, 59.

9. For a complete discussion of the convention, see Dyson, *Red Harvest,* 15–26.

10. Dyson, *Red Harvest,* 24; Klehr and Haynes, *American Communist Movement,* 41–42.

11. Charles Taylor interview by Dyson, 73.

12. Ibid., 74; "Farmer-Labor Party of the United States," June 24, 1924, 7, FBI Los Angeles File 61-1624-102, RIDS.

13. "Farmer-Labor Convention," June 20, 1924, FBI Minneapolis File 61-1624-1007, 10, RIDS. It is interesting to note that *New York Times* reporter Elmer Davis confirmed most of the FBI agent's statements in his article on the convention but did not mention Taylor's denial of having previously met Foster. Elmer Davis, "Farmer-Laborites Favor La Follette, But Won't Have Him," *New York Times,* June 19, 1924, A3.

14. Charles Taylor interview by Dyson, 57.

15. Charles Taylor interview by Dyson, 80–81; Dyson, *Red Harvest,* 24, 25. Waldron, *Montana Politics,* 196. Coolidge's plurality was 13,033 votes; had La Follette's vote not been split, at most he could have gained about 5,000 votes.

16. Klehr and Haynes, *American Communist Movement,* 42; Montana Department of Agriculture, *Montana Agricultural Statistics,* 4; *Producers News,* Mar. 31, 1922. Prices in Montana had been low for the previous two years as well. In Montana, the average prices for 1921–23 were ninety-eight, eighty-nine, and ninety-one cents, respectively. Montana Department of Agriculture, *Montana Agricultural Statistics,* 4; Shideler, *Farm Crisis,* 255; Waldron, *Montana Politics,* 174, 284. The 1920 census included in Sheridan County the population of what would become Daniels County. After 1930, the county's population steadily declined.

17. *Producers News,* Oct. 5, 1923, 6.

18. Ibid., Nov. 2, 1923, 4. The Placer was a hotel in Helena. The sixth floor of the Hennessy Building housed the offices of the Anaconda Copper Company. Emmons, *The Butte Irish,* 324.

19. *Producers News,* June 20, 1924, 4; ibid., June 6, 1924, 4.

20. See, for example, ibid., Apr. 25, 1924, 4; ibid., Sept. 5, 1924, 4; ibid., June 6, 1924, 4; ibid., Apr. 11, 1924, 1.

21. Ibid., June 23, 1924, 1.

22. Ibid., June 20, 1924, 4.

CHAPTER 8

1. *Plentywood Portrait,* 30.
2. Ibid.
3. *Producers News,* June 20, 1924, 1; ibid., Sept. 19, 1924, 1.
4. Ibid., Sept. 19, 1924, 4; ibid., Oct. 3, 1924, 1.
5. *Producers News,* Apr. 11, 1924, 4.
6. Ibid., Apr. 11, 1924, 4; ibid., May 16, 1924, 4.
7. Ibid., Feb. 3, 1922, 1.
8. Ibid., Mar. 30, 1923, 4; ibid., Apr. 20, 1923, 4.
9. Ibid., Nov. 17, 1923; ibid., Nov. 30, 1923.
10. *Sheridan County Farmer,* Feb. 8, 1924, 1; *Producers News,* Mar. 21, 1924, 1.
11. *Producers News,* Feb. 29, 1924, 1; ibid., Feb. 22, 1924, 4.
12. *Sheridan County Farmer,* May 2, 1924, 1; Dyson, *Red Harvest,* 20.
13. *Producers News,* May 16, 1924, 1.

14. *Sheridan County Farmer,* Sept. 12, 1924, 1.

15. *Producers News,* Sept. 19, 1924, 1.

16. Aasheim, *Sheridan's Daybreak,* 445.

CHAPTER 9

1. Klehr and Haynes, *American Communist Movement,* 37; *Producers News,* Feb. 1, 1924, 6. The Teapot Dome scandal involved bribery charges attached to members of Warren G. Harding's administration.

2. Klehr and Haynes, *American Communist Movement,* 42; *Producers News,* Feb. 22, 1924, 1; ibid., Apr. 4, 1924, 1; ibid., Jan. 23, 1925, 1.

3. *Producers News,* Nov. 7, 1924, 1; ibid., Nov. 14, 1924, 1, 4; Waldron, *Montana Politics,* 200, 202.

4. *Producers News,* Nov. 14, 1924, 1; ibid., Dec. 12, 1924, 4; ibid., Dec. 5, 1924, 4.

5. Dyson, *Red Harvest,* 11, 35–36; Charles Taylor interview by Dyson, 33, 93.

6. *Producers News,* Jan. 22, 1926, 2.

7. Dyson, *Red Harvest,* 30; Charles Taylor interview by Dyson, 94; Taylor to Knutson, Feb. 10, 1926, delo 687, RGASPI; Knutson to Keikkinen, Nov. 27, 1926, RGASPI.

8. *Producers News,* May 8, 1925, 4; Flowers to Puro, March 8, 1933, delo 3376, RGASPI; *Producers News,* July 10, 1925, 1. By September 4, Taylor was back to Sheridan County, reportedly for three or four weeks. The *Producers News* story on his visit quoted his claim that his company was growing rapidly and that it would "become one of the fastest successes in the history of this kind of business in America." *Producers News,* Sept. 4, 1925, 1. According to Lowell Dyson, Radium Remedies went belly-up after the death of one of its promoters caused the company to lose its claim on the radium source. Dyson, *Red Harvest,* 209.

9. Dyson, *Red Harvest,* 37; *Producers News,* Oct. 15, 1926, 2; ibid., Oct. 29, 1926, 8. Charles Taylor claimed that Wallace was not a Communist Party member, but Lowell Dyson concluded that he may have been. Dyson, *Red Harvest,* 38–39.

10. Charles Taylor interview by Dyson, 96–97.

11. *Producers News,* Oct. 15, 1926, 2; ibid., Sept. 24, 1926, 2.

12. Waldron, *Montana Politics,* 202; Aasheim, *Sheridan's Daybreak,* 11.

CHAPTER 10

1. The account of the robbery is taken from Engrebret Thorstenson's testimony that was reprinted in the *Plentywood Herald,* Oct. 25, 1928, 11; ibid., Dec. 3, 1926, 1; and Aasheim, *Sheridan's Daybreak,* 73. Thorstenson's name is often misspelled in both the *Plentywood Herald* and the *Producers News.* The spelling given here is as found in his entry in the history of the county, *Sheridan's Daybreak.*

2. *Producers News,* Dec. 3, 1926, 1; *Medicine Lake Wave,* Dec. 3, 1926, 1. It was an interesting coincidence that, in the six weeks preceding the robbery, the *Producers News* featured four stories on robberies in Montana and neighboring

states. According to the paper, it was an "epidemic of bank wrecking." Three more stories on robberies in other cities appeared in the weeks following the heist. During the same period, the other major Sheridan County newspaper, the *Plentywood Herald,* ran only one story on robberies that occurred outside Plentywood. See *Producers News,* Oct. 15, Nov. 12, 19, 26, Dec. 10, 17, 1926, Jan. 7, 1927; *Plentywood Herald,* Nov. 26, 1926, 1.

3. *Daniels County Leader,* Dec. 2, 1926, 1, 2.

4. Aasheim, *Sheridan's Daybreak,* 11; *Producers News,* Dec. 10, 1926, 2. For rumors around town, see, for example, Marron interview.

5. *Daniels County Leader,* Dec. 21, 1967, 1.

6. Ibid., 4.

7. Ibid., 4; ibid., June 28, 1923, 4.

8. Ibid., Feb. 21, 1924, 1; ibid., Dec. 21, 1967, 4; *Producers News,* Apr. 25, 1924, 4.

9. Waldron, *Montana Politics,* 176.

10. *Producers News,* Feb. 22, 1924, 1; ibid., Mar. 7, 1924, 4; ibid., Mar. 21, 1924, 1.

11. *Sheridan County Farmer,* Feb. 8, 1924, 1; *Daniels County Leader,* Mar. 13, 1924, 1.

12. *Daniels County Leader,* Mar. 13, 1924, 3.

13. Ibid., May 15, 1924, 4.

14. Ibid., Oct. 23, 1924, 1.

15. Ibid., Nov. 6, 1924, 6, 7.

16. Waldron, *Montana Politics,* 196. It should be noted that, even with this modest showing, Daniels County was fourth among Montana's then fifty-five counties in terms of F-LP votes.

17. *Producers News,* June 20, 1924, 4; *Daniels County Leader,* May 6, 1926, 1.

18. *Daniels County Leader,* July 15, 1926, 1.

19. Ibid., July 29, 1926, 1.

20. Ibid., Nov. 4, 1926, 2.

21. Aasheim, *Sheridan's Daybreak,* 669–70.

22. *Plentywood Herald,* June 10, 1921, 1.

23. Ibid., May 28, 1926, 1.

24. Ibid., Oct. 22, 1926, 3.

25. Ibid., Oct. 29, 1926, 6, 7.

26. *Producers News,* May 27, 1927, 4.

27. *Plentywood Herald,* Nov. 10, 1971, 1.

28. Aasheim, *Sheridan's Daybreak,* 589, 11; U.S. Department of Commerce, U.S. Bureau of the Census, *U.S. Census of Agriculture, 1930,* 121; Montana Department of Agriculture, *Montana Agricultural Statistics,* 4–5.

29. *Producers News,* May 25, 1928, 8.

30. *Plentywood Herald,* Oct. 22, 1926, 3.

31. Ibid., Jan. 7, 1927, 1; *Producers News,* Jan. 7, 1927, 8.

32. *Producers News,* May 11, 1928, 1.

33. *Plentywood Herald,* June 21, 1928, 4.

34. Ibid., June 28, 1928, 4.

35. Ibid., July 12, 1928, 4.

36. *Producers News,* May 25, 1928, 1, 8; *Plentywood Herald,* Aug. 16, 1928, 1; ibid., Aug. 23, 1928, 4.

37. *Producers News,* Aug. 31, 1928, 2; Oct. 12, 1928, 2; Sept. 7, 1928, 2.

38. *Plentywood Herald,* Oct. 11, 1928, 1.

39. Ibid., Sept. 20, 1928, 3.

40. Charles Taylor interview by Dyson, 48, 54–55.

41. *Plentywood Herald,* Oct. 25, 1928; Nov. 1, 1928, 4.

42. Ibid., Oct. 25, 1928, 1.

43. *Producers News,* Sept. 28, 1928, 2; Oct. 26, 1928, 1.

44. *Plentywood Herald,* Sept. 20, 1928, 3.

45. Ibid., Oct. 18, 1928, 4.

46. *Producers News,* Nov. 2, 1928, 1.

47. The unopposed candidate was the incumbent county clerk and recorder, Niels Madsen. Ibid., Nov. 23, 1928, 7.

CHAPTER 11

1. Ruthenberg to Knutson, Feb. 10, 1926, delo 686, RGASPI; Lovestone to Charles Taylor, Nov. 33, 1927, delo 1060, RGASPI; Lovestone to Taylor, Jan. 5, 1928, delo 1344, RGASPI; Knutson to Lovestone, Sept. 21, 1927, delo 1069, RGASPI.

2. *Producers News,* June 1, 1928, 2; ibid., Feb. 3, 1928, 1, 8; Charles Taylor interview by Dyson, 89.

3. *Producers News,* quoted from the *Butte Miner,* Nov. 28. 1927, 1; *Producers News,* Jan. 6, 1928, 1; *Daniels County Leader,* Feb. 9, 1928, 2; *Producers News,* Dec. 14, 21, 1928, 1.

4. *Producers News,* Dec. 27, 1929, 5; Charles Taylor interview by Dyson, 124; *Producers News,* May 23, 1930, 2.

5. *Plentywood Herald,* June 5, 1930, 1; *Daily Worker,* Oct. 15, 1930, 1.

6. Dyson, *Red Harvest,* 46–47; Montana Department of Agriculture, *Montana Agricultural Statistics,* 5; Aasheim, *Sheridan's Daybreak,* 11. While the average yields were falling, so too were the prices of wheat. The average price per bushel in 1929 was ninety-eight cents; in 1930, it plunged to fifty-seven cents.

7. *Plentywood Herald,* Aug. 6, 1931, 3; ibid., Aug. 27, 1931, 1; ibid., Sept. 10, 1931, 2; *Daniels County Leader,* Sept. 3, 1931, 3.

8. *Producers News,* Aug. 7, 1931, 1; ibid., July 31, 1931, 1; ibid., Oct. 16, 1931, 1.

9. Bloor to Weinstone, Jan. 30, 1932, delo 3041, RGASPI.

10. Unsigned letter to District 9 Secretariat, Dec. 22, 1932, delo 3041, RGASPI.

CHAPTER 12

1. Klehr and Haynes, *American Communist Movement,* 45–46.

2. *The Program of the Communist International,* 87.

3. *Theses and Resolutions for the Seventh National Convention of the Communist Party of the USA,* 81.

4. Zahavi, "'Who's Going to Dance?" 285n62; "Communist Activities in the State of Montana," p. 83, FBI Butte File 100-721-50, RIDS.

5. Bert to Agrarian Department, Jan. 24, 1932, delo 3041, RGASPI; Carl Taylor interview; Bert to Harju, n.d., delo 3041, RGASPI; Bert to Puro, n.d., ibid.; Bert to Schneiderman, various dates, ibid.

6. Harju to Puro, n.d., delo 3041, RGASPI.

7. *Producers News,* Nov. 20, 1931, 1; ibid., Nov. 27, 1931, 1.

8. Ibid., Dec. 11, 1931, 3.

9. Ibid., 3; Dec. 18, 1931, 3; *Plentywood Herald,* Dec. 10, 1931, 1; ibid., Dec. 17, 1931, 1. Gerald Zahavi fittingly describes the trial as a "clash of cultures." Zahavi, "Who's Going to Dance?" 269.

10. Zahavi, "Who's Going to Dance?" 272; *Producers News,* Feb. 19, 1932, 4; ibid., Jan. 1, 1932, 4.

11. Klehr, *Heyday of American Communism,* 305, 306.

12. *Producers News,* July 22, 1932, 4; Charles Taylor interview by Dyson, 33, 147.

13. *Producers News,* Apr. 15, 1932, 1. The Young Pioneer's pledge was as follows: "Stand ready for the cause of the working class. Are you ready? Always ready! I pledge allegiance to the workers' Red Flag and to the cause for which it stands. One aim thruout [*sic*] our lives—Freedom for the working class." Quoted in *Producers News,* Mar. 11, 1932, 1.

14. Kavon interview. Charles Taylor, who had been dubbed "Red Flag" by local residents, symbolized the Communist movement in Sheridan County, hence, the epithet "Taylor."

15. Lane, letter to editor, *Sheridan County News,* Apr. 17, 1996, 2. Lane's letter was written in response to the visit of a would-be filmmaker from western Montana who hoped to make a motion picture based on Sheridan County's Communist period. He was quoted in the newspaper as saying that what he was "trying to do is make you proud of your history and also tell a good story." *Sheridan County News,* Apr. 3, 1996; Bjork interview. Violet Chandler also recalls the song, "Let's all run to the Communist way / Wave the Scarlet banner triumphantly / For Communism and for liberty." Fay and Chandler interview.

16. *Producers News,* Oct. 25, 1918, 4.

17. Ibid., Oct. 25, 1918, 4; ibid., Dec. 20, 1918, 1; ibid., May 2, 1924, 4. Ware is described in Dyson, *Red Harvest,* 3.

18. *Producers News,* Oct. 20, 1922, 6; ibid., Jan. 11, 1924, 4; ibid., Apr. 14, 1922, 2.

19. *Plentywood Herald,* Dec. 12, 1929, 2; ibid., Feb. 27, 1930, 2; ibid., Mar. 27, 1930, 1; ibid., Dec. 4, 1930, 2; ibid., Feb. 11, 1932, 2; ibid., Mar. 10, 1932, 2.

20. *Producers News,* Aug. 7, 1931, 2.

21. Ibid., Nov. 2, 1932, 1.

22. Ibid., Mar. 11, 1932, 1.

23. *Plentywood Herald,* Nov. 3, 1932, 1; *Producers News,* Apr. 15, 1932, 1.

24. *Producers News,* May 27, 1932, 2; *Plentywood Portrait,* 35.

25. *Producers News,* Mar. 21, 1919, 1; ibid., Jan. 15, 1926, 2.

26. Ibid., Feb. 19, 1932, 4; ibid., Sept. 2, 1932, 1; ibid., Sept. 19, 1932, 1, 8.

27. *Plentywood Herald,* Dec. 12, 1929, 2; ibid., Feb. 13, 1930, 2.

28. *Producers News,* Nov. 2, 1932, 3; ibid., July 22, 1932, 1.

29. Ibid., Nov. 27, 1931, 4; ibid., Jan. 29, 1932, 4; ibid., Oct. 28, 1932, 4.

30. See, for example, *Plentywood Herald,* Feb. 11, 1932, 2; ibid., Mar. 10, 1932, 2; ibid., Nov. 3, 1932, 1.

31. Haynes, *Red Scare or Red Menace?,* 4. See also Sally Taylor, *Stalin's Apologist.*

32. *Producers News,* Aug. 30, 1918, 4. See also ibid., Sep. 27, 1934, 3; and Dec. 18, 1931, 5.

33. Ibid., Nov. 2, 1932, 4; ibid., Mar. 9, 1934, 4; ibid., Nov. 27, 1931, 1.

34. Erik Bert to Secretariat, n.d., delo 3041, RGASPI.

35. *Producers News,* July 11, 1930, 2; ibid., Dec. 18, 1931, 5.

36. Ibid., May 13, 1932, 1; ibid., Dec. 11, 1931, 1; ibid., Jan. 1, 1932, 2; ibid., Aug. 19, 1932, 1; ibid., Feb. 26, 1932, 1.

37. Ibid., Apr. 29, 1932, 1.

38. Dyson, *Red Harvest,* 74–75; *Producers News,* Aug. 12, 1932, 1, 4; *The Communist Position on the Farmers' Movement,* 29, 32.

39. *Producers News,* Sept. 9, 1932, 1; *Daily Worker,* June 4, 1931, 1.

40. *Producers News,* Sept. 2, 1932, 1; Bert to Agrarian Department, Jan. 24, 1932, delo 3041, RGASPI.

41. The CPUSA advertised the *News* on the back cover of *The Communist Position on the Farmers' Movement.*

42. It seems clear that Taylor, not the farmers themselves, was very much in control of the *Producers News.* Nor, according to a 1965 interview, was he given orders from CPUSA headquarters. "Nobody ever tried to direct the policy of the paper over my head," he said. Charles Taylor interview by Dyson, 95, 99, 100.

CHAPTER 13

1. *Plentywood Herald,* Feb. 13, 1930, 2. Although the *Herald* did not specify how Taylor had been "disowned," Charles Taylor's second family was aware that his first son, Francis, had changed his name from Taylor to his mother's maiden name, Smith. This assertion is supported by census records. In the 1910 census, Francis and his mother, Mary, reported their surname as Taylor; by 1920, the census listed them as Smith. Carl Taylor interview; "Mary R. Smith," *1920 U.S. Federal Census,* http://www.ancestry.com.

2. *Plentywood Herald,* Feb. 13, 1930, 2.

3. Ibid., Sept. 25, 1930, 1; ibid., Jan. 29, 1931, 2; *Producers News,* June 5, 1931, 1, quoted in ibid., June 12, 1931, 2.

4. *Plentywood Portrait,* 32; Aasheim, "Chicken Ranch"; *Plentywood Herald,* Jan. 23, 1930, 1. A schoolmate of Delores Pickett's recalls that Pickett and two of her classmates were known to frequent the Chicken Ranch. Magnus Aasheim also claimed that high school girls employed at the Chicken Ranch provided sexual favors for two dollars. Waller interview; Aasheim, "Chicken Ranch."

5. *Plentywood Herald,* Jan. 30, 1930, 2; *Producers News,* Jan. 24, 1930, 1, quoted in *Plentywood Herald,* May 1, 1930, 2.

6. *Plentywood Herald,* Sept. 4, 1930, 1; ibid., Nov. 5, 1931, 1.

7. Martinazzi, *Albert Rice Chapman,* 134, 135; Jensen interview.

8. *Producers News,* Sept. 8, 1922, 5.

9. Martinazzi, *Albert Rice Chapman,* 135.

10. *Plentywood Herald,* Aug. 7, 1930, 2; ibid., Mar. 20, 1930, 1.

11. *Producers News,* Sept. 11, 1931, 1; ibid., Sept. 2, 1932, 3, 4.

12. Martinazzi, *Albert Rice Chapman,* 137.

13. Althoff interview; Aasheim, *Sheridan's Daybreak,* 514.

14. Knutson to Lovestone, Mar. 14, 15, 1927, delo 1069, RGASPI; Knutson to Bedacht, July 10, 1927, delo 1069, RGASPI.

15. Hass's daughter was aware of no lingering resentment related to her mother's replacement by Marie Hansen. Althoff interview; *Producers News,* June 27, 1930, 2.

16. *Producers News,* Apr. 11, 1930, 1, 8.

17. Ibid., Apr. 11, 1930, 8. Hass's daughter remembers her parents discussing the case "vehemently." She indicates that the *Producers News* printed lies and that "there was no baby." Althoff interview.

18. *Plentywood Herald,* Apr. 17, 1930, 1.

19. Taylor captured 23 percent of the ballots in his hometown of Plentywood. *Producers News,* Nov. 14, 1930, 2; Waldron, *Montana Politics,* 232.

20. *Plentywood Herald,* July 21, 1932, 2.

21. Ibid., Oct. 20, 1932, 2.

22. Waldron, *Montana Politics,* 240, 246; *Plentywood Herald,* Nov. 10, 1932, 8; Aasheim, *Sheridan's Daybreak,* 12; *Plentywood Herald,* Nov. 10, 1932, 1.

23. *Producers News,* Nov. 25, 1932, 2.

CHAPTER 14

1. Aasheim, *Sheridan's Daybreak,* 11–12; Montana Department of Agriculture, *Montana Agricultural Statistics,* 5, 64.

2. Stadstad, *Growing Up in the Great Depression,* 13; Montana Department of Agriculture, *Montana Agricultural Statistics,* 4–5.

3. Aasheim, *Sheridan's Daybreak,* 11–12, 329.

4. Stoner to author, March 1993.

5. Ibid., 12; Stoner to author, March 1993; Timmerman interview.

6. Klehr, *Heyday of American Communism.*

7. *Producers News,* Jan. 6, 1933, 1; ibid., Aug. 11, 1933, 3; Tiala to Puro, Aug. 14, 1933, delo 3376, RGASPI.

8. Tiala to Puro, Aug. 31, 1933, delo 3376, RGASPI.

9. *Producers News,* Sept. 19, 1933, 1; Charles Taylor interview by Dyson, 234; Lerner to Puro, Sept. 30, 1933, delo 3379, RGASPI.

10. Lerner to Puro, Sept. 27, 1933, Oct. 1, 1933, Oct. 4, 1933, all in delo 3379, RGASPI. Lerner mistakenly refers to Bill "Hess." Lerner served as a kind of informer for Puro, head of CPUSA's agricultural department, and Tiala, UFL secretary, both of whom were antagonistic toward Charles Taylor.

11. *Producers News*, Dec. 1, 1933, 3; Tiala to Puro, Dec. 6, 1933, delo 3376, RGASPI.

12. Klehr, *Heyday of American Communism,* 47; *Producers News,* Jan. 26, 1934, 3; ibid., Feb. 23, 1934, 1.

13. According to the FBI, Miller was born in Germany in 1903 and entered the United States in 1928. "Alfred Miller," Mar. 3, 1943, 2, FBI Philadelphia File 100-18264, Department of Justice File 100-88799, RIDS; "Alfred Fortonueller [*sic*]," *1930 U.S. Federal Census,* http://www.ancestry.com; *Producers News,* Feb. 23, 1934, 4.

14. *Producers News,* Apr. 27, 1934, 2; ibid., May 31, 1934, 2; ibid., June 7, 1934, 2.

15. Althoff interview; *Producers News,* Jan. 26, 1934, 3.

16. *Producers News,* Jan. 26, 1934, 3.

17. "The Story of the Sell Out of the Producers News," undated item in possession of author.

18. *Producers News,* May 4, 1934, 2. Klehr and Haynes describe Communist Party factionalism in *American Communist Movement,* chap. 2.

19. Dyson, *Red Harvest,* 73; *Producers News,* July 12, 1934, 2.

20. *Producers News,* Sept. 27, 1934, 3; ibid., Oct. 11, 1934, 2.

21. Charles Taylor interview by Dyson, 189; Dyson, *Red Harvest,* 119, 120; Tiala to Puro, Oct. 9, 1933, delo 3376, RGASPI; Flowers to Taylor, March 1, 1933, delo 3376, RGASPI; Klehr, *Heyday of American Communism,* 143.

22. Charles Taylor interview by Dyson, 209, 132–33.

23. Ibid., 209, 132–33, 181, 186; Dyson, *Red Harvest,* 125; Shover, *Cornbelt Rebellion,* 174.

24. *Producers News,* June 14, 1934, 1; *Plentywood Portrait,* 38.

25. Aasheim, *Sheridan's Daybreak,* 589; *Plentywood Portrait,* 40; *Plentywood Herald,* Dec. 27, 1934, 1.

26. *Producers News,* Oct. 11, 1934, 2.

27. *Plentywood Herald,* Nov. 8, 1934, 1; *Producers News,* Nov. 23, 1934, 3; ibid., Nov. 9, 1934, 2. In a four-man race, the Communist candidate received the plurality of votes in Raymond and Dagmar, 36 and 43 percent, respectively. *Producers News,* Nov. 23, 1934, 3.

28. "Alfred Miller," Department of Justice File 100-88799 from FBI Philadelphia File 100-18264, March 3, 1943, 4; *Producers News,* Apr. 5, 1935, 1; ibid., Apr. 19, 1935, 1; ibid., Apr. 26, 1935, 2. The *News*'s last story about Miller indicated that he was being held on Ellis Island under an order of deportation in 1936. *Producers News,* Mar. 27, 1936, 1.

29. Taylor had a long history of deviating from the Communist Party line. He claims to have left the party for one year, probably 1929. He reentered party life but occasionally fell out of favor with the leadership over various issues, such as his sympathy for Leon Trotsky. He finally quit paying dues in 1935. Charles Taylor interview by Dyson, 138, 232.

30. Ibid., 234; *Producers News,* July 26, 1935, 2.

31. *Producers News,* Sept. 13, 1935, 1; ibid., Mar. 27, 1936, 5.

32. Ibid., Mar. 27, 1936, 4.

33. Waldron, *Montana Politics,* 264.

34. *Plentywood Herald,* Apr. 29, 1937, 1.

CHAPTER 15

1. Charles Taylor interview by Dyson, 159; Carl Taylor interview.

2. "Charles Edwin Taylor," March 30, 31, 1961, 2–5, FBI Seattle File 100-7258, in "Charles Taylor" file 100-55987, RIDS; Carl Taylor interview. The informant who claimed to have been recruited by Taylor indicated that he had been recruited in 1935 or 1936, which is unlikely since Taylor was in Plentywood at the time.

3. Dyson, *Red Harvest,* 119; "Eric Bert [*sic*]," May 11, 1942, and July 20, 1978, FBI St. Paul File 100-70994, RIDS; Klehr, *Heyday of American Communism,* 261, 457.

4. *Daniels County Leader,* Dec. 21, 1967, 2; Hoover to Bowler, July 20, 1959, Department of Justice File 94-52612-1, RIDS.

5. Aasheim, *Sheridan's Daybreak II,* 674; Gilluly, *Press Gang,* 113; *Plentywood Herald,* Nov. 10, 1971, 1; Nistler to author, January 2004.

6. Martinazzi, *Albert Rice Chapman,* 136; *Plentywood Herald,* June 16, 1938, 1.

7. *Plentywood Herald,* June 16, 1938, 1; "Communist Activities in State of Montana," FBI Butte File 100-721, June 16, 1941 (it should be noted that the report was mistaken as to the year in which Salisbury died, listing it as 1937); Martinazzi, *Albert Rice Chapman,* 136; Jardis [Salisbury] Hughes, quoted in Zahavi, "Who's Going to Dance?" 286n78.

8. Kelly to Pratt, Aug. 8, 1995; Martinazzi, *Albert Rice Chapman,* 137, 140.

9. *Producers News,* June 5, 1925: 1; ibid., Jan. 13, 1928, 1; Johnson interview; "Arthur Rueber," Social Security Death Index, http://www.ancestry.com.

10. Aasheim, *Sheridan's Daybreak,* 925; "Communist Activities in State of Montana," June 16, 1941, Butte FBI File 100-3-51-16, 103; Aasheim, *Sheridan's Daybreak,* 925.

11. Ransdell interview; Aasheim, *Sheridan's Daybreak,* 560; Ransdell to author, Nov. 10, 2002.

12. Dyson, *Red Harvest,* 73; "Communist Activities in State of Montana," June 16, 1941, 86–87.

13. "At Home," *New International,* Mar. 1939, 66; ibid., Oct. 1939, 290; "John Boulds," July 25, 1949, 1, 3, Butte FBI File 100-1622, RIDS; "John Boulds," 4; Aasheim, *Sheridan's Daybreak,* 605.

14. Althoff interview; Stoner interview.

15. "Communist Activities in State of Montana," June 16, 1941, 103, 108; *Plentywood Portrait,* 204.

16. Doig, *Bucking the Sun,* 174; Boswell, "Plentywood's Red Days Remembered," *Billings Gazette,* Oct. 9, 1989, 5A; Aasheim, *Sheridan's Daybreak,* 10; Peterson interview.

17. It should be noted that three important works describing Sheridan County's radicalism were published during the Cold War years. They are Vindex, "Radical Rule" (1968); Dyson, *Red Harvest* (1982); and Klehr, *Heyday of American Communism* (1984). Other treatments of the county's farm movement include Pratt, "Rural Radicalism" (1992), 42–55; Vichorek, *Hi-Line Profiles* (1993); Baxter, *Next Year Country* (1992); Zahavi, "Who's Going to Dance?"

(1996), 251–86; and McDonald, "A Paper of, by, and for the People" (1998), 18–33.

18. Hovland to author, Aug. 8, 2003, Mar. 25, 2005; U.S. Census Bureau, "County Population Estimates," U.S. Census Bureau, http://www.census.gov/popest/counties/CO-EST2008–05.html. Between July 1, 2007, and July 1, 2008, for instance, the county recorded twenty-eight births and fifty-one deaths.

19. Waldron, *Montana Politics,* 240–46, 254, 248. Two Democratic senators were elected that year: Burton K. Wheeler for a six-year term and James E. Murray for a two-year term to replace Thomas Walsh who had been appointed U.S. attorney general by President Roosevelt. Walsh died en route to Washington, D.C., to accept his appointment. "Biographical Directory of the United States Congress," http://bioguide.congress.gov/scripts/biodisplay.pl?index=W000104. One notable exception was the county's vote for Richard Nixon over George McGovern in 1972. Waldron, *Montana Politics,* 264, 286, 306, 326, 356, 384. In 2000, Bush received 1,176 votes to Gore's 702. Hovland, email to author, Aug. 8, 2003; ibid., Mar. 25, 2005; Sheridan County Clerk and Recorder, "Unofficial General Election Results—Nov. 4, 2008 Sheridan County Montana," http://www.co.sheridan.mt.us/2008_general_results.htm.

20. The phrase "to move movements" is from Lucas, "Coming to Terms with Movement Studies," 265.

21. Burgchardt, "Two Faces of American Communism," 383.

22. Klehr, *Heyday of American Communism,* 414, 415; Klehr and Haynes, *American Communist Movement,* 178.

23. Burke, "Revolutionary Symbolism," 271.

BIBLIOGRAPHY

BOOKS AND ARTICLES

Aasheim, Magnus, ed. *Sheridan's Daybreak.* Great Falls, Mont.: Blue Print and Letter Company, 1970.

———, ed. *Sheridan's Daybreak II.* Aberdeen, S.Dak.: North Plains Press, 1984.

Anderson, Arlow W. *The Norwegian-Americans.* Boston: Twayne, 1975.

Arnesen Eric, Julie Green, and Bruce Laurie, eds. *Labor Histories: Class, Politics, and the Working Class Experience.* Urbana: University of Illinois Press, 1998.

"At Home." *New International,* March 1939: 66.

Barnes, Donna A. *Farmers in Rebellion: The Rise and Fall of the Southern Farmers Alliance and People's Party in Texas.* Austin: University of Texas, 1984.

Baxter, Don. *Next Year Country: The Story of Eastern Montana.* Boulder, Colo.: Fred Pruett Books, 1992.

"Beloit Scores on Purple Team." *Chicago Daily Tribune,* October 15, 1905, A1.

Bison Men's Basketball, 2008–2009. Grand Forks: North Dakota State University, 2008.

Boswell, Evelyn. "Plentywood's Red Days Remembered." *Billings (Mont.) Gazette,* October 9, 1989, 5A.

Brazier, Richard. "The Story of the IWW's 'Little Red Song Book.'" *Labor History* 9 (Winter 1968): 91–107.

Buell, Jennie. *The Grange Master and the Grange Lecturer.* New York: Harcourt, Brace and Co., 1921.

Burgchardt, Carl R. "Two Faces of American Communism: Pamphlet Rhetoric of the Third Period and the Popular Front." *Quarterly Journal of Speech* 66 (1980): 375–91.

Burke, Kenneth. "Revolutionary Symbolism in America." In *The Legacy of Kenneth Burke.* Edited by Herbert W. Simons and Trevor Melia. Madison: University of Wisconsin Press, 1989.

Calvert, Jerry W. *The Gibraltar: Socialism and Labor in Butte, Montana, 1895–1920.* Helena: Montana Historical Society Press, 1988.

Carlson, Peter. *Roughneck: The Life and Times of Big Bill Haywood.* New York: Norton, 1983.

Carruthers, Bruce G., and Sarah Babb. "The Color of Money and the Nature of Value: Greenback and Gold in Postbellum America." *American Journal of Sociology* 101 (May 1996): 1556–91.

Carter, David A. "The Industrial Workers of the World and the Rhetoric of Song." *Quarterly Journal of Speech* 66 (1980): 365–74.
Clinch, Thomas A. *Urban Populism and Free Silver in Montana.* Missoula: University of Montana Press, 1970.
The Communist Position on the Farmers' Movement. New York: Workers Library Publishers, 1933.
Crawford, Paul. "The Farmer Assesses His Role in Society." In *The Rhetoric of Protest and Reform, 1878–1898.* Edited by Paul H. Boase. Athens: Ohio University Press, 1980.
Davis, Elmer. "Farmer-Laborites Favor La Follette, But Won't Have Him. *New York Times,* June 19, 1924, A3.
———. "Foster's Red Group Easily Dominates St. Paul Convention." *New York Times,* June 18, 1924, A1, A3.
Doig, Ivan. *Bucking the Sun.* New York: Simon and Schuster, 1996.
Draper, Theodore. *The Roots of American Communism.* New York: Viking, 1957.
Dubofsky, Melvyn. *"Big Bill" Haywood.* New York: St. Martin's, 1987.
———. *We Shall Be All: A History of the Industrial Workers of the World.* Chicago: Quadrangle Books, 1969.
Dyson, Lowell K. *Red Harvest: The Communist Party and American Farmers.* Lincoln: University of Nebraska Press, 1982.
Ecroyd, Donald H. "The Populist Spellbinders." In *The Rhetoric of Protest and Reform 1878–1898.* Edited by Paul H. Boase. Athens: Ohio University Press, 1980.
"Eighteenth Year." *Time,* June 19, 1944, 20.
Emmons, David M. *The Butte Irish: Class and Ethnicity in an American Mining Town, 1875–1925.* Urbana: University of Illinois Press, 1989.
Everett, Paul M. "Lutherans in Montana: From Immigrant to American Church." In *Religion in Montana: Pathways to the Present.* Edited by Lawrence F. Small. Helena, Mont.: Falcon Press, 1995.
Foley, Barbara. *Spectres of 1919: Class and Nation in the Making of the New Negro.* Champaign: University of Illinois Press, 2003.
Foner, Philip S., ed. *Fellow Workers and Friends: IWW Free-Speech Fights as Told by Participants.* Westport, Conn.: Greenwood, 1981.
Gieske, Millard L. *Minnesota Farmer-Laborism: The Third Party Alternative.* Minneapolis: University of Minnesota Press, 1969.
Gilluly, Sam. *The Press Gang: A Century of Montana Newspapers, 1885–1985.* Great Falls, Mont.: Artcraft Printers, 1985.
Gjerde, Jon, and Anne McCants, "Individual Life Chances, 1850–1910: A Norwegian-American Example." *Journal of Interdisciplinary History* 30 (Winter 1999): 377–405.
Goodwyn, Lawrence. *Democratic Promise: The Populist Moment in America.* New York: Oxford University Press, 1976.
Haynes, John E. *Red Scare or Red Menace? American Communism and Anticommunism in the Cold War Era.* Chicago: Ivan R. Dee, 1996.
Hegne, Barbara. *Border Outlaws of Montana, North Dakota, and Canada.* Eagle Point, Ore.: Self-published, 1993.

Hofstadter, Richard. *The Age of Reform: From Bryan to F.D.R.* New York: Alfred A. Knopf, 1972.

Howard, David H. *People, Pride and Progress: 125 Years of the Grange in America.* Washington, D.C.: National Grange, 1992.

Jefferson, Thomas. "Letter to James Madison." In *The Papers of Thomas Jefferson.* Edited by Julian Boyd and Kaveh Azar. Volume 8. New Brunswick, N.J.: Princeton University, 1972.

———. "Notes on the State of Virginia." In *Thomas Jefferson: Writings.* Edited by Merrill D. Peterson. New York: Library of America, 1984.

Klehr, Harvey. *The Heyday of American Communism: The Depression Decade.* New York: Basic Books, 1984.

———, and John Earl Haynes. *The American Communist Movement: Storming Heaven Itself.* New York: Twayne, 1992.

Kornbluh, Joyce L. *Rebel Voices: An IWW Anthology.* Ann Arbor: University of Michigan, 1968.

Kraditor, Aileen S. *The Radical Persuasion 1890–1917: Aspects of the Intellectual History and the Historiography of Three American Radical Organizations.* Baton Rouge: Louisiana State University, 1981.

Limerick, Patricia Nelson. "Making the Most of Words: Verbal Activity and Western America." In *Under an Open Sky: Rethinking America's Western Past.* Edited by William Cronon, George Miles, and Jay Gitlin. New York: Norton, 1992.

Lucas, Stephen E. "Coming to Terms with Movement Studies." *Central States Speech Journal* 31 (Winter 1980): 255–66.

Malone, Michael P., Richard B. Roeder, and William L. Lang. *Montana: A History of Two Centuries.* Rev. ed. Seattle: University of Washington Press, 2003.

Manifesto and Principal Resolutions Adopted by the Eighth Convention of the Communist Party of the USA. New York: Workers Library Publishers, 1934.

Manifesto of the Communist Party. New York: International Publishers, 1986.

Martinazzi, Toni. *Albert Rice Chapman, 1866–1948, and His Descendants.* Glenview, Ill.: Self-published, 1993.

McDonald, Verlaine Stoner. "'A Paper of, by, and for the People': The *Producers News* and the Farmers' Movement in Northeastern Montana, 1918–1937." In *Montana Legacy: Essays on History, People, and Place.* Edited by Harry W. Fritz, Mary Murphy, and Robert R. Swartout Jr. Helena: Montana Historical Society Press, 2002. Previously published in *Montana The Magazine of Western History* 48 (Winter 1998): 18–33.

McIntyre, Jerilyn S. "Rituals of Disorder: A Dramatistic Interpretation of Radical Dissent." *Journalism Monographs* 112 (May 1989): 1–33.

McMath, Robert C., Jr. *American Populism: A Social History, 1877–1898.* New York: Hill and Wang, 1993.

———. *Populist Vanguard: A History of the Southern Farmers' Alliance.* New York: Norton, 1975.

Miller, Worth Robert. "Farmers and Third-Party Politics." In *The Gilded Age: Essays on the Origins of Modern America.* Edited by Charles W. Calhoun. Wilmington, Del.: Scholarly Resources, 1996.

Minnesota Legislative Manual 1911. St. Paul: Office of the Secretary of State, 1911.

Montana Bureau of Agriculture, Labor, and Industry. *Montana.* Helena: Independent Publishing Co., 1912.

Montana Department of Agriculture. *Montana Agricultural Statistics: State Series, 1867–1976.* Bozeman: Colorworld of Montana, 1978.

Morlan, Robert L. *Political Prairie Fire: The Nonpartisan League, 1915–1922.* St. Paul: Minnesota Historical Society Press, 1985.

"News Notes." *Sporting Life,* April 14, 1906, 11.

Plentywood Portrait: Toil, Soil, Oil. Aberdeen, S.Dak.: Midstates Printing, 1987.

Pratt, William C. "Rural Radicalism on the Northern Plain, 1912–1950." *Montana The Magazine of Western History* 42 (Winter 1992): 42–55.

The Program of the Communist International. New York City: Workers Library Publishers, 1928.

Ross, Steven J. *Workers on the Edge: Work, Leisure, and Politics in Industrializing Cincinnati, 1788–1890.* New York: Columbia University Press, 1985.

Salerno, Salvatore. *Red November Black November: Culture and Community in the Industrial Workers of the World.* Albany: State University of New York, 1989.

Sandvig, Earl. "Stage on the High Line." *Montana The Magazine of Western History* 29 (Autumn 1979): 67–70.

Schwantes, Carlos A. "Landscapes of Opportunity: Phases of Railroad Promotion of the Pacific Northwest." *Montana The Magazine of Western History* 43 (Spring 1993): 38–51.

Segars, Loretta. *One Hundred Years in Culbertson, 1887–1987.* [Culbertson, Mont.]: Self-published, 1986.

Shearer, John. *Moc's Football: A History.* Signal Mountain, Tenn.: Mountain Press, 2000.

Shideler, James H. *Farm Crisis: 1919–1923.* Berkeley: University of California Press, 1957.

Shover, John L. *Cornbelt Rebellion: The Farmers' Holiday Association.* Urbana: University of Illinois Press, 1965.

Smith, Henry Nash. *Virgin Land: The American West as Symbol and Myth.* New York: Vintage, 1950.

Soden, Dale. "One Hundred Years Later." *Whitworthian,* December 14, 2008: 4.

"Stacks o' Facts." *Montana Magazine,* November/December 2002: 18.

Stadstad, Curtis. *Growing Up in the Great Depression.* n.p.: Self-published, n.d.

Stark, Rodney, and Kevin J. Christiano. "Support for the American Left, 1920–1924: The Opiate Thesis Reconsidered." *Journal for the Scientific Study of Religion* 31, no. 1 (1992): 62–75.

Stone, Albert E. "Introduction" to *Letters from an American Farmer and Sketches of Eighteenth Century America.* Edited by Albert E. Stone. New York: Penguin, 1981.

Swibold, Dennis L. *Copper Chorus: Mining, Politics, and the Montana Press, 1889–1959.* Helena: Montana Historical Society Press, 2006.

Taylor, Sally J. *Stalin's Apologist: Walter Duranty: The* New York Times*'s Man in Moscow.* New York: Oxford University Press, 1990.

Theses and Resolutions for the Seventh National Convention of the Communist Party of the USA. New York: Workers Library Publishers, 1930.

U.S. Bureau of the Census. *Decennial Censuses of Population* (title varies per census), *1890–2000.* Processed by the Census and Economic Information Center, Montana Department of Commerce, Helena. Updated November 2002.

U.S. Department of Agriculture, Soil Conservation Service. *Soil Survey of Sheridan County, Montana.* Washington, D.C.: U.S. Department of the Interior, 1977.

U.S. Department of Commerce, Bureau of the Census. *U.S. Census of Agriculture, 1930.* Washington, D.C.: U.S. Government Printing Office, [1931].

———. *U.S. Population Census 1920.* Washington, D.C.: U.S. Government Printing Office, [1921].

Vichorek, Daniel N. *The Hi-Line Profiles of a Montana Land.* Helena, Mont.: American and World Geographic Publishing, 1993.

Vindex, Charles. "Radical Rule in Montana." *Montana The Magazine of Western History* 18 (January 1968): 1–18.

Vivian, James F. "The Last Roundup: Theodore Roosevelt Confronts the Nonpartisan League, October 1918." *Montana The Magazine of Western History* 36 (Winter 1986): 42, 48.

Waldron, Ellis L. *Montana Politics since 1864: An Atlas of Elections.* Missoula: Montana State University Press, 1958.

Wells, Merle W. "The Western Federation of Miners." *Journal of the West* 12 (1973): 18–35.

Winters, Donald E., Jr. *The Soul of the Wobblies: The IWW, Religion, and American Culture in the Progressive Era, 1905–1917.* Westport, Conn.: Greenwood Press, 1985.

Woods, Thomas A. *Knights of the Plow: Oliver H. Kelley and the Origins of the Grange in Republican Ideology.* Ames: Iowa State University, 1991.

Zahavi, Gerald. "'Who's Going to Dance with Somebody Who Calls You a Mainstreeter?' Communism, Culture and Community in Sheridan County, Montana, 1918–1934." *Great Plains Quarterly* 16 (Fall 1996): 251–86.

INTERVIEWS

Althoff, Paula Hass. Interview by author. Oakland, California, August 30, 1994. Telephone interview by author, January 27, 2004.

Bjork, Harriet. Telephone interview by author, April 1, 1994.

Chandler, Fay, and Violet Chandler. Interview by Jackie Day, May 1985. Tape recording. Small Town Montana Oral History Project. Montana Historical Society, Helena.

Jensen, Anneva Hansen. Telephone interview by author, December 19, 2002.

Johnson, Raymond. Telephone interview by author, July 16, 2009.

Kavon, Louise. Interview by Jackie Day, May 1985. Tape recording. Small Town Montana Oral History Project. Montana Historical Society, Helena.

Marron, Nancy. Interview by Jackie Day, May 1985. Tape recording. Small Town Montana Oral History Project. Montana Historical Society, Helena.

Peterson, Clifford. Interview by Jackie Day, May 1985. Tape recording. Small Town Montana Oral History Project. Montana Historical Society, Helena.

Ransdell, Lucille Stoner. Telephone interview by author, October 30, 2002.

Stoner, Helen Wagnild. Interview by author. Outlook, Montana, July 6, 2003.

Syrstad, Ellen Taylor. Interview by author. Spanaway, Washington, March 21, 1995.

Taylor, Carl. Interviews by author. Spanaway, Washington, September 3, 1993; September 4, 1994; March 21, 1995.

Taylor, Charles E. Interview by Lowell K. Dyson, August 2–3, 1965. Columbia Oral History Collection, Oral History Research Office, Columbia University, New York.

Timmerman, Irwin. Interview by Jackie Day, May 1985. Tape recording. Small Town Montana Oral History Project. Montana Historical Society, Helena.

Waller, Myrtle. Interview by author. Plentywood, Montana, July 7, 2003.

Welter, Mona Boulds. Telephone interview by author, August 5, 2009.

UNPUBLISHED MANUSCRIPTS AND CORRESPONDENCE

Aasheim, Magnus. "The Chicken Ranch." December 2002. Copy in possession of author.

Bryan, Shelley (Valley County, Montana, Clerk of Court). E-mail to author, July 8, 2009.

Burleson, Brian (National Weather Service). Letter to Helen Stoner, February 14, 2003.

Hovland, Milton (Sheridan County, Montana, Clerk and Recorder). E-mails to author, August 8, 2003, and March 25, 2005.

Kelly, Camilla Salisbury. Letter to William Pratt, August 8, 1995.

Klumpp, James. "The Populists." Unpublished lecture notes in possession of author.

Nistler, Joe. E-mail to author, January 2004.

Nyquist, Lynne (Valley County, Montana, Clerk and Recorder). E-mail to author, July 9, 2009.

Olson, Cheryl (Sheridan County, Montana, Clerk of Court). E-mail to author, July 2, 2009.

Ransdell, Lucile Stoner. Letter to author, November 10, 2002.

Stoner, Ray. Letter to author, March 1993.

NEWSPAPERS

Antelope (Mont.) Independent Daily Worker

Medicine Lake (Mont.) Wave

New York Times

Plentywood (Mont.) Herald

Plentywood (Mont.) Producers News

Plentywood (Mont.) Sheridan County (Mont.) Farmer

Scobey (Mont.) Daniels County Leader

GOVERNMENT ARCHIVES

"Alfred Miller." FBI Philadelphia File 100-18264. March 3, 1943. Department of Justice File 100-88799, 2 (FBI-FOIA). Department of Justice, Record Information/Dissemination Section, Washington, D.C.

Bert, Erik. Letter to Agrarian Department. January 29, 1932, and various other dates. Russian State Archive of Socio-Political History Fond 515, Opis 1, Delo 3041, Library of Congress, Washington, D.C.

Bloor, Ella Reeve. Letter to William Weinstone. January 30, 1932. Russian State Archive of Socio-Political History Fond 515, Opis 1, Delo 3041, Library of Congress, Washington, D.C.

"Call for National Farmer-Labor Convention." March 13, 1924. Russian State Archive of Socio-Political History Fond 515, Opis 1, Delo 248 and Delo 373, Library of Congress, Washington, D.C.

"Charles Edwin Taylor." FBI Seattle File 100-7258. March 31, 1961, and April 30, 1963. Contained in "Charles Taylor" file 100-55987, 2-5 (FBI-FOIPA). Department of Justice, Record Information/Dissemination Section, Washington, D.C.

"Charles Taylor." FBI Minneapolis File 100-55987-38. May 28, 1953, 3 (FBI-FOIA). Department of Justice, Record Information/Dissemination Section, Washington, D.C.

"Communist Activities in the State of Montana." FBI Butte File 100-721-50. Contained in "Summary of CP Activities," 100-3-51-16, 94 (FBI-FOIA). Department of Justice, Record Information/Dissemination Section, Washington, D.C.

"Communist Party USA, Record of the CPUSA." Russian State Archive of Socio-Political History. Library of Congress, Washington, D.C.

"Eric Bert [*sic*]." FBI St. Paul File 100-70994 (FBI-FOIA). Department of Justice, Record Information/Dissemination Section, Washington, D.C.

"Farmer-Labor Convention." FBI Minneapolis File 61-1624-100. June 20, 1924, 7, 10 (FBI-FOIA). Department of Justice, Record Information/Dissemination Section, Washington, D.C.

"Farmer-Labor Party." FBI Butte File 61-1624-92. November 15, 1923, 2 (FBI-FOIA). Department of Justice, Record Information/Dissemination Section, Washington, D.C.

"Farmer-Labor Party of the United States." FBI Los Angeles File 61-1624-102. June 24, 1924, 7 (FBI-FOIA). Department of Justice, Record Information/Dissemination Section, Washington, D.C.

Flowers, James. Letter to Charles Taylor. March 1, 1933. Russian State Archive of Socio-Political History Fond 515, Opis 1, Delo 3376 Library of Congress, Washington, D.C.

———. Letter to Henry Puro. March 8, 1933. Russian State Archive of Socio-Political History Fond 515, Opis 1, Delo 3376, Library of Congress, Washington, D.C.

Hoover, J. Edgar. Letter to Burley Bowler, July 20, 1959. Department of Justice File 94-52612-1 (FBI-FOIPA). Department of Justice, Record Information/Dissemination Section, Washington, D.C.

"John Boulds." FBI Butte File 100-1622. July 25, 1949, 4. (FBI-FOIA). Department of Justice, Record Information/Dissemination Section, Washington, D.C.

Knutson, Alfred. Letter to Jay Lovestone, September 21, 1927. Russian State Archive of Socio-Political History Fond 515, Opis 1, Delo 1069, Library of Congress, Washington, D.C.

———. Letter to K. E. Keikkinen, November 27, 1926. Russian State Archive of Socio-Political History Fond 515, Opis 1, Delo 687, Library of Congress, Washington, D.C.

———. Letter to Max Bedacht, July 10, 1927. Russian State Archive of Socio-Political History Fond 515, Opis 1, Delo 1069, Library of Congress, Washington, D.C.

Lerner, Abe. Letter to Henry Puro, March 14 and 15, 1927; September 27, 1933; September 30, 1933; October 1, 1933; October 4, 1933. Russian State Archive of Socio-Political History Fond 515, Opis 1, Delo 3379, Library of Congress, Washington, D.C.

Lovestone, Jay. Letter to Charles Taylor, November 22, 1927. Russian State Archive of Socio-Political History Fond 515, Opis 1, Delo 1060, Library of Congress, Washington, D.C.

———. Letter to Charles Taylor, January 5, 1928. Russian State Archive of Socio-Political History Fond 515, Opis 1, Delo 1344, Library of Congress, Washington, D.C.

"Report of the Worker's Party of America to the Executive Committee of the Communist International," October 20, 1923. Russian State Archive of Socio-Political History Fond 515, Opis 1, Delo 199, Library of Congress, Washington, D.C.

"Report on the Federated Farmer Labor Party and Our Party Situation," October 3, 1923. Russian State Archive of Socio-Political History Fond 515, Opis 1, Delo 200, Library of Congress, Washington, D.C.

"Rodney Salisbury Main File." Correspondence from J. Edgar Hoover, Department of Justice File 62-15962-2. November 30, 1927 (FBI-FOIA). Department of Justice, Record Information/Dissemination Section, Washington, D.C.

Ruthenberg, Charles. Letter to Alfred Knutson, February 10, 1926. Russian State Archive of Socio-Political History Fond 515, Opis 1, Delo 686, Library of Congress, Washington, D.C.

Taylor, Charles. Letter to Alfred Knutson, February 10, 1926. Russian State Archive of Socio-Political History Fond 515, Opis 1, Delo 893, Library of Congress, Washington, D.C.

———. Letter to K. E. Keikkinen, November 27, 1926. Russian State Archive of Socio-Political History Fond 515, Opis 1, Delo 687, Library of Congress, Washington, D.C.

Tiala, Alfred. Letter to Henry Puro, August 14, 1933, and August 31, 1933. Russian State Archive of Socio-Political History Fond 515, Opis 1, Delo 3376, Library of Congress, Washington, D.C.

INTERNET SOURCES

"Alfred Fortonueller [*sic*]." *1930 United States Federal Census.* http://www.ancestry.com (accessed July 15, 2009).

"Arthur Rueber." *Social Security Death Index.* http://www.ancestory.com (accessed July 9, 2009).

"Biographical Directory of the United States Congress." http://bioguide.congress.gov (accessed August 16, 2007).

Bureau of Land Management. "Land Patent Details." Bureau of Land Management. http://www.glorecords.blm.gov/PatentSearch (accessed July 1, 2009).

"Francis M. Taylor." *Minnesota Territorial and State Censuses, 1845–1905.* http://www.ancestry.com (accessed July 10, 2009).

"Mary R. Smith." *1920 United States Federal Census.* http://www.ancestry.com (accessed July 15, 2009).

Michigan Department of Information Technology. "Michigan State Grange Commemorative Designation." Michigan Department of Information Technology. http://www.mcgi.state.mi.us/hso/sites/38395.htm (accessed June 24, 2009).

Miller, Worth Robert. "Farmers and Third-Party Politics." http://history.missouristate.edu/WRMiller/Populism/texts/farmers_and_third_party_politics.htm (accessed June 24, 2009).

Montana Department of Agriculture. "Montana Agricultural Statistics, 2001 report." Montana Department of Agriculture. http://www.nass.usda.gov/mt/bulletin/BulletinDist2001.pdf (accessed January 9, 2003).

National Grange. "Birth of an American Treasure." National Grange. http://www.nationalgrange.org/about/history.html (accessed July 12, 2009).

"Precipitation." U.S. Department of the Interior and U.S. Geological Survey. http://www.nationalatlas.gov/printable/images/pdf/precip/pageprecip_nv3.pdf (accessed July 1, 2009).

Sheridan County Clerk and Recorder. "Unofficial General Election Results—Nov. 4, 2008 Sheridan County Montana." Sheridan County Clerk and Recorder. http://www.co.sheridan.mt.us/2008_general_results.htm (accessed June 27, 2009).

U.S. Census Bureau. "County Population Estimates." U.S. Census Bureau. http://www.census.gov/popest/counties/CO-EST2008–05.html (accessed July 9, 2009).

U.S. Census Bureau. "Sheridan County, Montana." U.S. Census Bureau. http://quickfacts.census.gov/qfd/states/30/30091.html (accessed July 9, 2009).

U.S. Census Bureau. "USA Counties 1998." U.S. Census Bureau. http://www.census.gov/statab/USA98/30/091.txt (accessed January 9, 2003).

INDEX

D

E

F

G

L

M

N

R

S

T

U

V

W

Y